A

PICTORIAL HISTORY

OF

DEAF BRITAIN

Peter Jackson

First published in Great Britain 2001

Copyright © Peter Jackson 2001

Published by
Deafprint Winsford
PO Box 93
Winsford
Cheshire CW7 3FU
ENGLAND

The right of the Peter Webster Jackson to be identified as the author of this work has been asserted by him in accordance with the Copyright, Designs and Patents Act, 1988

All rights reserved
No part of this publication may be reproduced by any means, or stored in or introduced into a retrieval system, or transmitted in any form or by any means (electronic, mechanical, photocopying, recording or otherwise) without the prior written permission of the copyright owner and the above publisher of this book.

British Library Cataloguing Data

ISBN 0-9532206-4-8

Printed in Great Britain by Palladian Press Limited, Unit E, Chandlers Row, Port Lane, Colchester, Essex CO1 2HG

*This book is dedicated to all Deaf Activists and Pioneers
who have contributed so much to the British Deaf Community
and to friends and colleagues in the British Deaf History Society
who try to preserve our heritage*

Other Books by Peter Jackson
Britain's Deaf Heritage
Deaf Crime Casebook
Deaf to Evidence
Deaf Murder Casebook

A History of the Deaf Community in Northwich and Winsford 1880-2000
(With Maureen Jackson)

CONTENTS

Chapter		Page
	Acknowledgements	vii
	Foreword	ix
	Introduction	1
I	Deaf People Before 1760	3
II	British Sign Language	25
III	Deaf Education 1760-1900	51
IV	Deaf Art	77
V	Deaf People 1760-1900	111
VI	Missions and Centres for Deaf People	139
VII	Deaf Organisations	161
VIII	Social Life and Events	199
IX	Deaf Sport	213
X	Literature, Theatre and Television	231
XI	Deaf Schools in the War Years	245
XII	Deaf Education Today	251
XIII	Deaf People 1900-2000	265
XIV	Deaf Technology	293
	Picture Gallery 1	300
	Picture Gallery 2	304
	Picture Gallery 3	306
	Sport Picture Gallery	308
XV	The Deaf Community: The Future?	315
	About the Author	318
	Footnotes	320
	Bibliography	321
	Name and Subject Index	327
	Schools Index	336

ACKNOWLEDGEMENTS

The publication of my first book *Britain's Deaf Heritage* pre-dated what was to be a remarkable growth of interest in Deaf Studies among both Deaf and hearing people, especially sign language students. Unfortunately the book was quickly sold out and difficult to obtain through library loan sources. I used to get hundreds of enquiries per year from students, colleges and others desperate to obtain a copy. The recent set-up of many Level 3 BSL classes as well as courses in Deaf Studies in a number of universities only added to the demand. It was because of this that the decision was made to write a new book in a different format, suitably updated and corrected where appropriate.

It was not an easy decision to take because I was only to well aware of the enormous amount of work and time that was needed with the first book which was three years in the making. I am greatly indebted to many people for the encouragement and help that was given to complete this book in a much shorter time span. Of course technology has enormously improved since the late 1980s when the first book was written. The Internet and the use of e-mail has made research so much easier. Even so I would like to record my thanks to a number of individuals who gave their time and help freely.

First I must mention my wife Maureen and assistant, Cheridah Sword, who both make up our independent company. They both helped with the typing, picture collation and research.

I also owe a great deal to a number of colleagues in the British Deaf History Society especially Raymond Lee who gave tremendous support, making a number of suggestions regarding content and layout. Raymond also devoted considerable time to proof-reading the book. Others in the BDHS who helped include Geoffrey Eagling, Peter Brown, Christopher Marsh and Doreen Woodford.

There were a number of people who, in the interests of accuracy, I requested that they contribute articles or information. These include Jeff McWhinney (Chief Executive, BDA), John Young OBE (ex-Chair, BDA), Gillian Winstanley (Services Director, Breakthrough) and Arthur F. Dimmock MBE. Other individuals that contributed are Arthur Groom, Sharon Ridgeway and Irene Hall.

There were also organisations that helped to build an accurate picture. These include SENSE, Hearing Dogs for the Deaf and the National Hearing Aid Museum. Outside of the Deaf world there were individual organisations, records offices and people who also contributed valuable information, for example, the present owner of Bourton House, Gloucestershire.

There are many others and if I have not mentioned them here, please accept my sincere apologies for the omission.

Last but not the least I must mention Ian Anstice, Librarian at Winsford. Nothing was too much trouble for him and he was of tremendous assistance in tracing elusive books and material. It was through him that I finally secured the picture of Sir John Gaudy, which I had been looking for over ten years.

Any errors or omissions in this book are mine.

FOREWORD

Peter Jackson's *Britain's Deaf Heritage,* published in 1990, was a pioneering work in the field of Deaf history; it aroused an interest among members of the British Deaf community to research and to look into their history. Up to the time of publication of *Britain's Deaf Heritage,* the history of the Deaf of Britain, its community, its language and its culture was very little known and deliberately removed, and perhaps banned was the most suitable word, from the curricula of Deaf education in schools for the Deaf. Under the terrifying and suppressive rule of Oralism, Deaf children were not allowed to know anything about the history of other Deaf people and their communities and consequently Deaf people were made to feel like a people without any aims in life.

What, indeed, is a people without a history? They are nothing, and if they are anything at all, they are second-class citizens. History is many things. It is not just a rolling snapshot of past occurrences, recording people and events that contributed to and shaped the world. For many communities and their own members, history is a source of pride. And where people have pride, they develop self-confidence and where they have self-confidence, they are able to take pride in their own community, language and culture and face life with determination and positive outlook. That is one of the amazing ways that history can inspire and assist people. Deaf history is no different.

Time marched on since *Britain's Deaf Heritage* came out and the situation in Britain changed dramatically for the Deaf. The iron grip of Oralism has been smashed and Oralism is now nothing but a shadow of its evil self. British Sign Language slowly gained respect as many hearing people started to study it. Sign Language classes sprung up all over the country and universities established Deaf Studies degree courses. People cried for information on Deaf History. After one hundred and ten years under Oralism, it was not possible to gather over 1,200 years worth of information on Deaf history in a short period. It was with that in mind that the British Deaf History Society was established in 1993 to encourage interested individuals, Deaf or hearing alike, to assist in establishing a full picture of the history of the British Deaf community.

However, Peter Jackson has taken to update his original work and present it in a different format. The present book goes some way farther than his original classic; the author has skilfully made his present work serve a twofold purpose; one is as a sweeping history of the Deaf in Britain that would make interesting reading and the other as a source of reference for those studying Deaf history as a part of Deaf Studies course.

A Pictorial History of Deaf Britain has more to offer than *Britain's Deaf Heritage* in that recent research by the author yielded some interesting facts, events and Deaf characters that were not known barely three or four years ago. For all his efforts and determination to bring Deaf history to society and academia, Peter Jackson deserves admiration. But for his efforts to bring Deaf history to Deaf people of Britain, he deserves thanks. However, it is his relentless pursuit of facts and his dismissal of "unfounded traditional facts" that should earn him praise – and there is no greater praise than his present work, *A Pictorial History of Deaf Britain.*

Raymond Lee
Co-Founder – *British Deaf History Society*
Editor-in Chief – *Deaf History Journal.*

INTRODUCTION

It is incredibly difficult to write about Deaf History, particularly *Deaf people,* prior to 1600. There are a number of reasons for this. In an era when the majority of the population of Britain (and other countries) could not read or write and were classified as serfs or peasants, people who happened to be deaf and unable to speak found themselves on a lower scale still.

Furthermore, Deaf History has a heritage that largely relies on the expressive visuality of British Sign Language, and unless it is written about, or painted, or is built as a permanent structure, or has some other form of reference such as a notation in a legal document (for example, a record of a wedding or a funeral), very little can be known about it.

Thus, we come to rely on the writings of other people like Richard Carew's *Survey of Cornwall* (1595), John Bulwer's *Philocophus;* or the *Deafe and Dumbe Man's Friende* (1648), or even further back, the Hebrew book *Talmud* to learn something about the existence of deaf people and the kind of lives they led. In this, we are also helped by stories of deaf persons that have been passed down in legend, like John Dyott, Princess Katherine Plantagenet and Princess Joanna, the Royal Princess of Scotland. In families where deafness was hereditary, we find deaf folklore passed down through the generations. Unexpected anecdotes about deaf people would also come from diarists such as Samuel Pepys, John Evelyn or Dorothy Osborne in the mid-1600s.

It was the emergence of interest in Deaf Education that laid the foundation for more detailed records of Deaf History. People like two eminent (and feuding) Doctors of Divinity named William Holder and John Wallis extolled the successes of Deaf subjects who were (supposedly) taught to speak; the founding of schools in France (Charles Michel de l'Epee), in Germany (Samuel Heiniecke) and Scotland (Thomas Braidwood) were the catalysts which set off the modern Deaf History trail.

One such trail lies in tracing the existence of various nationalistic sign languages through old documents like alphabet charts or references to sign language itself. The more common trails, however, lie in unearthing stories of deaf people and deaf events either because of the Deaf Education system or because of what Deaf people became in life, and how events influenced the lives of Deaf people.

This book is selective because of lack of space and the style of its layout in the stories it presents of Deaf History. Wherever possible, a fuller study of any particular subject may be found by references made at the end of the book.

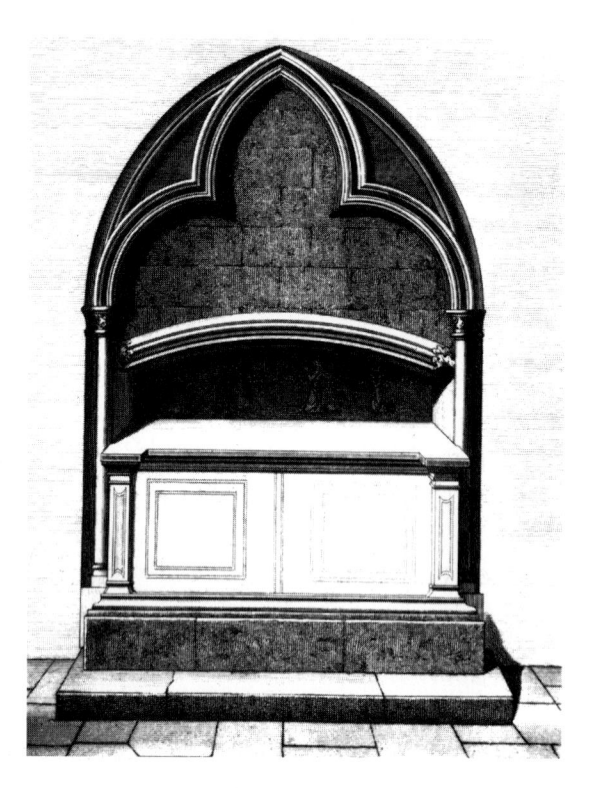

Tomb of Princess Katherine Plantagenet, Westminster Abbey
Photo: By courtesy of the Dean & Chapter of Westminster

The Morton Monument Effigies of the Earl of Morton & Princess Joanna
The Proceedings of the Society of Antiquaries of Scotland, 1862

CHAPTER I:

DEAF PEOPLE BEFORE 1760

The earliest known deaf person mentioned by name in British history was one of the daughters of King Henry III of England.

Princess Katherine Plantagenet (1253-1257)

Princess Katherine was born on November 25 1253 in the Palace of Westminster. Her feast held on her christening on 5 January 1254 has come down in history for its magnificence. All the English nobility was invited and the Archbishop of Canterbury officiated at the christening. Afterwards, those assembled consumed 14 wild boars, 24 swans, 135 rabbits, 250 partridges, 50 hares, 250 wild duck, 1650 fowls, 36 female geese and 61,000 eggs.

Up the age of two, which was when Princess Katherine first saw her father, the King, who had been away fighting wars in France, the royal child was looked after by a royal lady-in-waiting in the village of Swallowfield in Berkshire, near Windsor Castle. It was quite apparent when her father first saw his daughter that the Princess was deaf, and unable to speak. Nonetheless, the king was captivated by her extraordinary beauty and proud of his daughter.

A sickly child, she was subject to frequent spells of illness and she died at Windsor Castle on 3 May 1257, only 3 years and 5 months old. She was buried in Westminster Abbey where there is a tomb in her memory.

Had she lived a few years longer, who knows that being a Princess and greatly loved by her father, she might have been given an instructor and supplied another chapter in the education of deaf children?

Princess Joanna of Scotland (1426-1486?)

Another early deaf royal was Princess Joanna, one of the daughters of King James I of Scotland. She was born in 1426 and Scottish records indicate that she was fragile but beautiful. She may have been educated in France between 1445 and 1458, where she may have picked up monastic sign language. She was gifted at embroidery and could communicate with her younger sister, Princess Eleanor, by signs. She married James Douglas, Lord of Dalkeith in May 1459 and bore him 4 children. Her tomb is known as the Morton Monument and can be found in the ruins of the Dalkeith Collegiate Church Chancel, attached to the present St. Nicolas Buccleuch Parish Church.

A Deaf Marriage 1576

One of the earliest deaf people whose name is known was a man named Thomas Tilsye. The Parish Book of St. Martin's Church, Leicester contains a record of his marriage to Ursula Russel, who from all accounts was not deaf herself.

The extract from this record dated 5 February 1576 reads:

> "Thomas Tilsye and Ursula Russel were maryed; and because the sayde Thomas was and is naturally deafe, and also dumbe, so that the order of the forme of mariage used usually amongst others which can heare and speake, could not for his parte be observed. After the approbation had from Thomas the bishoppe of Lincolne, John Chippendale, doctor in lawe and commissarye, as also Mr. Richard Davye, then the mayor of the towne of Leicester, with others of his brethren, with the rest of the parishe; the sayde Thomas, for the expression of his minde instead of words, of his own accorde used these signs; first he embraced her with his armes, and took her by the hande, putt a ring upon her finger, and layed a hand upon his hearte, and then upon her hearte; and held up his hands toward heaven; and to shewe his continuance to dwell with her to his lyfes ende, he did it by closing his eyes, and digginge out of the earth with his foote, and pullinge as though he would ring a bell, with diverse other signes approved."

This is the first known written record of the acceptance of the use of sign language in a church ceremony.

Chapter I   A Pictorial History of Deaf Britain

A Deaf Wedding 1576

A computer-generated picture by the author

Chapter I A Pictorial History of Deaf Britain

Edward Bone & John Kempe in Signed Conversation
A computer-generated picture by the author

Edward Bone (c.1570-?) and John Kempe (c.1578-?)

It was about 1595, and the scene was the marketplace in the old town of Truro in Cornwall, and the Town Crier was about to give one of his regular announcements. A young man with a sharp instinct for news pushed his way through the crowd and planted himself directly in front of the speaker. The townsfolk were used to his ways and let him through to stand in his usual place. As the Town Crier spoke, the young man watched him intently, taking in all that was said. Once the speeches were over, the young man would leave and hurry to his Master, Peter Courtney (1559-1605), who was the Member of Parliament for the county, and repeat to him in very effective sign language what had been said in the marketplace. In this manner, his Master was kept well informed of the goings-on in his constituency.

When his immediate services were no longer needed, he would walk the eight miles across to the nearby village of Merther and meet with another young man. Together, these two young men would communicate with much hearty laughter in a style of sign language different to that which the first young man had used to communicate with his Master.

This young man was Edward Bone, and he was Courtney's manservant. He had a Deaf brother who had what nowadays would be called 'learning difficulties'. He was unpopular with the rest the servants because he would report to the Master any lewd behaviour. His Deaf friend was John Kempe, who was related to the Courtneys by marriage, and their meetings were recorded in a book written by Richard Carew (1555-1620) *A Survey of Cornwall*. His disinterested observation is the first written independent account in Britain of how a deaf person could lip-read, communicate with his hearing employer by signs and seek out another deaf person and communicate in a sign language not readily understood by most hearing people.

Bone is said by Carew to be 'assisted with so firme a memorie, that hee would not onely know any partie whome hee had once seene, for ever after, but also make him knowne to any other by some speciall observation, and difference', and his sign language conversation with Kempe is referred to by Carew as 'strange and often earnest tokenings' which were not understood by hearing people.

The use of these phrases, and description of communication systems, suggest that Edward Bone, although an ordinary manservant, had language and intelligence enough to adapt his daily lifestyle so that he could lip-read well, use a form of Signed English with his employer, and BSL with other deaf people, and as Deaf people do today, give people signed names for easy reference in conversation with others.

Sir Edward Gostwicke, 3rd Bart. (1620-1671): William Gostwicke (1630-1696)

Sir Edward Gostwicke was the sixth child of Sir Edward Gostwicke, 2nd Baronet of Willington, Bedfordshire, and his wife, Anne Wentworth, and became the heir when his elder brother William died as a child.

Born deaf, he succeeded to the baronetcy when aged 10 on the death of his father a few months before the birth of his youngest brother – also named William who was also deaf.

Sir Edward was described by John Hacket, Archdeacon of Bedford between 1631 and 1637, as a "sweet creature of rare perspicuity of nature whose behaviour, gestures and zealous signs have procured and allowed him admittance to sermons, prayers, the Lord's Supper and to the marriage of a lady of a great and prudent family, his understanding speaking as much in all his motion as if his tongue could articulately deliver his mind."

Sir Edward, and his brother William, were both given to pursuing women of their fancy, even after marriages (Sir Edward to a Mary Lytton, and William to a Joanna Wharton).

Sir Edward for many years pursued the affections of diarist Dorothy Osborne who was later to complain: "Just now, I was called away to entertain two dumb gentlemen. They have made such a tedious visit and I am tired of making signs and tokens for everything I had to say! Good God! How do those that always live with them? They are brothers; and the elder is a baronet, has a good estate, a wife and three or four children. He was my servant [*suitor*] heretofore and comes to see me still for old love's sake but if he could have made me mistress of the world I could not have had him. And yet I'll swear he has nothing to be disliked in him except for his want of tongue."

It is a pity, perhaps, that Dorothy Osborne rejected Sir Edward – her family was ruined by the Civil War whereas Sir Edward's deafness prevented him being involved and his estate came through unscathed, and he was quite a rich man.

John Bulwer dedicated *Philocophus, or the Deafe and Dumbe Man's Friende* to the Gostwicke brothers for their lip-reading abilities, yet we can see from Hacket's and Dorothy Osborne's letters that they used sign language. Because Sir Edward was rich and could travel, he undoubtedly met many other deaf people, and gave their names to Bulwer.

Chapter I   A Pictorial History of Deaf Britain

Sir Edward Gostwicke
By an unknown artist
Reproduced by the kind permission of the owner, S.C.Whitbread

Chapter I   A Pictorial History of Deaf Britain

Freeford Manor, Lichfield, ancestral home of the Dyott family

The Gun used by John Dyott at the Siege of Lichfield to kill Lord Brooke
Both photographs from the author's collection

John Dyott (1606 – 1664)

John Dyott, well-known locally as "Dumb" Dyott, was 37 years old when the Civil War between the Royalist forces of King Charles I and Oliver Cromwell's Parliamentarians reached the town of Lichfield in March 1643. Lichfield was being held for the Royalists by Captain Sir Richard Dyott, the father of John Dyott (not the brother as some historians have said). Sir Richard had been Stafford's MP since 1638, and was a strong Royalist supporter.

At the time the Parliamentarians laid siege to Lichfield, the Royalist garrison was small and weak, but they were determined to deny access to the Commanding Officer of the Parliamentary Army, General Robert Greville, the Lord Brooke, who had vowed to reduce Lichfield Cathedral to rubble.

John Dyott was one of only three men who were up on the castle battlements when the Parliamentarians began their assault on the morning of 2 March 1643. Those three men caused such havoc to the Parliamentarians that the assault was held up.

During a lull, a horseman expensively clad in ermine rode into view. It was Lord Brooke, who had come to see for himself what was holding up what should have been an easy assault. Almost immediately, John Dyott fired his gun, and the bullet went through Lord Brooke's right eye into the brain and the General fell dead from his horse. The assault died away with the death of Lord Brooke, and John "Dumb" Dyott was led down from the battlements to a hero's reception from the townsfolk of Lichfield.

Despite this setback, however, the parliamentary forces captured Lichfield three days later on 5 March 1643 with a renewed assault, but the Cathedral was spared destruction.

Very little is known of John Dyott after this incident that earned him fame, as he seems to have been ignored by the rest of his wealthy family. He is not mentioned in his father's Will, or in any other family Wills. He is not buried in the family vault in the Dyott Chapel in Lichfield, but is stated to have been buried in Temple Church, London in 1664. What we do know, however, is that he married a deaf and dumb girl called Katherine after the Civil War who bore him four daughters and a son. This must be one of the earliest ever-recorded marriages between two born-deaf people.

The gun with which John "Dumb" Dyott felled Lord Brooke is still in possession of the family at the ancestral home, Freeford Manor in Lichfield. It occupies pride of place on the mantelpiece in a room adorned by family portraits of long-dead soldiers, including some that fought at Waterloo and in many of Britain's foreign battles.

Samuel Pepys and the Link with Martha's Vineyard

The great diarist, Samuel Pepys, had a close encounter with a deaf boy on 9 November 1666 at a dinner where he was a guest and received news of a fire near Whitehall not long after the Great Fire of London.

> *"By and by comes news that the fire is slackened; so then we were a little cheered up again, and to supper and pretty merry. But above all, there comes in that Dumb boy that I knew in Oliver's time, who is mightily acquainted here and with Downing, and he made strange signs of the fire and how the King was abroad, and many things they understood but I could not – which I am wondering at, and discoursing with Downing about it, "Why" says he, "it is only a little use, and you will understand him and make him understand you with as much ease as may be." So I prayed him to tell him that I was afeared my coach would be gone and that he should go down and steal one of the seats out of the coach and keep it, and that would make the coachman stay. He (Downing) did this so that the Dumb boy did go down, and like a cunning roague went into the coach, pretending to sleep; and by and by fell to his work, but finds the seats nailed to the coach; so he did all he could, but could not do it; however, stayed there and stayed the coach, till the coachman's patience was quite spent, and beat the Dumb boy with force and so went away. So the Dumb boy came up and told him (Downing) all the story, which they below could see all that had passed and knew it to be true."*

Clearly, the boy's "strange signs" were not just gestures or mime, but proper sign language. Downing Street, the official residence of the British Prime Minister, is named after the man Pepys wrote about, Sir George Downing who was a government minister at the time. It is interesting to note that Downing grew up in Kent Weald in the 1630s. It was from here that the first settlers emigrated to Martha's Vineyard between 1634 and 1644, which led to British Sign Language being used for centuries on the island. In the Kent Weald, use of sign language must have been quite commonplace in the 1630s for Downing to become so familiar with it that in 1666 as a politician, he could communicate with a deaf boy with ease.

Chapter I   A Pictorial History of Deaf Britain

Samuel Pepys

Chapter I   A Pictorial History of Deaf Britain

Main Entrance, Bourton House, Bourton-on-the Hill, Gloucestershire
Little has changed since Alexander Popham lived there in the late
17th century
Photo: Richard Parris

Bourton House, from the back gardens
Photo: Author's Collection

Alexander Popham (1649 – 1708)

Alexander Popham shares with Daniel Whalley, the dubious distinction of being the first born-deaf person in Britain to have supposedly been taught to speak.

Alexander was the second-born son of Colonel Edward Popham, a Member of Parliament for Minehead, Somerset, and Anne Wharton.

Alexander's father died at sea of a fever in 1651, and his uncle, Colonel Alexander Popham, then brought up the boy.

Alexander was sent at the age of 11 in 1659 to Dr. William Holder, FRS (1616-1698) at Oxford after this eminent gentleman had undertaken to teach the boy how to speak. This appears to have had enough success to enable Dr. Holder explain at length in his *Elements of Speech etc. with an Appendix concerning persons Deaf and Dumb*, published in 1669.

However, his family were apparently not happy with the progress made by Dr. Holder, so in 1661, Alexander was sent to another Doctor of Divinity, Dr. John Wallis (1616-1703) who had already been teaching a young man named Daniel Whalley for about a year. Evidently, Alexander did not like Dr. Wallis very much and forgot much of what he had learnt through Dr. Holder's instruction.

Nonetheless, Dr. Wallis took the opportunity to present both Popham, then aged 14, and Whalley, then aged 25, before the Court of King Charles II in May 1662 where both young deaf men were said to have spoken before the King.

However, Alexander apparently uttered only one or two words and was taciturn and ill disposed in front of the King. It may be that the young lad still had strong feelings towards Royalty given his family's strong Parliamentary links.

After this event, nothing more is heard of Alexander until 1679 when he married Brilliana Harley, the daughter of Sir Edward Harley of Hereford, and went to live with her at Bourton Manor, Bourton-on-the-Hill, Gloucestershire which his family purchased for him.

He had three daughters and one son, Francis, by Brilliana. Family documents do not record whether Brilliana or any of the four children were deaf, only that one daughter died in infancy, the other two daughters remaining unmarried throughout their lives, and Francis dying without any male issue.

Alexander Popham died in early 1708 and was buried on 9 February 1708 aged 59. He left little by way of family documents, apart from some land deeds and a Will, which is rather indecipherable. The latter gives some credence to the fact that Alexander was indeed taught to read and write, and had an education of sorts, which enabled him to get married to a presumably hearing person and manage a Manor House. (Daniel Whalley's life subsequent to the presentation before the King in 1662 is poor in comparison).

Daniel Whalley (1636 – 1695)

Daniel Whalley has a special place in British Deaf History as being one of the first two *named* prelingually deaf persons to be taught to speak. Dr. John Wallis, who subsequently wrote about these experiences, taught Daniel Whalley. Dr. Wallis took the opportunity to present Daniel, together with another youth he was teaching, Alexander Popham, to the a special gathering in Whitehall in May 1662 of the court of King Charles II. Daniel Whalley was then 25 years old. The king was reported to have asked both young men their names, which were mouthed by Dr. Wallis, and the two youths told their names and where they lived.

Daniel Whalley was the sixth child of Peter and Hannah Whaley** of Northampton, who had total of 13 children, four of who died in infancy. His father was a wealthy stationer and bookbinder who was a freeman of the town of Northampton and served as Mayor in 1646-7 and again in 1655-6, during which term he died in office. At the time of his death, Peter Whaley was also MP for Northampton. Peter Whaley's wealth is evident by the bequests in his Will. Apart from the third-born son, also named Peter who evidently fell out with his father and only received £20, all the other surviving children <u>with the exception of Daniel himself</u> received handsome legacies, including land and sums of money not less than £200. In contrast, Daniel was left an annuity of £15 per annum out of the rents of Tower House.

In the Will of Hannah Whaley, his mother, who died in 1671, all children also received handsome bequests and legacies except Daniel, who only received a silver spoon and one of his mother's little silver cups, plus a burial plot.

Hannah's Will concludes with this injunction: - *". And I charge you all my children with whom I have travailed in birth that you take especial care of your poor brother Daniel, and if any affliction befall him, that you succour and comforte him all the dayes of his life.."*

For all that Dr. Wallis is supposed to have taught Daniel Whalley to read, write and to speak, it is evident that this education was insufficient to enable Daniel to support and look after himself (unlike Alexander Popham).

Daniel Whalley never married, and died at Cogenhoe, Northampton, in March 1695 and was buried in his brother, Rev. Peter Whaley's, church.

** The family name was spelt Whaley with one 'l' up to the deaths of Peter and Hannah Whaley. Some of their children spelt the family name Whalley, including Daniel – others retained the original spelling.

**Alexander Popham (aged 12), front right, and
Daniel Whalley (aged 25), behind Popham, demonstrating
Their "education" before the court of King Charles II in
May 1662 after being presented by
Dr. Wallis (facing the King and Queen)**
A computer-generated picture by the author.

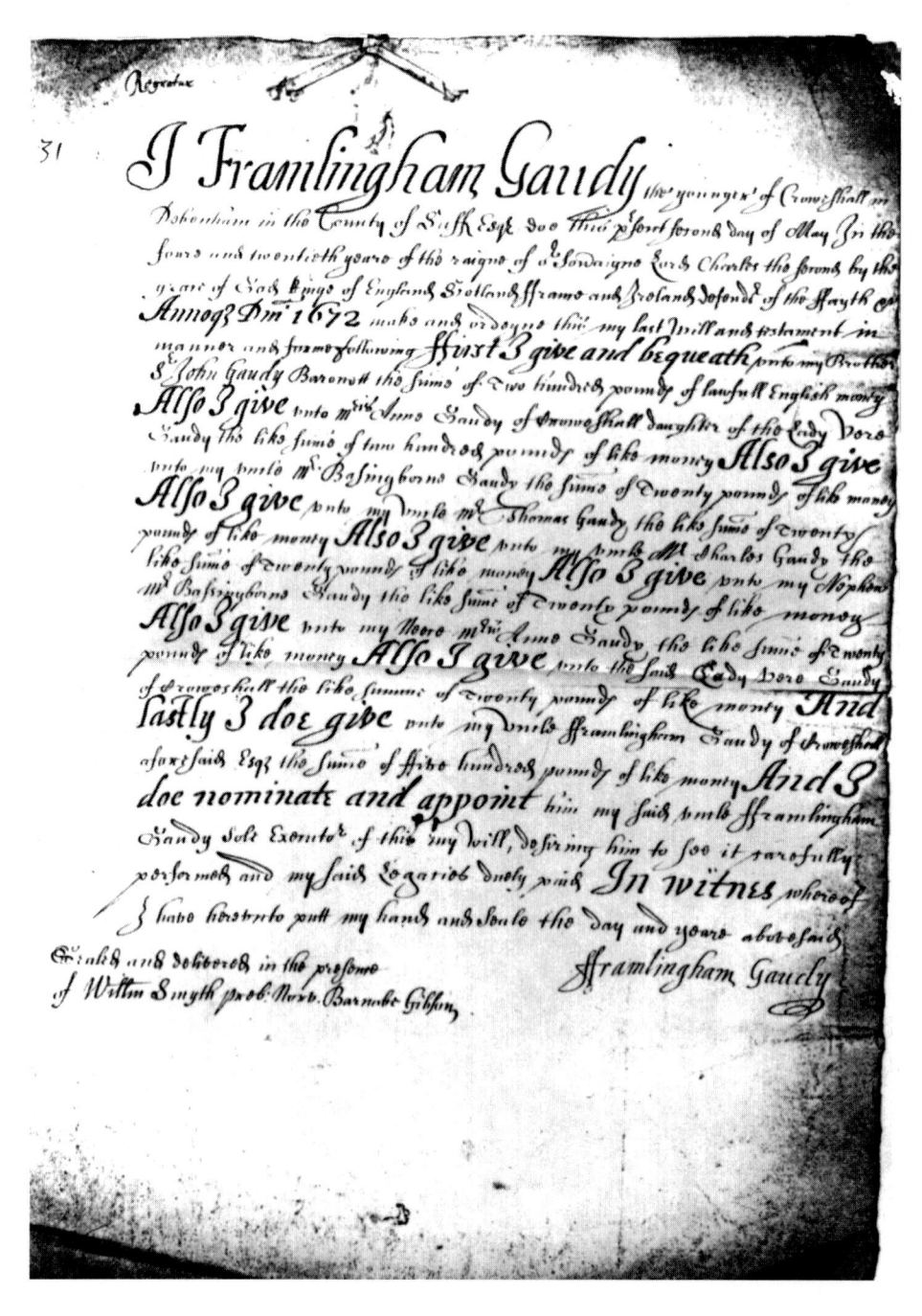

The Will of Framlingham Gaudy
The first known Will written by a Deaf person, 1672
Reproduced by the kind permission of Norfolk County Records Office

Sir John (1639 – 1708) and Framlingham Gaudy (1642 – 1673)

The deaf brothers Sir John and Framlingham Gaudy came from a wealthy family residing in Norfolk with ancestors who were at times Members of Parliament or High Sheriffs of Norfolk. They were the second and fourth of four sons of Sir William Gaudy, 2nd Baronet and his wife Elizabeth who also had a daughter Mary, but when the eldest and third brothers both died in the smallpox epidemic of 1660, John inherited the baronetcy.

All four brothers, and their sister, received an excellent education at home, and the two hearing brothers also went to Bury St. Edmunds Grammar School. After this, the two hearing brothers went on to university and the deaf brothers went to study art in the school run by Sir Peter Lely intending to become professional artists. However, the death of his elder brother in 1660 followed by his father in 1669 caused Sir John to paint for amusement only whilst Framlingham Gaudy got such a severe attack of smallpox at the height of his excellent academic progress that he retired to the family home, and after a long illness, died unmarried, aged only 31.

Framlingham Gaudy's Will, proved at Norwich on 5 September 1673, is interesting in that it is the first **known** Will to have been written by a deaf person, and contains a certificate to validate this, which says: *"These instruction for a Will were written with the proper handwriting of the said Framlingham Gaudy, who is a person both deafe and dumbe and soe not able otherwise to express his minde and this was written of his proper motion, the second day of May 1672, in the presence of William Smyth, Preb. Norv. B. Gibson."* The Will is reproduced opposite and shows the excellent quality of Framlingham's handwriting and English Grammar.

Sir John Gaudy married a Anne de Grey and had by her four children, and in a visit to Bury St. Edmunds in 1677, the diarist John Evelyn reported that *"there dined this day at my Lord's one Sir John Gaudy, a very handsome person but quite dumb, yet very intelligent by signs and a very fine painter; he was so civil and well-bred, as it was not possible to discern any imperfection in him. His lady and children were also there, and he was at church in the morning with us."*

By this, we see that Sir John, and presumably his deceased brother as well, used sign language.

Sir John and Framlingham Gaudy were given to writing a lot of letters, to their father from London, and to their invalid sister and to friends. After Framlingham's death, Sir John Gaudy appears to have done a fair amount of socialising and travelling, and seems to have been quite well known in East Anglia and in London.

The Gaudy Letters 1660-1708

The Deaf brothers, Sir John and Framlingham Gaudy, have left a legacy for Deaf historians in the wealth of correspondence that they left. These two brothers are the earliest known born-deaf sign language users who were inveterate correspondents.

Framlingham, who was probably the more academic of the two deaf brothers, wrote to his father, brothers and his sister regularly while he was studying at Sir Peter Lely's school in London, and some of these letters are preserved and wait to be discovered in the museums of Norfolk and the British Museum. In one of these letters, he wrote to his elder brother William in 1660 making reference to his invalid sister Mary (who was disfigured with goitre), *"The swelling in here face is more swelled than evere, it was quite down and is lately increased verye much. I would have you ask the King's Surgeon what hee would advise you."* In another, to his father dated 2 October 1667, he refers to his sister again and tells his father that there has been no medical benefit to Mary from the consultation by a Dr. Bokenham.

The British Museum also holds several letters written by Sir John Gaudy, many of them in poor and ink-splattered handwriting, which makes them difficult to read.

As the Gaudy brothers lived long before the start of Deaf Education in 1760, and were academically gifted **before** Alexander Popham and Daniel Whalley were presented to King Charles II in 1662, it follows that the person who taught them to read and write is probably the first true teacher of the Deaf in Britain. This person was most certainly John Cressener, the rector of West Harling, who is mentioned several times in correspondence.

Although both were painters, no paintings done by Framlingham can be traced but there are three paintings supposedly still in existence in Bury St. Edmunds by Sir John, a self-portrait of himself, and two of his wife.

There are also detailed mentions of the Gaudy brothers in other correspondence including those by their father, their art teacher Sir Peter Lely, and Sir John's son-in-law, Oliver de Neve.

Sir John's use of sign language has been recorded by the diarist John Evelyn, and is also mentioned in the Le Neve family papers particularly with regard to Sir John's grandson, Jacky, who was "retarded" (as the correspondence calls him) and brought up by his grandfather. Jacky was taught by his grandfather to communicate in *sign language* and apparently used sign language until he died at an early age. As for Framlingham, there is a mention in his father's correspondence that whilst Framlingham was seriously ill with smallpox, the family were looking for a woman able to sign to take care of him and converse with him.

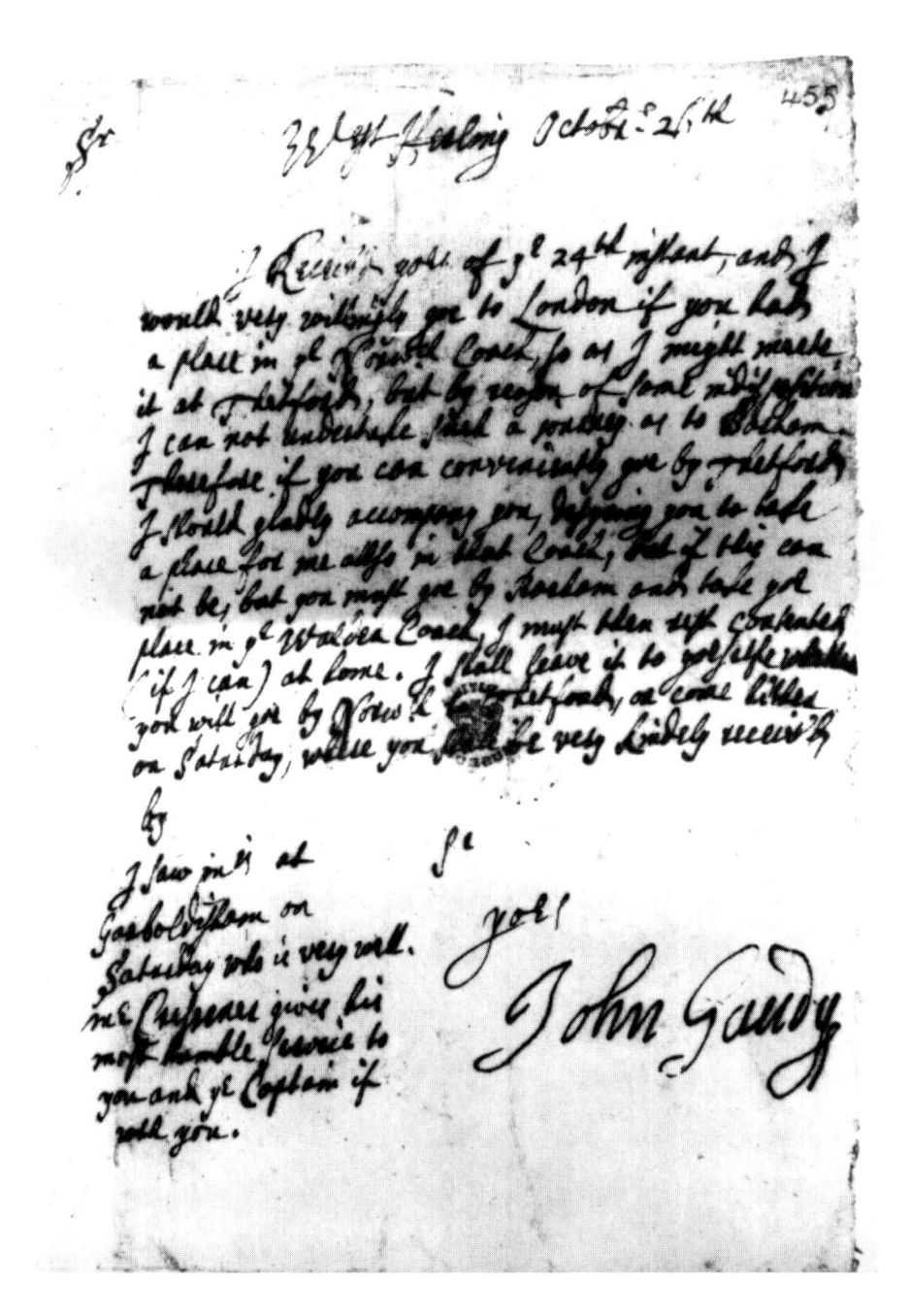

One of the letters written by Sir John Gaudy
Reproduced by the kind permission of the British Museum, London

John Bulwer's *Philocophus*
Mention is made of over 25 Deaf people in this book.

Social Interaction in the 1600s and early 1700s

Traditionally, it has always been accepted that the Deaf Community – as we know it – started with the establishment of residential schools for the Deaf. However, it is clear that there was some kind of social interaction by sign language users before the start of Deaf Education, though much of this evidence is circumstantial and not hard fact.

Sir John Gaudy, for example, mentions in some of his correspondence a family named Lukes. This family was also acquainted with the Gostwicke brothers, more specifically Sir Edward Gostwicke, so it is probable that the two baronets had known, and perhaps, met each other given that both liked to travel extensively.

It is also interesting to note that the wife of Sir Edward Gostwicke's brother William, Joanna Wharton, was the niece of Anne Wentworth, mother of Alexander Popham, so there is another link in relationships and social intercourse between deaf people of the 1660s. Popham was of course in turn acquainted with Daniel Whalley with whom he studied for over a year as Dr. John Wallis' pupil.

We also have the evidence of the marriage between John Dyott and a "deaf and dumb" girl named Katherine in 1647 who gave birth to four children, and the evidence of Edward Bone regularly meeting with John Kempe. Further evidence of some social interaction comes from Samuel Pepys of the chance meeting between the Deaf boy and Sir George Downing, and Downing's upbringing in the Kentish Weald from where the emigrants to Martha's Vineyard Island, America, originated.

Another connection between Pepys and Deaf people comes from Pepys' close friendship with fellow diarist John Evelyn, who had met and written about Sir John Gaudy.

When John Bulwer wrote his *Philocophus or the Deafe and Dumbe Man's Friende* in 1648, he mentioned the existence of over 25 sign language users in, mostly, south-east England. In this book, Bulwer makes a dedication to Sir Edward Gostwicke which is more of a treatise on lipreading but given that Sir Edward and his brother William were regular travellers, it was probably Sir Edward who gave Bulwer the names of the deaf persons mentioned in the book.

Similarly, when Daniel Defoe wrote the *Life and Times of Duncan Campbell* in 1720 (and also produced a manual alphabet chart), he mentioned the existence of several Deaf people.

That so many people knew of sign language, or the manual alphabet (with its various versions), or of other Deaf people, cannot but prove the existence of some form of social interaction between Deaf people long before the advent of Deaf Education.

Chapter II   A Pictorial History of Deaf Britain

A sign language poster on the theme of liberation
Produced by the Cheshire Deaf Society

CHAPTER II

BRITISH SIGN LANGUAGE

A Proud Heritage

Sign Language has been called 'the noblest gift God has given to deaf people' by George W. Veditz, the seventh president of the United States National Association for the Deaf.

British Sign Language (BSL) is the language of Britain's deaf community. It is a language rich in movement and space, of the hands, eyes, and body; of abstract communication as well as iconic story telling.

More importantly, BSL is also a story. It is story of a language rich in its history for the study of its people. It is a story of oppression, of despair and of renaissance. It is a battleground epitomised of man's inhumanity to man. BSL is not; contrary to what some people may think a new language although like many other languages it is constantly evolving according to society's needs, e.g. Information Technology, political correctness, space exploration – to name a few.

BSL has been around for centuries. It is a naturally occurring form of communication among people who do not hear. Although, unlike the spoken word, there is no definite record of its use prior to the sixteenth century, this is because BSL is a visual-gestural language containing no written form. Unless it is written about in other people's writings or preserved in art form, no record exists.

This lack of a long, documented history (prior to 1600 at any rate) concerns all historians interested in Deaf people and their language.

As we start the 21st Century, there is widespread recognition amongst linguists of BSL as a unique language in its own right. It is different, often strikingly so, from English but it shares with many other languages features and grammatical processes. It differs in that it has no spoken or written components.

Although it has achieved a status amongst all forward–thinking people, thanks to its exposure on television, there is still one area of prime concern to all Deaf and hearing people proud to be associated with BSL. It still has to be accorded official language status by the British government.

Early History of Sign Language

The earliest mention of the existence of any form of sign language comes in 422 BC. The ancient Greek philosopher, Socrates, had this comment to make, "If we have no voice or tongue and wished to make things clear to one another, should we not try, as the dumb actually do, to make signs with our hands, head and person generally?" This was an acknowledgement that Deaf people could communicate in an understandable form.

The Hebrew book, *Talmud*, records that deaf-mutes can hold conversation by means of gestures. This statement suggests that the rabbis who wrote the book had such conversations interpreted for them by hearing members of a deaf person's family. This is the earliest recorded statement of any visual form of language amongst deaf people; it was, even then, probably a form of Yiddish Sign Language though not recorded as such.

As it is, the earliest recorded use of sign language can be traced back to the religious order founded by St. Benedict (A.D.529). These monks were required to take vows of partial or perpetual silence, but although spoken words were considered unacceptable, signs were not, and so it came about that signs were created and passed down generations of monks. It was a Benedictine monk, Pedro Ponce de Leon of Spain, who is universally regarded as the first teacher of deaf pupils. This was *circa* 1550.

It was not until 1595 that the first recorded observation in England of sign language communication in use between two deaf people when Carew wrote about Edward Bone and John Kempe. The fluency of the observed communication suggests that use of sign language by Deaf people was well established by then. For instance, Scottish Royal Court records indicate the Princess Joanna, daughter of James 1 of Scotland, communicated by signs in the 1450s.

Interestingly, a 1450s book titled *Anngiers History of the Zion Monastery at Lisbon and Brentford* describes signs for words that are still in use! For example:

Hammer – make a signe with thyne hande up and down as thou did knockke.
Kepying (keeping) – putte thy right hande under thy left
Man – putte and holde thy berde in thy right hande.

Taking into account the nature of British lifestyle at the time, with most people rarely venturing more than 25 miles from where they lived, it is likely that many forms of early BSL were localised or based on family signs. Edward Bone, for instance, had a Deaf brother.

Without concrete documented proof, it cannot be said that sign language flourished wherever Deaf people met, but it is possible to suggest from collaboratory evidence that Deaf people would know other Deaf people in their locality, and would gravitate together to communicate as did Edward Bone and John Kempe. By these means, knowledge of the existence of Deaf people and their language would get to those who would write about them. John Bulwer, for example, mentions the existence of over 25 Deaf persons as far apart as Cheshire and Essex in *Philocophus* in 1648.

Chapter II   A Pictorial History of Deaf Britain

**Above and Below: 2 charts from John Bulwer's
Chirologia (1644)**

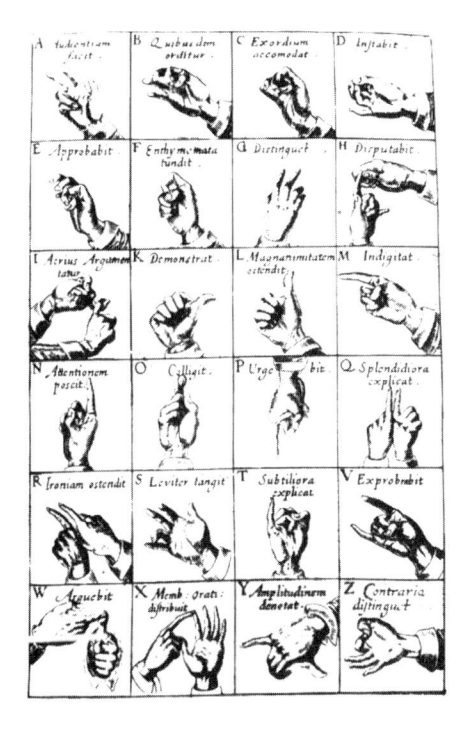

Chapter II   A Pictorial History of Deaf Britain

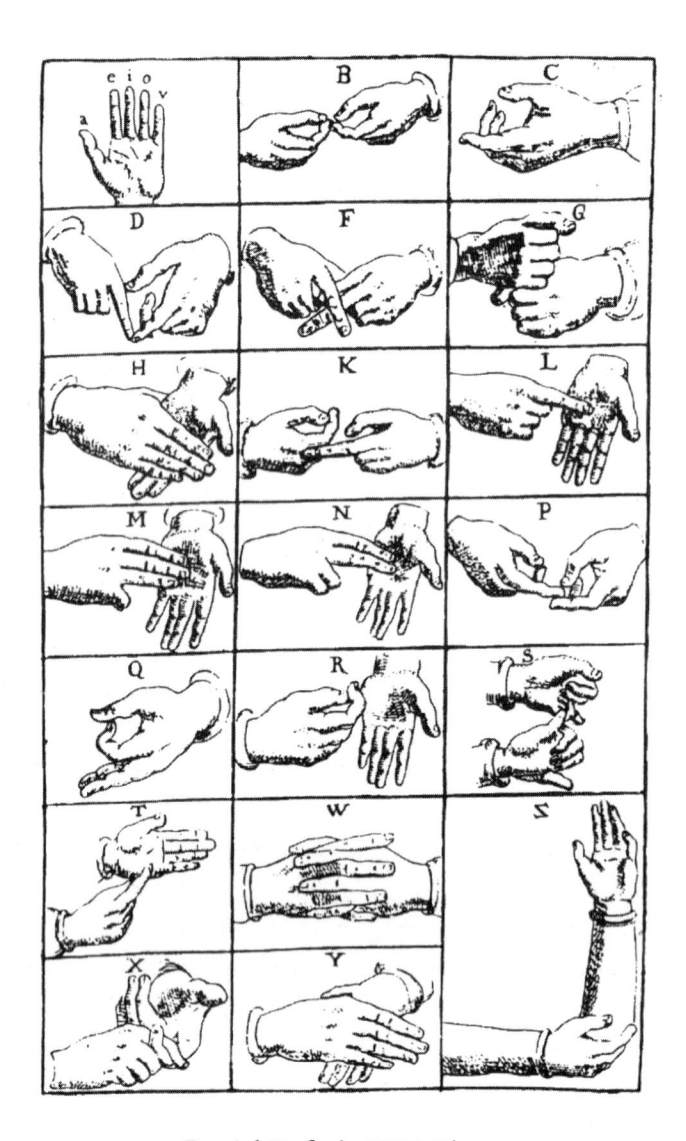

Daniel Defoe's 1720 Chart

Earliest evidence of BSL & Manual Alphabets

It is during the seventeenth-century, especially between 1640 and 1680, that we begin to see numerous references to the use of sign language in Britain. These were all independent observations from writers or diarists.

Inference can be taken from many early writings that sign language was a fact of life in 16th/17th century Britain. We know from two separate sources, the diaries of Dorothy Osborne and John Hacket, Archdeacon of Bedford, that the Gostwicke brothers, Sir Edward and William, were fluent in an early form of BSL. Likewise, we learn from another famous diarist, John Evelyn that Sir John Gaudy (who also had a Deaf brother, Framlingham) conversed fluently in sign language with his family. Sir John Gaudy is also credited in the *Le Neve Correspondence* with the education of his nephew through the use of signs. This mentions that the nephew had severe learning difficulties. Although he could hear, he could not speak or function intelligibly and had been given up as a lost cause before Sir John informally adopted him. The nephew is recorded as showing considerable improvement following this adoption.

We also learn from unexpected sources such as a quote in a letter written by George Freeman, an Art Master in Sir Peter Lely's famous art school at the time Framlingham Gaudy was there, and stricken with smallpox: *"..I should wish Mr. Bull to be carefull of him and gett him a good nurse who can signe…."*

We have evidence from Samuel Pepys that a government minister, Sir George Downing, used fluent sign language with a young, unnamed Deaf boy. It was also from the same area where Downing spent his childhood (the Kent Weald) that many of the inhabitants sailed as pilgrims to the New World, eventually setting in Martha's Vineyard where BSL flourished into the late 1800s.

It was in 1644 that John Bulwer wrote *Chironomia* and included a diagram of hand-language. Three years earlier a clergyman the Rev. John Wilkins published a book in which he explained how the letters of the alphabet were formed on the hands.

The mid-1600s was a popular period for the study of Arthrologia amongst scholars. The young Christopher Wren (later, the architect of St. Paul's Cathedral, London) was among those who studied the manual alphabet. Others included his brother-in-law, the Rev. William Holder and a Scotsman from Aberdeen named George Dalgarno who published *Didascalocophus*, or *The Deaf and Dumb Man's Tutor*.

In 1698, a booklet – *Digiti Lingua* – was published in London containing a two-handed manual alphabet chart from which the one in present day use derives. The author is unknown but is believed to be a deaf man.

Daniel Defoe, writing *The History of the Life and Adventures of Duncan Campbell* in 1720, included in this book a modified, London-based manual alphabet chart. This alphabet seems to have been used by Henry Baker, who taught a Deaf girl named Jane Forster to read and write between 1720 and 1729.

It was not until the deaf education system started in Britain in the eighteenth century that use of sign language became more widely documented.

British Sign Language: The Blossoming

From the day the first school for deaf children in Britain was established by Thomas Braidwood in Edinburgh in 1760, sign language amongst the pupils, if not amongst the staff, was in common use. Braidwood himself may have not at first known any sign language, but it is certain that he did later pick it up from his pupils and adapt his teaching methods accordingly to use a form of total communication (e.g. speech, writing, sign language and reading). The members of his family who carried on after his death, both at Edinburgh and then at Hackney, and at the newly-established schools in Birmingham and Edinburgh, all used sign language as a means of communication with their pupils. One person who trained under the Braidwoods, Robert Kinniburgh, was to become an interpreter one occasion in a court of law.

As more and more deaf schools were formed, use of sign language flourished. Many educationalists were strong advocates of the use of sign language. For example, Charles Baker, Headmaster at the Yorkshire Institution for the Deaf (Doncaster), was a prolific contributor to newspapers and magazines about the use of sign language in education.

Teaching methods in the early deaf schools in Britain relied heavily on manual communication methods. It is likely that around this period, a lot of signs of "abstract" nature (non-iconic) were created to replace long-winded fingerspellings, i.e, adjectives, adverbs, to speed up teaching.

The use of manual communication methods became more profound when these schools started to use pupil-teachers and junior teachers from suitable and gifted children who came through their ranks. People like Walter Geikie, the famous artist, and Edward Kirk, the headmaster of Leeds School for the Deaf, were pupil-teachers at their respective schools (the Edinburgh and the Yorkshire Institutions) before they moved elsewhere to carve out other careers for themselves. Practically all schools for the deaf prior to 1880 had deaf people on the teaching staff; often these outnumbered the hearing members of the staff.

It was not just in the schools that sign language and fingerspelling flourished. The era from the 1830s to the 1880s saw the establishment of many adult Deaf missions and societies. In these gatherings, the use of sign language and fingerspelling was dominant.

This emphasis on manual communication was one of the reasons that led to the establishment of pure oral schools in this country, starting with Arnold's school at Northampton in 1868. Some parents and educators felt that no effort was made, or little attention was given, to the teaching of speech in these schools.

The spread of schools where pure oralism was in use forced the manual schools to respond by implementing a combined system, i.e. using articulation as well as manual communication. However, the biggest change to use of sign language in Deaf education came after the Milan Congress of 1880 which voted to outlaw the use of sign language in the education of deaf children in favour of the pure oral method (known at that time as "The German Method").

Chapter II   *A Pictorial History of Deaf Britain*

**The Rev. Stainer delivering a church service using
sign language in the 1850s**

Services in Deaf churches such as St. Saviour's Church and the
Edinburgh Congregational Church for the Deaf and Dumb were
attended by many prominent Deaf people including
Royalty (i.e. The Prince and Princess of Wales)

Queen Victoria & Mrs. Tuffield, née Groves

The use of fingerspelling by the Royal Family was hated by those
who supported the Oral Method.

Chapter II   A Pictorial History of Deaf Britain

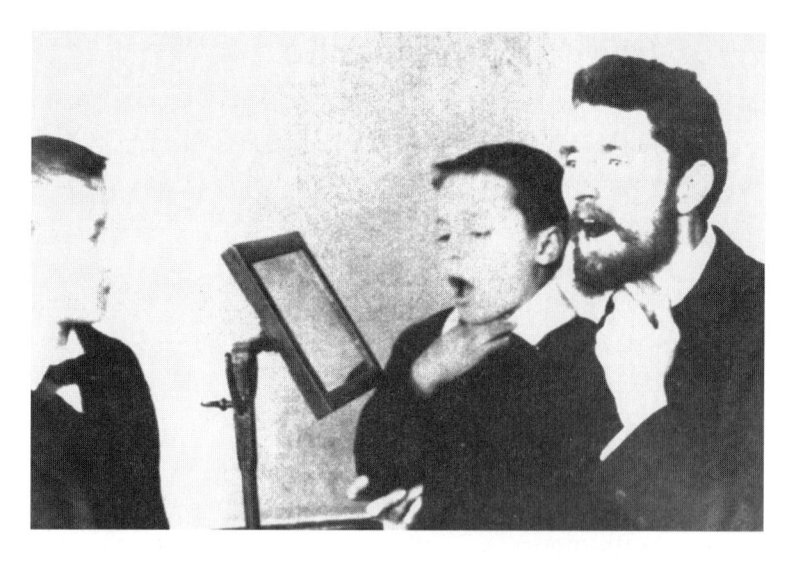

An oral method speech lesson in the 1890s
Photo: Royal West of England School for Deaf Children, Exeter

Classroom session using Oral Method
Note all the children with hands behind their backs!
This was common in oral education schools with children
trying very hard not to use their hands, which would
otherwise get smacked or whacked with a cane or a ruler.
Children would also often sit on their hands to stop themselves signing.
Photo: Royal Cross School, Preston

British Sign Language: The Rise of Oralism

It is difficult for many sign language students now at the onset of the 21st century to understand the controversy between sign language and oralism, a war, which has lasted well over a century. To compare, parallels could perhaps be drawn with the attempts to suppress the Catholic faith by rabid Protestantism in the Middle Ages when Catholic people faced a wide range of oppression, legal or otherwise.

The beliefs in oralism arose from those who considered deaf people inferior unless they were able to speak. They saw the use of sign language as the root cause of perpetuating a lower class leading to stigmatisation.

There are of course deaf people who could speak, and there always have been. That is not to say, however, that all Deaf people could use intelligible speech or that the spoken word is always the best method of educating them or giving information to them. One of the first oral schools in Britain, the Northampton School for Deaf Children set up by Arnold in 1868, was quite successful but it was very selective in its intake of pupils. The success of this elitist group was held up as a fine example of oral teaching.

Unfortunately it was seized upon as the only way forward in Deaf education, particularly in Germany and latterly in Italy and France. This gave rise to the German Method.

Much of this method was quite cruel. Deaf pupils were made to contort their faces in exaggeration of exhibiting tongue positions. Slow learners had their tongues grabbed and rulers forced into their mouths to manipulate their tongues into required positions. Hapless pupils strained themselves, particularly their lungs, in the enforcement of a means of communication, exposing them to consumption, which was a killer at that time. For instance, out of 20 pupils in a Leipzig school 17 died of the disease.

One consequence of the German Method was that the acquisition of knowledge, a proven statistic with sign language instruction was poor in comparison.

Sign language, needless to say, was ruthlessly suppressed as the German Method won the approval of parents of Deaf children and educators.

Supporters of the German Method, the oralists, saw the employment of Deaf teachers as a hindrance to their movement and philosophy and sought to remove them from their posts. They began to form a group of like minded oralists and started to campaign for the acceptance of oral-only method of educating the Deaf. The true battle on their part was for the monopolisation of Deaf education; the ridding of Deaf teachers was the paramount move to pave the way for the growth of the Oralist movement and doctrine.

The International Congress of Teachers of Deaf–Mutes, Milan 1880

What came to be viewed as the greatest injustice ever to be perpetrated against deaf people occurred in September 1880 when the highly misleading International Congress of teachers of deaf-mutes was convened in Milan, Italy.

This Congress had its roots planted in Paris in 1878 at the French Universal Exhibition when a hastily assembled meeting of twenty-seven mainly French teachers of deaf children was arranged. It was no coincidence that most of the French delegates were members of the little-known *Le Societé Peréire*, which sought to recognise Peréire as the first teacher of the deaf in that country, Peréire being a man who practised teaching by the oral method. The objective of this association was to promote the adoption of the education of deaf through oral methods to the total exclusion of sign language altogether.

The Paris meeting appointed a committee of twelve from those present to make arrangements for a second international conference. Of these twelve, eleven were from France (and naturally *Le Societé Peréire*).

Milan was chosen because of the presence of two schools, which had pursued the German Method for the previous ten years. To help to give the Congress credibility, they chose as the President one of the schools' headmasters, while the other school's headmaster was made Secretary. In addition, they appointed four Vice-Presidents and four Vice-Secretaries of whom seven were staunch supporters of the German Method.

It was easy for the congress organisers to ensure that once assembled, it would exude a strong oralist flavour. Not only was it a condition of the principal financial backer that there had to be an overwhelming vote in favour of an oral system, most of the delegates themselves were carefully selected to guarantee this vote. Out of 164 participants, eighty-seven were Italians and fifty-three were French. The only truly representative delegation was that of the United States whose five delegates had been chosen by vote earlier that year at a convention in Cincinnati.

The Deaf persons attending were Claudius Forestier, director of the Lyon School for the Deaf in France and James Denison, principal of the Columbia Institution in Washington D.C.

There were very few delegates representing large schools known to favour the combined system. For example, none of the great institutions in Edinburgh, Glasgow, Manchester, Birmingham or Yorkshire – which had in their employ a considerable number of deaf teachers of the deaf – were even present. In reality, none had even been invited, as the organisers made sure that delegates opposed to the oral system were in the minority.

Front page of the Final Report of the International Congress of Teachers of Deaf-Mutes, Milan 1880

Dr. Richard Elliott, Headmaster of the Asylum for the Deaf and Dumb, Margate from 1875 to 1908.

He was the only British delegate to vote against the resolution at Milan that sign language should no longer be used in schools.

Benjamin St. John Ackers, one of the British delegates at Milan.

Very wealthy and very tyrannical, he had a deaf daughter who he educated at home, refusing to send her to any deaf school because of what he called 'uncouth' signing. He totally abhorred sign language and had no experience at all of deaf schools.

His daughter was never heard of again after 1881, until 1932 when she was found to be leading a reclusive life in Somerset, totally unable to converse orally. She was still fearful of her sign language-hating father even though he was long dead!

Milan: The British Delegation and the Resolutions

The British sent a delegation of eight. These comprised of two Principals of Oral Schools for the Deaf, which had a combined total of less than 25 students! They were the Rev. Thomas Arnold and Susannah Hull. Another was Arthur A. Kinsey, the Principal of the Ealing College for Training of Oral teachers of the Deaf. His Secretary, Dr. David Buxton, accompanied him. He was formerly headmaster at the Liverpool Institution for the Deaf and Dumb, who had become a convert to oral methods.

Two others, a Mr. and Mrs. Ackers, were parents of a deaf girl who had been orally educated by them at home. They had no experience whatsoever of any deaf school.

Only Richard Elliott, Headmaster of the Asylum for the Deaf and Dumb at Margate, could be said to be a representative of the dominant sign language education system then prevailing in British schools.

Eight resolutions were put before the Congress, the most crucial being the first two which proposed that since education of deaf children by the *proven* German Method was far superior, the use of sign language in education should no longer be used.

The first of these two resolutions were carried by a massive 160 votes to 4 – these four being three Americans along with Richard Elliott. The second resolution, which stressed that sign language was a disadvantage, injuring speech, lip-reading and the formulation of ideas, was carried 150 votes to 16.

Thus the Congress had met the objectives of its financial backers. Under the pretext of giving speech to deaf children, the Congress had obtained through manipulation of delegates and presentation of papers sanction to ban sign language.

These declarations were sent to all existing schools for the Deaf and to those in authority in government.

The Milan Consequences

The consequences arising from Milan Congress were appalling. It not only severely retarded the development of generations of deaf children for whom the Oral Method was totally inappropriate, it also caused the loss of hundreds of teaching jobs held by deaf people throughout the world in schools for the deaf children.

In the 20 years after Milan 1880, the number of Deaf schools that allowed teaching through sign language fell throughout the world. In 1850, there were 26 schools for deaf children in the USA – all used sign language; by 1900, there were 139 schools, and in every one the use of American Sign Language was forbidden to the point of pain. It was a similar story in France (160 schools and French Sign Language allowed in none of them) and Britain (87 schools and BSL allowed in none of them). An entire generation of educators who were themselves Deaf were kicked out of teaching posts and thrown into unemployment and poverty. It is estimated that in the decade after Milan, at least 2000 Deaf teachers of deaf children lost their employment throughout the world, mainly in Europe and the North American continent.

In Britain, the appointment of Edward Kirk to the post of Principal at the Leeds School for Deaf Children in 1881 was unique. It was to be over 100 years before another Deaf person was appointed Head of a School for Deaf Children in Britain.

In order to suppress sign language, oral educators did everything they could to kill it. The co-operation of parents was sought, Deaf teachers were refused employment, and Deaf children were told that using signs was bad and degrading. They were told that they would not grow up to be 'normal' people if they could not speak or lip-read; many children were told that if they went to deaf centres, they were failures for deaf clubs were dens of depravity where sign language flourished.

A sizeable number of Deaf children for whom the Oral System was totally inappropriate ended up in mental institutions for life. Some methods of suppressing the use of sign language were extremely harsh; punishments frequently included rapping children's hands with stiff sticks or rulers, tying up the children's hand behind their back or in brown paper bags. Other forms included making them sit on their hands to keep them from going astray and forming signs; depriving children of amenities; making them write out ' I must not sign' repeatedly for up to an hour, or even more. Even natural gestures as innocent as describing, for example, the size of a fish incurred the wrath of the teachers.

It was the greatest injustice ever done to Deaf People.

The Reverend William Stainer, Head of the London Day Schools Board for Deaf Children, who attended the Milan Congress as an observer.

He embraced the Congress resolutions with such enthusiasm that he implemented the policy in his classes as soon as he could.

Jane Elizabeth Groom (1839-1908)

Born in Wem, Shropshire and educated at the Manchester Institution for the Deaf and Dumb, she had a career as a Deaf Teacher for over 25 years.

She was one of those dismissed by the Rev. Stainer following the Milan Congress. More than 2000 Deaf teachers all over the world lost their jobs as a result of Milan

Satirical cartoon
British Deaf magazines around 1890 fought a losing battle to prevent the spread of oralism in deaf education. Many resorted to satire to make their points against the influence of oralists and those in government.
This cartoon is from the *British Deaf Mute*.

British Sign Language: The Government Backs Suppression

In 1889, the government of the day published a report by the Royal Commission on the Education of the Blind, and the Deaf and the Dumb. It was a review of the prevailing education of children with sensory disabilities. It accepted at face value the entire recommendations of the Milan Congress.

It pandered to the evidence presented by those in favour of the introduction of the oral system, and the suppression of sign language. Any evidence submitted by Deaf people, or by teachers in favour of the use of sign language was ignored. A typical statement, or point of view, offered by a supporter of oralism was one by Dr. David Buxton, the former headmaster of the Liverpool Institute for the Deaf and Dumb:

'I am so thoroughly in earnest in my advocacy of the superiority of the oral system, that I should be very glad to see the other extinguished; but; know that must be a matter of time. The oral system is incomparably the best; it is not open to question at all, because it assimilates to deaf to the class with whom they live. If I want to communicate by signs to a deaf child I have to descend to his level, but by the oral I raise him to my level. For a time, perhaps, the combined system may struggle on; I think that is very probable. But that the sign system will last in itself, I have not the slightest expectation – I think sign language will die out'.

Many oral advocates held exactly the same view. Sign language was blamed for everything that was held to be 'bad' about Deaf people – it was blamed for their lack of speech, for their poor grasp of the English language, for the high rate of intermarriage amongst deaf people. If anything was wrong with Deaf people, sign language was the cause of it.

A Deaf man called Abraham Farrar, who was regarded by the oralist advocates as their greatest triumph, became so concerned over the intensity of the moves to suppress and outlaw sign language that he counselled for '…tolerance over the use of sign language in education'. It would be, he stated in an article to a newspaper, a grave mistake to regard oralism as the vehicle by which all Deaf people could make progress. Even he was contemptuously brushed aside. After all, when it really came down to it, Abraham Farrar was Deaf too, and Deaf people's views were of no consequence.

It was the greatest disservice ever done to Deaf people in Britain by any British government.

British Sign Language: Keeping the Spirit Alive During the Years of Oppression

All attempts to suppress sign language only caused Deaf people to defy them. Children would use it on the sly behind teachers' backs, or underneath desks, or in the lavatories. Unfortunately, such use also came to be associated with deceit, stigma and a negative, guilty attitude. It was like the forbidden fruit, and visits to adult deaf centres by Deaf schoolchildren became daring – children would in fact 'dare' each other to go, and those who would not were labelled 'chicken'. The deceit and the stigma slowly spread out amongst the general population who came to view deaf institutes and social centres as 'loony bins', and as such places to be avoided.

Those Deaf children who did not succeed in oral schools, and there were many of them, were labelled 'oral failures' and the standard of deaf education plunged. Children who did get through an oral education often felt misfits in the wider society. Many were so indoctrinated against going to deaf clubs or functions that they were psychologically damaged. They led lonely and isolated lives before they would 'discover' that the deaf way of life, the deaf sub-culture, was not as bad as it had been painted, that the deaf community and the deaf heritage were rich in opportunities for fulfilment.

Fortunately for British Sign Language, there were a number of issues, which ensured its survival despite all attempts to ruthlessly suppress it. First and foremost, many Deaf people left school with imperfect unintelligible speech, speech that was never going to be good enough to enable them to cope effectively in the wider society. In addition, many also had poor lip-reading skills. For those people, BSL was their most effective means of communication, and thus freed of the restraints imposed on them by schools and oralism, which blighted them during their youth, Deaf people began to use it in earnest.

Secondly, the Deaf Community had, and still has, a very firm core, which could never be eradicated by the oralists however hard they tried. This was the ten per cent who had deaf parents. In such families, the use of British Sign Language was an everyday fact of life. Often, especially in rural areas the homes of families where BSL was in everyday use, were attractions for other local Deaf people. Deaf people would seek out other Deaf people in the same way that Edward Bone would seek out John Kempe back in 1595.

Thirdly, the British Deaf and Dumb Association, despite its weak position and being practically taken over at the top and run by hearing people, nonetheless managed to weld together a social, leisure, welfare and educational infrastructure which maintained a fabric out of which the Deaf Community could plan its resurgence.

There were also some individuals, like Harry Ash of London, who attempted with little success to promote BSL to members of the public through a series of publications. His *Guide to Chirology* written, designed and printed by himself during the First World War was the first attempt at creating Deaf Awareness among the public.

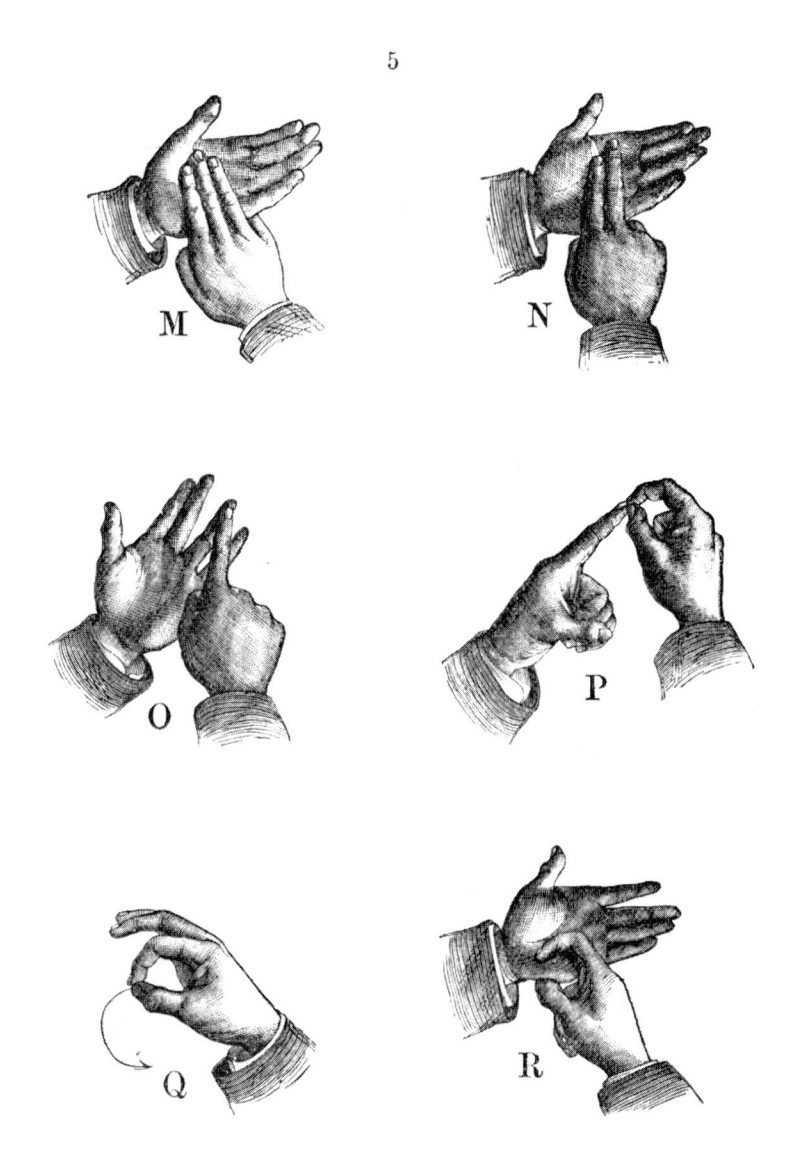

Q is executed by putting the hand in the position represented in the engraving, and by moving it in the direction of the curved line with the arrowhead.

Part of a manual alphabet booklet
issued by the
Asylum for the Deaf and Dumb, Margate in
1830 promoting the use of the sign language.
Note the "Q" and how it differs today.

Chapter II   A Pictorial History of Deaf Britain

Allan Brindle Hayhurst, M.B.E.
Secretary-Treasurer of the British Deaf Association

Started a project to create a British Sign Language dictionary he would not live to see finished.
Photo: Author's Collection

British Sign Language: The Renaissance

Although for many years Deaf adults like George Healey, James Paul, Francis Maginn and William Agnew, all highly respected pillars of the community, fought a tough battle to stop the suppression of British Sign Language, few made any impact. Agnew, in particular, was extremely well read and a compulsive letter writer. He bombarded many influential newspapers and magazines about sign language. He drew tremendous pride from the fact that he could communicate as an equal with Queen Victoria.

Not even the British Deaf and Dumb Association could halt the tide of the onslaught of oralism and the threat to sign language.. At its very first Congress in 1890, a resolution was passed that the Congress *'…indignantly protests against the imputation that the finger and sign language is barbarous. We consider such a mode of exchanging our ideas as most natural and indispensable, and that the combined system of education is by far preferable to the so-called Pure Oral'*.

However, despite some schools tolerating it (usually out of the classroom), BSL remained for many years a 'forbidden fruit', its users shunned and relegated to a sub-human class by society. It was not until developments in the 1950s by Dr. William Stokoe initiated research into American Sign Language that most, if not all, sign languages began to come out of their years of oppression.

Dr. William Stokoe was a linguist who became fascinated by the language of signs in use on the Gallaudet College campus, and started his own research. He proved that American Sign Language had all the necessary ingredients that made up a language: the points of contrasts, the morphemes, and the syntactical patterns. He was the first linguist to subject sign language to all the tests of a real language, and it withstood all the tests. However, when he published his initial findings in 1960, few people paid attention. He was nearly alone in his belief that sign language was a language in its own right.

Dr. Stokoe's research into sign language excited Allan Brindle Hayhurst, the Secretary-treasurer of the British Deaf Association, so much that he started a project he was not to live to finish – a BSL dictionary. Hayhurst's work on this project was eventually taken over by Durham University as agents for the BDA.

British Sign Language: The Awakening, Manchester 1985

Perhaps more significantly for British Sign Language, Dr. Stokoe's work came to the attention of British linguists and psychologists like Margaret Deuchar and others at Moray House College, Edinburgh, and Bristol University. At Edinburgh Mary Brennan in 1980 and at Bristol Dr. J. Kyle in 1981 both formed teams to do research into British Sign Language. These teams both found that BSL was indeed a language and one of greater complexity than ever had been suspected.

By simply declaring that British Sign Language was a language, people's perceptions changed.

Deaf people now officially had something positive and attractive which for them was a matter of pride, a priceless heritage, a thriving sign language, vibrant and still alive more than a century after its death had been prophesied in 1889!

One of the little-known but most significant turns of the renaissance of Deaf people and their sign languages came at the International Congress on the Education of the Deaf, held in Manchester in July 1985.

There had been for the past decade considerable changes in attitudes to British Sign Language. These changes heralded into being, for example, the Council for the Advancement for the Communication of Deaf People (CACDP), sign language examinations, the training of sign language interpreters, and so forth.

None of these changes, however, had the same impact on British Sign Language as did the momentous events that took place in Manchester in that unique week of July 1985.

Literally hundreds of Deaf people ambushed the Congress.

Brilliantly co-ordinated jointly by the National Union of the Deaf and the Deaf Tribune Group of the BDA's North-West Regional Council, and well supported by Deaf American, Swedish and Danish friends, they held an Alternative Congress. This took place during the same week as the International Congress at Manchester Deaf Centre. Scores of delegates abandoned the official congress, which became a public relations disaster.

The highlight of the Alternative Congress was the presentation of a paper by Harlan Lane. The massive club hall was packed with hearing and Deaf people alike from all over the world who sat, riveted and enthralled, as Harlan Lane delivered his paper. The four interpreters alongside him sweated to keep in pace with the delivery – it was impossible without breaking the delivery even to relieve them. Standing room in the hall was also at a premium, with hardly room to move.

There are certain dates and times in the history of humanity which are vividly imprinted in people's minds. With respect to Deaf History, no one who was privileged to be at Manchester in 1985 will ever forget the re-birth of Deaf renaissance.

Making their points
Mabel Davis (above), a Deaf teacher and
Gloria Pullen (below), a Deaf researcher at Bristol University,
at the International Congress on Education for the Deaf,
Manchester, 1985

Marching for British Sign Language

In the summer of 1999, the Federation of Deaf People proposed a March through London for the recognition of BSL.

The concept took off and in 2000, another March was held in London. There were also Marches for BSL in Birmingham, Bradford and a host of other towns.

British Sign Language Today

BSL has come a long way since the earth-shattering events of Manchester 1985. A few months after this event, the first steps were taken by the BDA in conjunction with the University of Durham to address the shortage of trained teachers of sign language, needed to meet the mushrooming growth of sign language classes. This gave birth to scores of qualified teachers of BSL.

BSL is now a recognised teaching subject, with appropriate standards of qualifications set by CACDP, agreed by the government's Qualifications Curriculum Authority (Q.C.A.). In 1996-8, only people studying first aid courses topped the numbers of sign language students in the Further Education Funding Council list. The numbers of people studying BSL were more than French, German, Russian and Spanish combined.

Sign Language Marathons in the 1980's as a means of fundraising or promoting Deaf Awareness, exposure on television either through specific programmes for Deaf people or on the news, mentions in various legislation or official documentation have all helped to give BSL a status it has never previously held.

The issue of human rights and disability discrimination legislation has also elevated BSL into a quasi–legal status insofar as dissemination of information (via video or CD-ROM) and provision of interpreting is concerned. Government departments have to issue relevant information to Deaf people on an equal status to other spoken and written languages. The Police and Criminal Evidence Act stipulates that Deaf people arrested for a crime cannot be interviewed without proper and adequate sign language interpretation.

BSL still does not, however, hold official language status in the U.K., and consequently, in June 1999, a 'March for BSL' was organised by the newly formed Federation of Deaf People in London. It was attended by thousands of supporters who braved a torrential downpour. This did not dampen the enthusiasm of Deaf people for this campaign, and more Marches for BSL were held in 2000 in other towns and cities besides London.

Only time will tell if this will ever be achieved. Compared to the years of oppression BSL is now a vibrant, thriving language that gives pride to its users, and employment to hundreds of Deaf and hearing as teachers, interpreters, communication support workers in education, as well as linguists, researchers, care workers.

In short, it is the British Deaf people's greatest living heritage.

Chapter III   A Pictorial History of Deaf Britain

Duncan Campbell (1680-1730)
Privately educated, he had a high intelligence and a sharp mind but acquired a reputation as a "charlatan" and a "fake". He was also accredited with developing the manual alphabet into a more acceptable form.

CHAPTER III

DEAF EDUCATION 1760-1900

The Early Teachers of the Deaf

It is generally accepted that prior to 1600, there were no Deaf people who had been educated to any degree. There were no schools for deaf children and unless the deaf child came from a wealthy family, it was unlikely that any received any form of private tuition.

By the middle of the 17th century, following the publication of John Bulwer's two books on chirology, there was some interest in the theories of the teaching of speech and language to deaf people, which led to two different men to experiment with deaf subjects. They were a Dr. William Holder, and Dr. John Wallis. Dr. Holder, the brother-in-law of Christopher Wren, concentrated his efforts on speech teaching whilst Dr. Wallis made use of a manual alphabet taken from a Spanish source to teach English words.

Both Dr. Holder and Dr. Wallis may be said to be the first teachers of speech to the deaf. In reality, neither was really as successful as they made themselves out to be, as a study of their subjects Alexander Popham and Daniel Whalley show. At least Dr. Wallis did succeed in showing the Royal Society as well as the King and his court in 1662 what could be done with the speech of deaf people,

By their feud with each other, Holder and Wallis laid the groundwork for the future of education of the deaf. The groundwork was followed up by George Dalgarno of Aberdeen (who – as far as is known – never taught a deaf person, but nonetheless published in 1680 an account of how it could be done, using a manual alphabet as well as speech training). Forty years later, Henry Baker is reported to have taught a Miss Jane Forster from 1720 to 1729 to read, write, speak and understand the English language. He is also said to have taught a number of deaf people (this is recorded in Defoe's *Life and Times of Duncan Campbell)*. However, Baker left no indication of the method he used in his teaching.

Duncan Campbell himself was educated under Wallis' method by a doctor undertaking the role of a private tutor in 1685. The education he received served him well and he excelled in reading, writing and manualism. Campbell made a fortune as a "professional predictor" communicating mainly in writing.

Though the two eminent and feuding Doctors of Divinity are regarded as the first teachers for teaching deaf people in Britain to speak, there were in fact earlier records of Deaf people being educated. Bulwer, in his book *Philocophus*, published in 1648, actually names several deaf people who were able to write. It is unfortunately extremely difficult to find this evidence. However, one person not regarded as a teacher of the deaf is known to have taught two deaf brothers to read and write in immaculate English. He was not a learned man of letters with a keen desire to create fame for himself like Holder or Wallis – he was simply a rector and friend to the Gaudy family of Norfolk. Unfortunately, very little is known of him except where he is mentioned in Wills and family correspondence. His name was John Cressener, and his legacy to deaf heritage is that many of the letters written by the deaf brothers between 1658 and 1703 still exist. They can be seen in the British Library.

The First School for the Deaf

By 1760, there was still no school in Britain where deaf children could be educated. The few educated Deaf people at that time had been taught by private individuals like Henry Baker who never divulged the methods they used in their teaching. In the first quarter of that year, a wealthy Edinburgh merchant, Alexander Shirreff, approached Thomas Braidwood (1715 – 1806) the owner of a mathematical school in Edinburgh and asked him to educate his ten-year old deaf son with a view to his learning to write. Thus the first school for the deaf in Britain (or for that matter, the world) was started.[1]

Braidwood was fascinated by the concept and challenge of teaching deaf children and abandoned any further aspirations at teaching only mathematics, devoting the remainder of his life to the teaching of deaf children. These children were mostly those of wealthy parents.

The school was known as Braidwood's Academy for the Deaf and Dumb, and is mentioned in Sir Walter Scott's novel, *The Heart of Midlothian.*

In October 1773, Dr. Samuel Johnson visited the school on his way to the Western Isles of Scotland. He was impressed enough to write as follows: *'There is one subject of philosophical curiosity in Edinburgh which no other city has to show; a College for the Deaf and Dumb, who are taught to speak, to read and to write, and to practise arithmetic, by a gentleman whose name is Braidwood. It was pleasing to see one of the most desperate of human calamities capable of so much help: whatever enlarges hope will exalt courage. After having seen the deaf taught arithmetic, who would be afraid to cultivate the Hebrides'?*

Braidwood never published any account of his teaching methods, but we can gather enough from authentic sources to know that Braidwood used a form of total communication.

Braidwood had a number of pupils who went on to make remarkable achievements after they had left his Academy: Shirreff, John Goodricke, and Francis Mackenzie, to name a few. None of these people had any understandable speech in later life, and had to rely on sign language or writing for communication purposes.

The father of another pupil, Francis Green, however, published *Vox oculis subjecta: A Dissertation on the most curious and important art of imparting speech, and the knowledge of language, to the naturally deaf, and (consequently) dumb; with a particular account of the Academy of Messrs. Braidwood of Edinburgh.* The Latin title was the Academy's motto, and in this account, we learn that Braidwood included a fair amount of oral teaching.

Incidentally, the pupil referred to above, Charles Green, was the first deaf American to receive an education.

In 1783, the Braidwoods moved their school to Mare Street in Hackney, London, where it was carried on by Thomas Braidwood's daughter and her son after his death in 1806.

Chapter III   A Pictorial History of Deaf Britain

Braidwood's Academy for the Deaf
The first school for the Deaf

Chapter III   A Pictorial History of Deaf Britain

The Asylum for the Deaf and Dumb on Old Kent Road, London 1810's

The Old Kent Road School (re-built 1885)

The Asylum for the Deaf and Dumb

The first *public* school for the deaf was established in Grange Road in Bermondsey, London, with Dr. Joseph Watson, a distant relative of Thomas Braidwood, as Principal following the efforts of a distinguished Congregational minister, Rev. John Townsend, who had become acquainted with a Mrs. Creasy.

Mrs Creasy had a Deaf son named John who had formerly been educated at the Braidwood Academy, both in Edinburgh and in Hackney. The Reverend Townsend became so interested in the subject of the education of deaf children that he resolved to found a charitable institution for the indigent deaf. He succeeded in securing the interest of a wealthy man named Henry Thornton, and obtained subscriptions from a number of other people.

In November 1792, the new school was opened with six children and grew rapidly until it had 70 children in 1809.

The establishment of the Asylum for the Deaf and Dumb Poor at Bermondsey was such a success that demand for places always outstripped capacity.

This led the governors of the school to purchase a freehold piece of ground in Old Kent Road, London, for £1,800 in 1803 and building work commenced on a new school that could accommodate 120 pupils. The new school was opened in 1809 at a cost of £12,000 and the premises at Grange Road were eventually disposed of.

Queen Charlotte visited the school in 1817 with Princess Elizabeth, and presented the institution with fifty guineas and twenty guineas respectively. The Queen accepted the title of 'Protectress of the Asylum for the Deaf and Dumb'.

The school was enlarged in 1819 to accommodate 200 pupils, and had on its roll a total of 219 pupils with 4 hearing and 8 deaf teachers.

The first Headteacher of the school was Dr. Joseph Watson whose publication, *Instruction of the Deaf and Dumb* (1809), was the first of its kind since Dalgarno's work in 1661. The school taught trades such as shoemaking, tailoring, painting, bookbinding, cotton and twine spinning, sackmaking and ropemaking.

In 1830, the first link with Margate was made with the establishment of four beds at the sea-bathing hospital for the benefit of pupils of the school.

In 1860 the first branch school was opened in Margate and this saw such tremendous strides in the development of healthy deaf children that by 1873 it had been decided to transfer the whole school to Margate. This transfer was to take a number of years, and it was not until 1903 that the final transference of pupils from the Old Kent Road premises took place. (The building at Old Kent Road was incidentally taken over by the London Schools Board and continued as a deaf school until 1968).

In 1910, King George V and Queen Mary became Patrons, and an Act of Parliament was passed in 1915 to enable the Asylum to change its title to the 'Royal School for the Deaf & Dumb Children, Margate'. In 1975-6, the school was rebuilt on the same site with modern classrooms and accommodation and the old buildings were demolished.

The First Deaf Teachers of the Deaf

Braidwood's Academy in Hackney was the first Deaf school to employ ex-pupils as teachers of Deaf children, such as John Creasy. It was, however, the Asylum for the Deaf and Dumb in Old Kent Road that first trained and employed many Deaf people to become teachers of the children at the Asylum. William Hunter was the first teacher. He was trained by John Creasy and started teaching in 1804.

John Creasy (1774 –1855?)

John Creasy's date of birth is unknown but he was baptised at Deptford on 18 September 1774. The son of John and Mary Creasy, he was for almost ten years a pupil of Thomas Braidwood at his Academy, first at Edinburgh and then at Hackney.

On Sunday 20 May 1792, John Creasy and his mother met the Rev. John Townsend, the minister of a Congregational church in Bermondsey. During her conversation with Townsend, she suggested that a school should be founded for the education of poor deaf children. This had been the dream of Thomas Braidwood but he failed to receive public encouragement in 1769. In support of this, she presented before Townsend her tall young deaf son, John, for whom she had paid £1,500 in fees during his ten years of education at Braidwood Academy.

The new Asylum was founded on 14 November 1792 with the first six poor deaf children admitted in a humble building in Fort Place on Grange Road, Bermondsey. This grew into a large school that was to be famously known as the London Asylum for the Deaf and Dumb, Kent Road. As the school grew during its formative years, its principal, Joseph Watson, employed Creasy not only to teach his private pupils, but to train the bright Asylum pupils to become teachers. It is not known where or when he died but it is said that he lived on to a cheerful and active old age.

William Hunter (1785-1861) and George Banton (1812–1879)

William Hunter and George Banton were just two of the pupils who went on to become teachers at the London Asylum for the Deaf and Dumb during the period when Joseph Watson and his son Thomas were headmasters.

Born in Southwark to a poor wharfinger's clerk and his wife, William Hunter is noteworthy because he was among the second batch of pupils admitted to the institution in 1793, and was trained by John Creasey to be a teacher. He completed his teacher training in 1804, and was still teaching at the age of 76 when he died. His teaching career spanned an incredible 57 years.

George Banton was born in Finsbury, Middlesex on 7 July 1812, one of the three Deaf sons and two hearing daughters of George and Sarah Banton. After a short private education, he transferred to the London Asylum for the Deaf and Dumb in Old Kent Road, Southwark as a "pay-list" pupil.

After being chosen to train as a teacher, George Banton went on to serve the same school for 50 years before retiring in 1875, a year before his death.

George Banton, (1812-1879)
The Old Kent Road Asylum, Deaf Teacher of the Deaf

Chapter III   A Pictorial History of Deaf Britain

The Deaf and Dumb Institution, Canongate, Edinburgh

Donaldson's Hospital (now Donaldson's College for the Deaf), Edinburgh

Classroom at Donaldson's Hospital, Edinburgh: 1890s
Photo: Courtesy of the Governors of Donaldson's School.

Edinburgh: Institution for the Deaf and Dumb; Donaldson's Hospital

For a period of just over twenty years from 1760, the rich of Scotland had the means of obtaining education for their deaf children through Braidwood's Academy. However, for the poor no provision was made.

With the removal of the Academy to Hackney, London, in 1783 there was no education available in Scotland for deaf children, but during the first eighteen years of the London Asylum's existence few individuals Scotland were admitted to receive its benefits. However, the difficulty of gaining admission, together with the expense of removal to so great a distance and the disinclination of parents to have their children so far separated from them, showed the necessity of having a similar institution in Scotland.

In June 1810, an institution was established for the education of the deaf and dumb poor belonging to Scotland. A grandson of Thomas Braidwood, John Braidwood, was engaged as the first teacher. In May 1811, a new assistant was engaged to work alongside John Braidwood and his name was Robert Kinniburgh. However, barely two months later in July, John Braidwood abruptly left his post and departed for America. Consequently, the school had to be temporarily closed.

John Braidwood's behaviour outraged the committee of the Edinburgh Institution, and they made their feelings known to the Braidwood family in Hackney. Apparently, the committee and the Braidwood family came to an arrangement where Kinniburgh would be trained in the art of teaching the deaf by the Braidwood Academy free of charge, provided that Kinniburgh agreed to be bound by a bond under a penalty of £1000. This bond that he would not communicate his teaching methods to anyone, confining his teaching only to the poor, was to last for a duration of seven years. Having acquired a competent art of instruction, Kinniburgh returned to Edinburgh in December 1811 and took charge of the pupils, while John Braidwood having departed to America where he began teaching a private class of deaf children at Bolling Hall in Cobbs, Virginia.

Starting with a pupil roll of 10 children, the school moved four times as the student roll increased each year, until 1824 when it settled in Henderson Row where it remained for over a century until it merged with Donaldson's Hospital.

A little known and interesting account of a pupil's education at the Institution is contained in a book called *Memoirs of My Youth* by Alexander Atkinson published in 1865.

In 1830, a wealthy Edinburgh bookseller, James Donaldson, bequeathed the whole of his estate to the founding of a hospital to be named after him for poor boys and girls. As a result, Donaldson's Hospital was built and opened in 1850 – a building so magnificent that even Queen Victoria said she would like to live there. Donaldson's has an interesting history, in that it was the only boarding school in Britain where hearing and deaf children were educated together. In its heyday, it had around 300 children, of whom 120 were deaf and many of the hearing children became fluent in sign language.

When Donaldson's merged with the Royal Edinburgh Institution for Deaf and Dumb Children, the Hospital discontinued the practice of admitting hearing children and renamed itself Donaldson's School for the Deaf.

The building still stands to this day, still serving deaf education.

The Growth of Deaf and Dumb Institutions, 1812-1850

The success of deaf education was watched with interest in many other cities in Britain. Generally, there was an abundance of philanthropic people willing to embrace charitable causes, and the education of deaf children aroused great interest. The majority happened because a number of wealthy men (and women) came across deaf children in the street and found they were not in receipt of any form of education. In Manchester, for example, a Mr. Phillips found that in one large cotton factory, the workers between them had 19 deaf children of various ages without speech.

In the majority of cases, funds were obtained through public meetings, which were well reported in the local newspapers of the day, enabling many people to find a cause to subscribe to. This happened in Birmingham, Glasgow, Manchester, Liverpool, Exeter, Doncaster and Newcastle-upon-Tyne leading to the founding of some great institutions, some of which still remain to this day. The same developments happened in Northern Ireland and in Wales, but in the case of Northern Ireland, the school that was set up was known as the Ulster Institute for the Deaf and Dumb and the Blind, taking in children with both sensory impairments.

The education that deaf children received in these institutions was a good one, although some places found it difficult to start with. Although some institutions obtained their first teachers or headmasters from others that had been established before them, most teachers were dedicated rather than trained. For example, at the General Institution for Deaf and Dumb Children, Edgbaston, Birmingham (later to be known as the Royal School for Deaf and Dumb Children), the first headmaster was Thomas Braidwood. At that time, he was running his private Academy in Hackney, and by coming to Birmingham in 1812, he effectively terminated over 50 years continuous private instruction by his family, starting in Edinburgh in 1760.

Similarly, the Manchester Institution (later to become the Royal Residential Schools for Deaf Children) was able to start only because Dr. Joseph Watson, the Head Teacher at the London Asylum, allowed his principal assistant, William Vaughan, to leave and become the headmaster of that institution.

By the late 1820s, enough educational establishments for deaf children had been in existence to enable assistant masters at these first schools to be appointed headmasters of the new schools starting up. This happened at Exeter and Doncaster, where Henry Bingham and Charles Baker were appointed respectively to the new headmaster posts. Both these men had been assistant masters at the Birmingham Institution.

Many other teachers learned to do their job increasing well through experience, and trained on the job. At all times, both deaf and hearing teachers worked together as it was no bar in those days for a Deaf person to be able to be a teacher. John Creasy, who was so instrumental in helping to start the London Asylum, was himself a Deaf teacher of private pupils at the Asylum.

Chapter III A Pictorial History of Deaf Britain

The Manchester Institution
In Salford, 1823

The Manchester Institution at Old
Trafford, 1837 - 1967

Deaf and Dumb Institution,
Liverpool.

Yorkshire Institution for the Deaf
And Dumb, Doncaster.

Institution for the Deaf and Dumb,
Birmingham, 1852.

West of England Institution for
The Deaf and Dumb, Exeter, 1827.

Chapter III   A Pictorial History of Deaf Britain

Matthew Robert Burns
Founder of two schools for Deaf children

Schools started by Deaf people

Not all schools were started through public philanthropy. Some schools started off as small private schools. This happened in Derby. Others, such as Aberdeen School for the Deaf, were started through the encouragement of headmasters of other established schools. At least two schools, however, were founded through the efforts of Deaf people themselves, Dundee and Bristol.

Matthew Robert Burns (1798 – 1880)

No writing on the history of deaf education would be complete without the mention of Matthew Robert Burns, the first born-deaf person ever to be a school headmaster, and the founder of several schools. He was born on 10 November 1798 in Dundee to a major in the 84th regiment of Foot and his wife, the daughter of a Lombard Street banker.

Burns was initially educated by his mother but later attended a local hearing school where he became well educated. At the age of 10, his family moved to London and enrolled him as a private pupil at the Asylum for the Deaf and Dumb in Old Kent Road, London.

The next we learn of Matthew Burns is in 1830 when he appeared in Edinburgh and helped to form the deaf church in that city. In 1832, he opened a day school for deaf children in Carruber's Close Chapel, assisted by two other Deaf people, Charles Buchan and Alexander Campbell. He left after a short while to go to Dundee in 1833 to try and establish a Sabbath School. This did not last long, as in 1834, he was appointed the Headmaster of the Aberdeen Institution for the Deaf and Dumb where he remained for seven years.

In 1841, Matthew Burns went to Bristol where he helped to found the Bristol Institution for the Deaf and Dumb at Tyndall's Park, Bristol, as principal.

He did not stay long at the school in Tyndall's Park – a mere two years. The cause of his leaving is a mystery; Matthew Burns would only say that the 'heathen Bristol' did not contribute much to the institution of the deaf children.

After his departure, the institution at Bristol continued but never enjoyed a very good reputation for the quality of its education. Reports in 1884 and 1886 frequently expressed concern that no reading was taught at the school to children between 7 and 12 years old, and that no trades were taught to enable them to seek employment. The school finally closed in 1908 and was replaced by a new local authority school, which remains to this day, known as Elmfield School for the Deaf.

Matthew Burns never taught again except in bible classes. A religious man, he spent much of his remaining years preaching and acting as secretary to the Adult Institution for providing Employment, &c. for the Deaf and Dumb. This was the forerunner of the Royal Association for the Deaf. Matthew Burns died of bronchitis in Barnsbury on 21 January 1880.

Alexander Drysdale and the Dundee Institution for the Deaf

Another deaf school that was founded by a Deaf man was the Dundee Institution in 1846. Previously there had been two attempts to set up a school for the deaf in that city. In 1819, There was an attempt by a family called Rattray to establish a local institution. The principal movers were a minister, the Reverend Rattray and his younger Deaf brother. To give themselves some credence in the teaching of the Deaf, the younger brother was sent to the Edinburgh Institution for an education by Robert Kinniburgh but only stayed one year before leaving to join his brother in Dundee. The boy was said to have been of a dull and inanimate character who had difficulty learning the Edinburgh sign method, and the proposed Dundee Institution appears to have been short-lived. A second attempt at establishing a Deaf school in Dundee was made by Matthew Robert Burns in 1833. This was more of a Sabbath School, or Bible Class, rather than a proper school and it folded after a few months, with Burns moving on to Aberdeen.

It took another Deaf pioneer, Alexander Drysdale, to set up the first proper school for deaf children in Dundee in 1846, fourteen years after Burns had left the city to get on with his career. Drysdale had been a teacher at the Edinburgh Institution for over ten years before he came to Dundee.

Little is known of Drysdale's early years. He was either born deaf or became so at a very early age, receiving his education at the Deaf and Dumb Institution in Edinburgh. After finishing school, he was an assistant teacher for some years. In 1841 Alexander, then 29 years of age, started to apply for a new position. He wrote to the Directors of the Aberdeen Institution applying for the post that had been left vacant by Matthew Burns.

To support his application, Alexander sent testimonials from parents, clergymen and directors of the Edinburgh Institution referring to the success of his teaching and cuttings from local newspapers, which showed he often gave exhibitions and examinations of his pupils, as was customary at that time, with the help of an interpreter. The perfection of the pupils' finger-language was noted, but signs were also used. This was seen to be very expressive, and the pupils' knowledge of all their lessons excellent.

Unfortunately, he did not get the post in Aberdeen, but on March 9 1846 he and his wife, whom he had married in the previous year, opened the Dundee Institution in Meadow Street. They remained in charge for the next thirty-five years. The school rapidly grew and after two years moved to another leased building. There blind and deaf children were taught together, but, after ten years, a new building was opened for Deaf children only in Dudhope Bank, Logie Den.

Alexander Drysdale also started the Deaf Mission at Dundee, taking various church services before he died suddenly in his chair after a heart attack in April 1880. He had been headmaster for nearly 35 years. He was followed by another Deaf man, James Barland, as headmaster, an ex-pupil of the school.

Under Barland, the school relocated to Dunhope Castle where it remained until it closed in 1985. In one strange incident in 1914, a bomb planted by suffragettes was found in a doorway at the Castle and was defused just in time before it was due to explode!

Dudhope Castle, Dundee
The Dundee School for the Deaf and Dumb occupied an
unique position in Dundee. It was in Dudhope Castle,
built in 1298 in a park of the same name.
The Castle also housed the adult Mission to the Deaf and Dumb.
This picture was taken after discovery of the bomb placed by women's
suffragettes in one of the doorways of the castle. The policeman in
the foreground is guarding the castle.

Chapter III A Pictorial History of Deaf Britain

St. John's School for the Deaf, Boston Spa.
Founded by Monsignore De Haerne in 1869,
it is still the only Roman Catholic school for Deaf children in England.

Havering House, Milton Libourne, Wiltshire
The location of the Jewish School for Deaf children
from 1940 – 1946.

Religious and Secular Schools

In theory, all the established schools for deaf children prior to 1869 took in pupils of all different religious beliefs. In practice, many schools followed the Protestant faith, incorporating some religious teaching in their curriculum. There was no institution in England, Wales or Scotland where deaf children of Roman Catholics could be specifically educated in their own faith, although there were two in Ireland (Dublin), one each for boys and girls, both founded in 1849.

A Belgian priest, Monsignore de Hearne, who was a deputy in the Belgian Senate, learnt of this omission and came to Britain in 1869 with the purpose of establishing such a school. Procuring a cottage at Handsworth Woodhouse, near Sheffield, he provided a teacher and entrusted the running of the school to a management committee at his own expense.

He had previously already funded Catholic institutions for deaf children in Belgium, France and Portugal, and was to found one in India a few years later as well.

In 1874, the Roman Catholic Bishop of Beverley, Yorkshire, adopted the institution as a public school. The Bishops of England passed a resolution to recognise St. John's Institution for the Deaf and Dumb as a Catholic institution for England and resolved also to assist in its foundation and development.

In 1875, Boston Spa College, near Wetherby in Yorkshire, was purchased and this became the nucleus of the present day school and college. St. John's School for the Deaf is still the only residential school in England and Wales for Roman Catholic deaf children, although deaf children of other denominations are welcome.

Boston Spa was not, however, the *first* school for non-Protestant deaf children. This honour belonged to the Jews' Deaf and Dumb Home in Walmer Road, Kensington, London, run by a Mr. S. Scöhntheil (sometimes spelt Shontheil), a native of Hungary, which was established in 1866. The number of pupils on the roll varied between 24 and 30.

This home/school later relocated to 101 Nightingale Road, Clapham, where it remained for a number of years, eventually catering for about 50 Jewish deaf schoolchildren. During the war, the Jewish school took in a number of refugees from Europe and relocated to Havering House in Wiltshire, before returning to Clapham. The site is now occupied by Oak Lodge School for Deaf Children (founded 1905) which is non-Jewish.

In Scotland, the first Roman Catholic School for deaf children did not come into being until 1872. This was situated in an orphanage in Lanark and the pupil roll varied around 22-28 pupils. Later, this was transferred to the Tollcross Blind and Deaf-Mute Roman Catholic School in Shettleston, Glasgow, usually known as St. Vincent's, which is still in existence mainly as a Deaf-blind school.

The Rise of Oralism

The 1860s were a significant period in the history of deaf education due to the establishment of a number of schools, which were founded specifically for the purpose of teaching deaf children through the Oral System.

The teaching of deaf children through oral methods alone was not new; the earliest teachers of the deaf such as Holder and Wallis tried it in the 1660s with (as evidence shows) far less success than they wrote about in the publications that earned them fame. In the eighteenth century, teachers such as Henry Baker and Thomas Braidwood used oralism as part of a combined system nowadays known as Total Communication.

It was Samuel Heinicke who pioneered the pure oral system of teaching deaf children in Germany with the founding of his school in 1760, a method of teaching that has persisted in that country ever since and which in the nineteenth century came to be known as the 'German System.' It's introduction into British schools, first by the Reverend Thomas Arnold at Northampton in 1868, then by William Van Praagh at 11 Fitzroy Square, London, in 1872, rapidly spread, especially after 1880. It came to be both detested and feared by leading deaf people everywhere who saw that it could – as indeed it did – seriously damage the systems of education that had served so well since the growth of deaf education.

Arnold, founder of the Oral School for the Deaf at Northampton in 1868, first trained ironically under that great advocate for sign language, Charles Baker, at the Yorkshire Institution for the Deaf and Dumb, Doncaster, where he (Arnold) tried out the system in a special class, meeting only with limited success.

At Northampton, with no one to answer to except himself, Arnold implemented the oral system ruthlessly and he probably did more to establish the system in Britain than anyone else with the fine academic record of his school.

That the Oral School for the Deaf had a very distinguished record is not disputed. After all, the school produced the first Deaf Fellow of the Geological Society, the first Deaf Ph.D., as well as a host of other academic successes. However, weighed against this is the fact that neither Arnold nor his successor, Dixon, ever took more than 8 boys a time and most of them were very carefully selected, few being born deaf. This is not always appreciated by those who point to this success compared to the systems in use in large institutions.

Through the 'success' of their selective teaching, Arnold and Van Praagh's schools laid the foundations for over a century of controversy and the beginning of the end of sign language-dominated educational teaching.

Thomas Arnold 1816 – 1897
The founder of the first oral school for Deaf children in England
at Northampton.

Chapter III   A Pictorial History of Deaf Britain

The first Unit or Day Class for Deaf children, Greenock Academy.
This was where Alexander Graham Bell taught before he emigrated to America where he invented the telephone.

The First Unit

Today, the majority of deaf children are educated either in mainstream schools, or in units attached to ordinary schools, under various names such as 'deaf units', 'partially deaf/hearing units' or 'units for the hearing-impaired'. One such unit in existence today is the Garvel Deaf Centre in Greenock, Renfrewshire. It is a provision for deaf children, incorporating a small school, a secondary unit, and a peripatetic service. It is not, however, generally known that this was the first-ever 'unit' to be established in Britain, in 1873!

At the instigation of the Greenock Deaf and Dumb Christian Society, the local authority in Greenock approved the use of a room in Greenock Academy (which had been opened in 1855) for the teaching of the few deaf children that resided in the town. The first method used was sign language.

However, in 1878, deaf education in Greenock faced a crisis because there was no one able to continue to teach the children following the departure of the first teacher. Also, one parent was unhappy about having his child being taught in sign language. The person that this parent approached for help and advice was Alexander Graham Bell, the inventor of the telephone.

Bell was a supporter of the oral system. Upon learning of the difficulties faced by the Academy, he took over the teaching of the deaf children in the unit for two months until the arrival of a Mr. Jones all the way from the United States of America as a replacement teacher.

Bell, therefore, not only saved the deaf class at Greenock Academy from closure, but also introduced the oral method of teaching and laid the foundations for the present day Garvel Deaf Centre. It was the experience he gained in Greenock that enabled him to go to the United States and feature so prominently in American deaf education.

Greenock was not the only place in Britain that set up deaf classes in local hearing schools. In London, the Schools Board found that there were over 450 deaf children of various ages between 5 and 13. Of this number, only 150 were being educated in institutions, and the London Schools Board decided to do something about that situation. They would not build anything new but where a group of deaf children were living close enough to each other, a class was to be established in a local school for hearing children and special teachers were to be recruited to teach them.

The first class was set up in Bethnal Green in 1874 and although the first method of instruction was through sign language, the system quickly reverted to the oral system. By 1880, there were eight such classes operating across London, all of them using the oral system.

The day classes or Schools Board classes (as they were called) were not confined to London alone. Two classes were set up in local schools in Hull and another was set up in Sheffield.

After the Milan Congress of 1880, the setting up of day classes spread rapidly, with principal ones being established in Nottingham, Leicester and Airdrie (Scotland). Perhaps one of the most significant was the one established in April 1881 at Leeds with the local missioner, Joseph Moreton, as the first teacher.

Edward A. Kirk (1848 – 1917)

Edward Alfred Kirk was born on February 28 1855 in Doncaster. At the age of 7, he lost his hearing through scarlet fever, and was sent when aged eleven to be educated at the Yorkshire Institution for the Deaf and Dumb. Although he left school at age 16 with no employment, his abilities had so impressed the headmaster, the great Charles Baker, that he was offered a post at the school as an assistant teacher.

When the pro-oralist John Howard succeeded Charles Baker following the latter's death in 1874, he introduced the oral method. Edward Kirk witnessed the change from the manual system to the oral system but continued to take one of the two classes, which still used the manual system. Kirk was dissatisfied and wanted to move and waited for the opportunity to do so. In truth, he also wanted to get married and could not afford to do so on the salary he was receiving at the Yorkshire Institution – one of the worst paid in the country.

When the vacancy created by the resignation of Joseph Moreton at the newly created Leeds half-day classes arose, Edward Kirk applied for the position, ignoring the advice of John Howard, who felt he was unsuited to the position.

To his surprise, Edward Kirk was offered the position at a salary of £120 per year. His appointment was unique, as he was the first (and last) Deaf person to be appointed into a position as headmaster by a local authority for *over 100 years!*

Edward Kirk was to remain as Headmaster at Leeds until his death. In an era where deaf teachers were losing their jobs or being brushed aside to make way for progress, the word progress being defined as oralism, Edward Kirk was a shining example of what a deaf teacher could do with his charges. He was aware of the controversy over the employment of deaf teachers, and took the stance of one who showed that action spoke louder than words.

He saw his school grow from a small class of 6 pupils on a half-day basis into a fully-fledged school taking in boarders and day scholars with a roll of over 100 children, with a reputation second to none. Indeed, in a survey conducted in 1895, it was stated that Leeds School for the Deaf was the only day school which was a success in deaf education.

In total, Edward Kirk taught deaf children for an astonishing 53 years!

Kirk was also an active member of the National Association of Teachers for the Deaf, despite the isolation he felt at being the only Deaf teacher in a multitude of hearing teachers of deaf children.

Edward Kirk died in March 1924 after a three-week illness. The high esteem in which he was held was shown at his funeral where the Director of Education for the district paid a tribute to his great accomplishments for deaf education in Leeds.

Chapter III   A Pictorial History of Deaf Britain

Edward A. Kirk

Leeds School and Home for Blind and Deaf Children

Chapter III   A Pictorial History of Deaf Britain

Celebrating the Report of the Royal Commission on the Education of the Blind and the Deaf and Dumb.
Scene from a Period Play: 1930s
Photo: Northern Counties School for Deaf Children, Newcastle upon Tyne.

Elementary Education (Blind and Deaf Children) Act, 1893

The recommendations of the Royal Commission's report of 1889 were embodied in a Bill which was presented to Parliament, and needed to be introduced four times before it was finally accepted onto the Statute book.

The main reason for the first three failures to carry the Bill through Parliament was that the then Secretary of State for Education, George Kekewich, objected to the clauses in the Bill whereby it was not compulsory for local authorities to make any provision for the education of deaf children in their area.

Only when the Bill was amended to make it compulsory for local authorities to provide and maintain facilities for deaf children did the Liberal Government of the day allow the Bill to become law.

This was an important provision; the Act of 1893 now gave every deaf child the right to have an education. Previously, under the Poor Law Act of 1834, a clause empowered boards of guardians to use local rates to pay for deaf (and blind) children's education in asylums. In both 1845 and 1862 they were encouraged to assist their education by the same means and the 1870 Act created school boards and the London Schools Board. The latter did lead to the establishment of classes for deaf children, but because the provision of this education was not compulsory, many local school boards evaded their responsibilities and pleaded poverty.

Not only local school boards evaded responsibilities. Local workhouses were just as negligent regarding the education of deaf children in their care. For example, Northwich Union Workhouse only sent two deaf children to the Manchester Institution between 1836 (when it was built) and 1893, but the implementation of the Act saw them send no less than 6 children in 1893!

At the time the Act was being introduced, conditions in many deaf institutions and asylums were often grim and unhygienic. At Boston Spa, for example, there were no adequate washing facilities for 16 years. At Exeter, it was 1887 before the school got hot water facilities, more than 50 years after the school was first erected. At Old Kent Road, the installation of gas pipes which could have provided better lighting was rejected in 1833 on the grounds the cost was exorbitant and that the children could make do with candles. And so it went on: poor or non-existent sanitation, overcrowded dormitories, dull and unappetising food and workhouse conditions.

The 1893 Act sought to remedy this by allowing institutions a Parliamentary grant per pupil, but only if the institution/asylum met the standards set by the periodic visits of Her Majesty's Inspector. In order to meet these standards and obtain their grants, schools had to improve on the conditions in which the pupils were taught. While this was a good thing, such improvements were at first only superficial and it was a long time before everyday living conditions in deaf boarding institutions and day classes were of acceptable standard.

This Act remained in force until it was superseded by the Education Act of 1944, which made considerable changes in the education of deaf children.

Chapter IV   A Pictorial History of Deaf Britain

Court of Chancery
By Benjamin Ferrers
Picture courtesy of National Portrait Gallery, London

CHAPTER IV

DEAF ART

Deaf Art: Early History

Many of the earliest 'professional' Deaf people were artists. Through the years, art has provided the opportunity to escape from a humdrum life and provide an adequate living although many also painted for pleasure.

In the sixteenth century, Spain had produced Juan Fernández Navarette (1526-1579), known as El Mudo (the Mute). He could read, write and of course paint. He was painter to the Spanish king, Felipe II. Because of his splendid use of colouring, Fernandez is sometimes described as the Spanish Titian. However, Spain had produced even before Fernandez another painter named Jaime Lopez who flourished in the 15th century in Madrid, and was also known as El Mudo. Lopez painted mainly religious history subjects for churches.

Next in importance to Juan Fernandez Navarette as a painter was Hendrik Avercamp (1585-1663) of the Netherlands, who painted many landscapes, animal studies and charming scenes of townsfolk enjoying their winter amusements and merry carnivals on the ice.

Not until 1768 did Britain have a deaf person as a Royal painter, Sir Joshua Reynolds. He was followed in 1789 by a born-Deaf person, Richard Crosse.

However, Britain had been producing Deaf artists for over a century before then. Had he not died from smallpox at an early age, Framlingham Gaudy (see page 19) might have earned a good living from painting. Certainly, his studies under the renowned artist, Sir Peter Lely, earned him glowing reports. His brother, Sir John, also studied at the same school, but after becoming baronet, painted only for pleasure and not for a living.

It is Benjamin Ferrers (c1670-1732) who is our earliest recognised British Deaf Artist. Little is known about his personal life. Even the date of his birth is unknown, but he could certainly read and write. His earliest known painting is titled *Plant in a China Pot*, but Ferrers achieved fame mainly as a portrait painter specialising in Chancery Court scenes around Westminster in London where he lived.

Sir Joshua Reynolds (1723 - 1792)

A portrait and history painter and the dominant artistic personality in the reign of George III, Reynolds was born at Plympton, Devon, on 16 July 1723.

Whereas other deaf painters of the same era such as Crosse, Shirreff and Roche had been born deaf or had become so in early childhood, Reynolds did not lose his hearing until he was 26 years old as a result of a riding accident in Rome. Even so, he did not lose his hearing completely; he was able to hear shouted conversation with the aid of an ear trumpet.

By then, he was already an accomplished painter although his main work and fame was to come after he had lost his hearing and his ear trumpet had become a familiar sight.

> When they judged without skill, he was hard of hearing,
> When they talked of their Raphaels, Corregios and stuff,
> He shifted his trumpet and only took sniff'.
> *Goldsmith c 1730 - 1774*

By the time the first ever-public exhibition of art was held in 1760, Reynolds had established himself as the leading portrait painter in London. When King George III established the Royal Academy in 1768, Reynolds was the only possible candidate for the presidency even though the king found his style and personality unsympathetic. Indeed, Reynolds was not well liked by London society of the time.

A lot of this may have been due to his deafness that caused him to remain aloof. Also, people found the practice of having to shout into his ear trumpet rather tiresome, especially as there were often misunderstandings on Reynolds' part over what had been said to him.

In 1769, he was knighted and became Sir Joshua Reynolds. Then he was at his zenith, earning £6000 a year and in 1773, he became mayor of Plympton, his place of birth.

In 1789, Reynolds became blind and, unable to paint any more, he resigned as the President of the Royal Academy. In the same year, Richard Crosse was made Court Painter in Enamel.

Reynolds never married and died in 1792 a lonely man in Plympton.

Chapter IV   A Pictorial History of Deaf Britain

Himself as a Deaf Man
Self-portrait by Sir Joshua Reynolds
Reproduced by the kind permission of the Tate Gallery, London

Chapter IV   A Pictorial History of Deaf Britain

Richard Crosse
Self Portrait
Reproduced by the kind permission of the Royal Albert Memorial Museum, Exeter

Richard Crosse (1742 - 1810)

The last three decades of the eighteenth century were a golden age in the history of British miniature portrait painting. Some of the best miniature painters flourished at this time, and deaf art produced three such painters - Shirreff, Roche and Crosse. Of these three, Richard Crosse was regarded as one of the better of the second rank of British miniature portrait painters.

He was the second son of John Crosse and his wife Mary and was born at Knowle, near Cullompton, Devon on 24 April 1742.

He had a Deaf sister, Alice, and it is evident that both of them were fairly well educated although neither could speak. It is not known who educated them as a large part of the family records perished when the ancestral manor home of the Crosse family was destroyed by fire in the 1870s when a servant set alight some straw in the kennels where the Crosse hounds were kept. One of the manuscripts which survived the fire, however, was a well-written letter by Alice to her brother James complaining about a portrait that Richard Crosse had painted of her husband on wood instead of on canvas!

Bearing in mind some members of the family were lawyers, it would appear that the deaf siblings shared the same tutor(s) as the other children at the family home.

When aged 16, Richard Crosse won a premium at the Society of Arts in 1758 and went to study in London at Sibley's Drawing School and the Duke of Richmond's Gallery.

Richard Crosse was a prolific painter, painting hundreds of miniatures between $1^1/_2$ inches and 6 inches high. He kept a ledger in which he meticulously recorded every painting done and sold. In the space between 13 September 1776 and 30 January 1777, he painted and sold 56 small miniatures for eight guineas each, two of a medium size for ten and twelve guineas. He also sold a half-size portrait for fifteen guineas, and two large size portraits for thirty guineas each - total of 61 works for £572. This was an excellent income for those days. This ledger can be seen in the Victoria and Albert Museum, London.

Many of his paintings and miniatures were unsigned which resulted in his not getting the credit he deserved in latter years. Those, which he did sign, were either with his initials R.C. or in four different ways in full in careful handwriting.

In 1789, he was appointed Court Painter in Enamel to King George III.

He fell in love with his cousin, Miss Sarah Cobley, who refused his offer of marriage and instead married a Mr. Haydon, the father of B. R. Haydon, the painter. This left him embittered and turned him into a recluse in his later years, causing him to retire from painting in 1798, already a wealthy man. He lived for a time with Miss Cobley's brother, the Prebendary Cobley, at Wells, Somerset, before ending his final years at Knowle where he died in May 1810.

In his *Memoirs*, B. R. Haydon wrote about the final meeting between Richard Crosse and his mother, which is a lovely story and is reproduced on the next text page.

Richard Crosse and Sarah Haydon (Extract from the *Memoirs* of B. R. Haydon)

'My dear Mother felt her approaching end so clearly that she made every arrangement with reference to her death. She had passed a great part of her life with a brother (the prebend of Wells), who took care of a Mr. Crosse, a dumb miniature painter. Crosse (who in early life had made a fortune by his miniatures) loved my mother, and proposed to her, but she being at that time engaged to my father, refused him and they had never seen each other since. He retired from society, deeply affected at his disappointment. The day after leaving Exeter, we stopped at Wells, as my mother wished to see my uncle once more.

The meeting was very touching. As I left the room and crossed the hall, I met a tall handsome, old man; his eyes seemed to look me through; muttering hasty unintelligible sounds he opened the door, saw my mother, and rushed over to her, as if inspired of a sudden with youthful vigour. Then pressing her to his heart he wept, uttering sounds of joy not human! This was Crosse. They had not met for thirty years. We came so suddenly to my uncle's they had never thought of getting him out of the way. It seemed as if the great sympathising Spirit once again brought them together, before their souls took flight.

He was in agony of joy and pain, smoothing her hair and pointing first to her cheek and then to his own, as if to say "how altered!" The moment he darted his eyes upon my sister and me, he looked as if he *felt* we were her children, but did not notice us much beyond this. My sister, hanging over my poor mother, wept painfully. She, Crosse, my uncle and aunt were all sobbing and much touched; for my part my chest hove up and down, as I struggled with emotions at this singular and affecting meeting. What a combination of human feelings and suffering!

Disappointed in love, this man who, dumb by nature, can only express his feelings by the lightings of his eye been left for thirty years, brooded over affections wounded as for the mere pleasure of torture. For many months after my mother married, he was frantic and ungovernable at her continued absence, and then sank into sullen sorrow.

His relations and friends endeavoured to explain to him the cause of her going away, but he was never satisfied and never believed them. Now when the recollection of her, young and beautiful, might occasionally have soothed his imagination, like a melancholy dream, she suddenly burst on his with two children, the off-spring of her marriage with his rival - and so altered, bowed, weakened, as to root out the association of her youthful beauty with the days of his happy thoughts.

Such a moment was this. His anger, his frantic indignation, and his sullen silence at her long absence all passed away before her worn and sickly face. He saw her before him broken and dying; he felt all his affection return, and flinging himself forward on the table, he burst into a paroxysm of tears, as if his very heartstrings would crack. By degrees we calmed him, for nature had been relieved by this agonising grief, and they parted in a few moments for the last time'.

Sarah Haydon died the next day.

Two paintings by Richard Crosse
Above: Lady in Blue
Reproduced by the kind permission of the Royal Albert Museum, Exeter
Below: Officer in a Red Coat
Reproduced by the kind permission of the Holburne Museum, Bath

Chapter IV   A Pictorial History of Deaf Britain

A painting by Charles Sherriff
Thomas Wilkes of Overseal
Reproduced by the kind permission of the Victoria & Albert Museum, London

Charles Shirreff (1750 - 1831)

The name of Charles Shirreff (at times spelt variously as Sherrif, Sherriff and Shirref) has a special niche in British Deaf history. He was the first deaf pupil of Thomas Braidwood, and his progress was such that Braidwood forsook his previous calling as a private teacher, and devoted the rest of his life to the education of deaf children.

The son of Alexander Shirreff, a wealthy wine merchant of South Leith, Edinburgh, Charles left Braidwood's Academy at the age of 18 to go to the Royal Academy Schools in August 1769 from which he graduated with a silver medal in 1772 to make a career as a miniature painter. He successfully exhibited at the Free Society of Artists and at the Royal Academy, as well as others, and built up a clientele that was mainly theatrical.

He worked from London after graduating from the Royal Academy, and applied to go to India in 1778. In his application to the East India Company, he stated that he had no speech but was able to make himself understood by signs and requested that he be accompanied by his father and his sister Mary to act as interpreters. However, the failure of Fordyce's Bank ruined his father; and his plan to visit India was abandoned, as Charles had to stay to support his family.

He lived and worked in Bath from 1791 to 1795 where he was no doubt acquainted with two other deaf miniaturists, Sampson Towgood Roche and Richard Crosse. Certainly, all three shared at various times the same people whom they painted.

In 1795, he renewed his application to go to India, and left England in the *Lord Hawkesbury* which reached Madras in January 1797. He painted in Madras for some years before moving to Calcutta, where he worked on his *Illustrations of Signs*. In 1807, he announced it was nearly completed and would be available to subscribers as soon as possible. This work has never been traced and is presumed lost *en passage* from India, a great pity as it might well have been the first sign dictionary.

He returned from India in 1809, and painted in London for a number of years before retiring to Bath where he died unmarried in 1831.

Sampson Towgood Roche (1759 - 1847)

Sampson Roche was born deaf in Youghal, Ireland, and began to show an aptitude for art. He was sent to Dublin to study under painters who were practising there and also in Bath between 1784 and 1788. It is not known if he was educated, but he could write his name. His pictures were signed simply Roch or Roche, followed by a date. The letters were always separate and simple.

He married a Miss Roch (probably a cousin) in Cork in June 1788, then returned to live in Bath in 1792 where he and Charles Shirreff were contemporaries.

He had a flourishing practice painting miniatures, and lived in Bath until 1830, when he retired as a miniaturist and returned to Ireland where he died at Waterford in 1847.

Thomas Arrowsmith (1771-about 1831)

Thomas Arrowsmith was born in Newent, Gloucestershire, the fourth of six children of Nathaniel and Elizabeth, nee Cook, and christened on 23 January 1771.

He was educated at home by his family. Thomas' early years are chronicled in a book by his brother John Pauncefort Arrowsmith who published an account in *The Art of Instructing the Infant Deaf and Dumb* in 1819.

This education enabled Thomas to attend a local village school for hearing children where he learnt to read and write, though not to speak. In J.P.Arrowsmith's published account, he advocates the deaf being educated in ordinary schools as opposed to special institutions, citing his brother as an example – this is the first occasion anyone has advocated a *mainstreamed* educational system for deaf children.

However, Thomas Arrowsmith only remained at the village school until he was ten or eleven years old in 1782. There is a strong probability that he attended Thomas Braidwood's Academy for the Deaf and Dumb in Mare Street, Hackney for at least part of the time before he is next heard of in 1789. The reason for this conclusion is that Arrowsmith painted a number of old Braidwoodian pupils in his early years, and his acquaintance of these former pupils could be traced back to the time he shared his education with them.

Arrowsmith entered the Royal Academy Schools in 1789, and began to exhibit there from 1792 onwards.

He married Elizabeth Carpenter, who was illiterate and believed to be Deaf, at St. Marylebone on 17 September 1812, and they both left London afterwards to live and work in Liverpool, where his brother John Pauncefort was a solicitor. A number of his paintings are in the Walker Art Gallery, Liverpool.

Despite his brother's championing of Thomas Arrowsmith as a person who was educated in an ordinary school, there is no doubt that he mixed with other Deaf people. Apart from the portraits he painted of former Braidwoodian pupils, he was mentioned by a number of Deaf people in Manchester as living and working there between 1827 and 1830. Also, there is a portrait painted by him in the Yorkshire Residential School for Deaf Children in Doncaster, which he visited in 1829 according to the Visitor's Book. In this book, Arrowsmith puts down his residence as 'London'

Thomas Arrowsmith's last known work is dated 1829, and he is believed to have died in Manchester sometime in 1830-1, exact date unknown.

Chapter IV   A Pictorial History of Deaf Britain

Thomas Arrowsmith

Chapter IV   A Pictorial History of Deaf Britain

James Howe

Skirling Fair by James Howe
Reproduced with the kind permission of the Scottish National Portrait Gallery

James Howe (1780-1836)

James Howe was Scotland's first – and is arguably its greatest – animal painter. He drawings and paintings offer a richly detailed, often humorous, view of Scotland in the early nineteenth-century – of social custom, of transport, of life and town and country. He was fascinated by horses and came to be called 'The Man who Loved to Draw Horses'.

Born on 31 August 1780 in the village of Skirling in Peebleshire, James Howe attended the village school in Skirling but left still young and incompletely educated on account of his deafness. It has been suggested that despite his lack of education, James was considerably influenced by the schoolmaster Robert Davidson who had such neat handwriting that he was often asked to write people's names in their bibles and would do so, adorning them with little drawings of flowers and animals. James was always making drawing on every piece of paper he could lay hands on – even his father's sermons were not safe. He would sometimes open his notes in the pulpit when ready to preach and find that they had been decorated with James' latest drawings of animals.

When he was 14, he was apprenticed to the Edinburgh firm of Smiton and Chancellor, coach painters – hardly an ideal apprenticeship for what he wanted to be. When this ended, he set himself up first as a portrait painter. He did paint a number of portraits, but a painting of a piebald pony in the window of his studio was so lifelike that people started to ask him to paint animals.

Howe's reputation as animal painter was made when Sir John Sinclair of the Board of Agriculture commissioned him to draw details of various breeds of cattle, and he went on to paint hundreds more pictures, mostly of horses.

After the battle of Waterloo Howe visited the battlefield and on his return produced a panorama covering many feet of canvas, which depicted incidents in the fight. This was exhibited in various places with great financial success.

Flushed with success, however, Howe was turning into an alcoholic owing to his frequenting many alehouses around Edinburgh and this, coupled with his deafness, meant he was preyed upon by unscrupulous acquaintances so that when he died in 1836, he was almost a pauper. Prior to his death, he had returned to Skirling where he was born, in an attempt to have the country air restore his health but constant coughing made him weak and he died of a burst blood vessel on 11 July 1836. He is buried in Skirling churchyard quite close to the house where he was born. Relatives and admirers erected to his memory a tombstone, which contains a carved palette and brushes.

Deaf Art: The 19th Century

The early nineteenth century and the 1890s were probably the heyday of Deaf Art. Many deaf people painted in their leisure time and had their pictures exhibited, like William Agnew. Others painted professionally and relied on the sale of works of art to earn a living - these included Thomas Arrowsmith, Walter Geikie, John Howe, Thomas Davidson, Rupert Dent and William Trood.

There were so many Deaf artists around in the 1890s that Glasgow was able to hold the first-ever exhibition of Deaf art and other works. It was extremely popular and attracted over 6000 visitors during the week it was open. Many of the well-known Deaf artists like Davidson, Trood and Dent donated paintings to the exhibition, which raised over £5000 for Glasgow's new Deaf mission.

Many, other Deaf people found work as engravers or designers, such as Harry Ash, who won three prizes at the School of Art in King's College for the design of wallpaper patterns.

The 1890s was also the age of many illustrated newspapers and magazines such as the *Graphic* and *Punch* magazines – Trood and Dent sold much of their work to these publications, as did Davidson and others on occasion. Davidson, however, preferred to paint elaborate historical naval scenes.

In Scotland, Geikie and Howe mainly earned their living through commissions, with Howe becoming famous as the 'Man Who Loved to Draw Horses'.

Many of the nineteenth century artists were also prominent in the Deaf Community, like Geikie, one of the founders of Edinburgh Deaf Congregational Church; Agnew, the driving force behind the Glasgow Adult Deaf & Dumb Institute and Davidson, who was President of the Deaf Debating Society at St. Saviour's Church, London.

Not all Deaf artists were male. A Mrs. Jane A. North of Shepherd's Bush, London, made a good living out of painting and selling portraits of several well-known personalities. Some of her best paintings went for the same price as Davidson's masterpieces!

The twentieth-century has also produced notable artists such as Alfred Thomson, Roland Pitchforth and David Hockney. The first two were given appointments as Official War Artists during the 1939-45 war.

Deaf Art is not confined to painting. The late 19th century and early 20th century produced many Deaf men and women who made an excellent living as engravers and sculptors. These included Joseph Gawen and Dorothy Stanton Wise, who were prominent in the Deaf Community, and Kathleen Trousdell Shaw. In the second half of the 20th century, another engraver flourished in a different field – woodcarving. Martin Dutton of York built up a good business as a skilled woodcarver, producing many intricate wooden works, mainly for churches throughout the North of England.

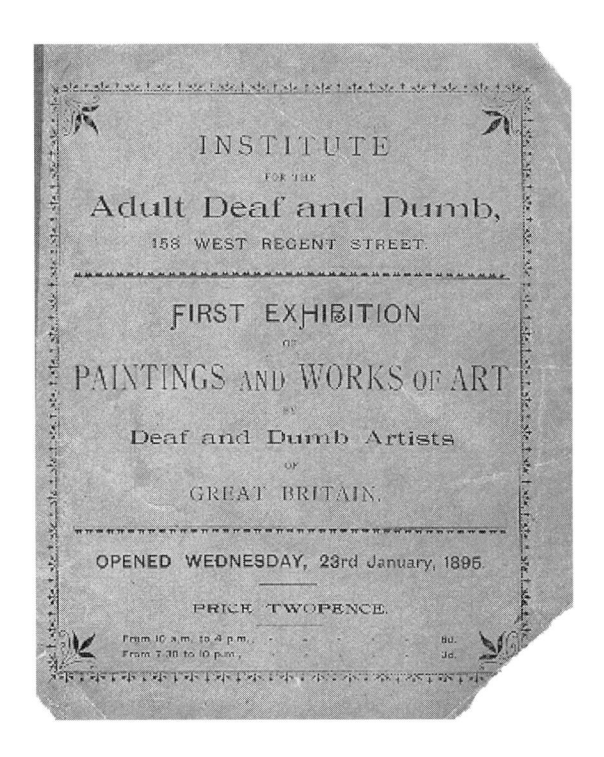

Programme Cover for the First Deaf Art Exhibition, Glasgow

A Typical satire cartoon in The Graphic Magazine
By W. H. H. Trood

Chapter IV   A Pictorial History of Deaf Britain

The Drunk Man
By Walter Geikie, R.S.A.
Reproduced by the courtesy of the Talbot Rice Gallery, University of Edinburgh

Walter Geikie, R.S.A. (1795 – 1837)

One of Scotland's most famous artists was the 'deaf and dumb Geikie', as he was commonly known. Walter Geikie was born on 9 November 1795 in Edinburgh, the elder son of Archibald Geikie, a pharmacist by occupation but a philosopher by inclination, and when still only two years old, contracted a 'brain fever' (probably meningitis) which left him deaf for life.

Archibald Geikie somehow learnt the manual alphabet, and there being no school for the deaf in Edinburgh at that time (Braidwood's Academy had moved to Hackney in 1783), undertook the teaching of his son himself. He was so successful that Walter was able to read, and write, and he did read many books.

When the new Institution for the Deaf and Dumb was opened in Edinburgh in 1810 with John Braidwood, grandson of Thomas Braidwood, as Principal, Walter Geikie was enrolled as one of the first students. He was then fourteen years old, a rather late age at which to start a formal education. However, Geikie was so well educated that Braidwood began to use him more as an assistant teacher.

When Braidwood left the Institution in 1812 to go to the United States, Archibald Geikie was asked to assume direction of the school with his son as an assistant teacher, but they would not assume the responsibility. Later that year, Geikie became a pupil of John Graham who had been the famous artist David Wilkie's teacher.

Geikie's drawings first appeared in the art markets in 1815 and during his lifetime he turned out an immense number of sketches, many of which were sold after his death when his fame had spread widely. He developed a talent for paying particular attention to individual traits of feature, form and character that appeared in the men and women he met. He could retain their features in his mind and produce a lifelike sketch from memory. He also developed the ability to sketch as he walked with his pad and pencil.

His friend Sir Thomas Lauder of Grange and Fountainhall tells of one humorous incident where Geikie once followed a particularly pompous, pot-bellied and self-assertive porter through the marketplace sketching as he went. Eventually, the victim got angry and chased Geikie into a house from whose attic window the artist completed the sketch with some extra touches to show features of indignation to perfect the picture.

In 1834, Geikie was made a Fellow of the Scottish Academy.

He never married, and had led a very healthy life, which caused him to have over-confidence in his constitution, and thus neglected to go to a physician at the onset of a serious illness, until it was too late. Five days before his death, he took to his bed and soon sank into a coma from which he never recovered and died on 1 August 1837 at the age of 41. He was buried in Greyfriars Churchyard.

After his death, his friend, Sir T. Lauder, published a volume of his etchings in 1841 with comments and a biographical introduction. Thus much of his work is preserved in print. This particular book *Etchings Illustrative of Scottish Character and Scenery* represents the first appearance of a deaf artist in pictorial literature.

Walter Geikie and the Edinburgh Deaf Community

Despite his fame, Walter Geikie never forgot the time he spent at the Edinburgh Institution for the Deaf and Dumb under John Braidwood. He was so proficient in sign language and fingerspelling that he always had time for Deaf friends. On at least two occasions, he drew and sold sketches of Deaf people.

Walter Geikie possessed great social qualities. A wonderful comic, his mirthful spirit and love of mimicry made him a great favourite not only of Deaf people, but also of his brother artists.

An avid reader of the Bible, he held a strong desire for the opportunity to attend church services in which he could fully participate. He got together with two other Deaf men, Matthew Burns and Alexander Blackwood, to start Sunday services for the deaf of Edinburgh in June 1830. They established the Congregational Church for the Deaf and Dumb in Edinburgh, the first meeting place being a small room with only one window in Lady Stair's Close, Lawnmarket.

The Edinburgh Congregational Church is the oldest Deaf church still in existence anywhere in the world, and it was Geikie's inspiration that got it started. He sometimes took his turn to conduct services, or deliver sermons and spiritual lectures, in sign language, for the Bible was one of his favourite books for reading.

His great friend Sir Thomas Lauder once attended such a service and was moved to comment that this assembling of the deaf was an affecting spectacle:

> 'not for the purpose of repining that they had been deprived of the important blessings of hearing and speech, but to manifest their love and gratitude to God for all those other things He permitted them to enjoy'.

Out of the Edinburgh Deaf Congregational Church's humble beginnings grew the Edinburgh Adult Deaf and Dumb Benevolent Society and the present-day Edinburgh and East of Scotland Society for Deaf people.

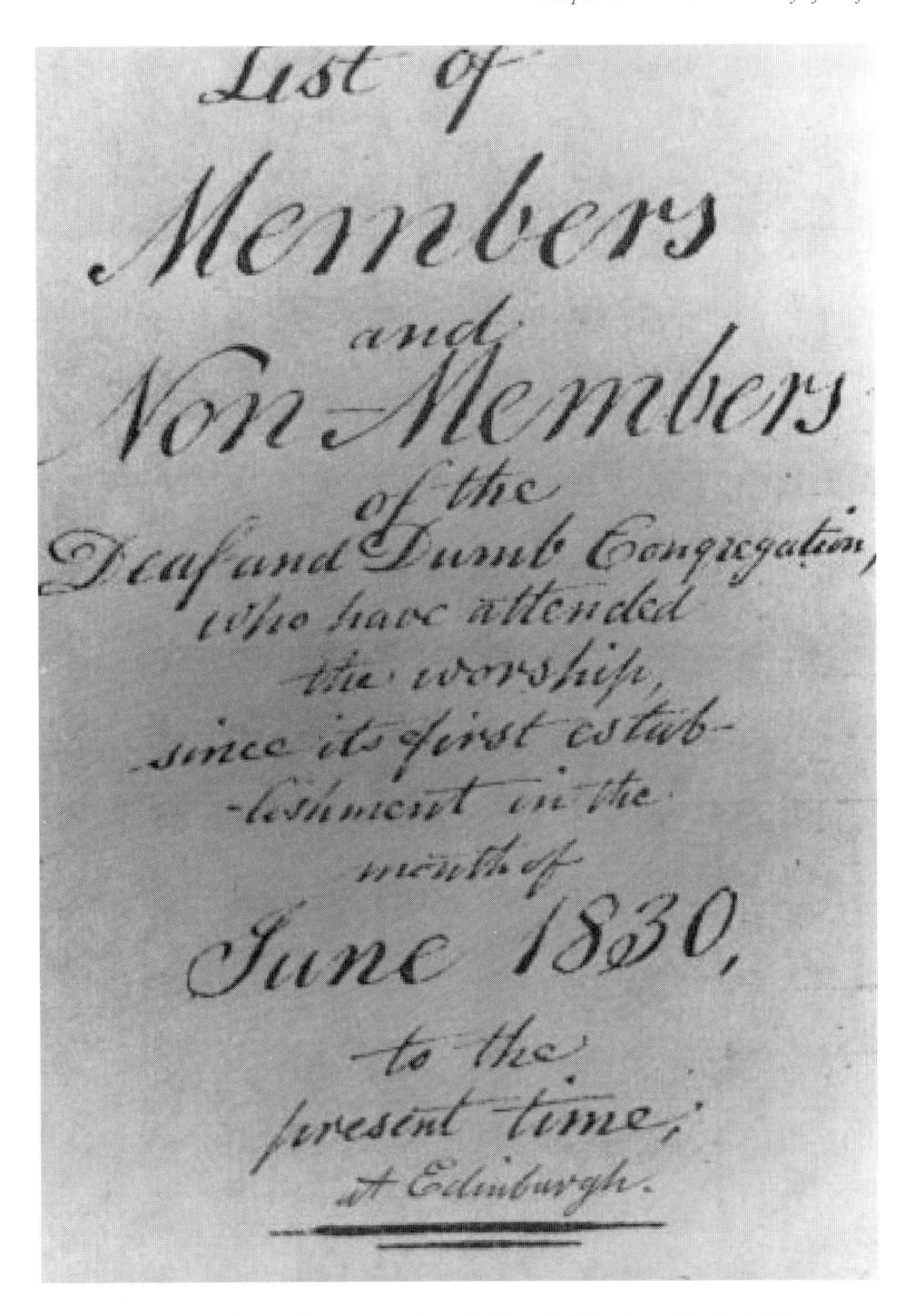

Edinburgh Deaf Congregational Church Members Book 1830
From: Edinburgh and East of Scotland Society for the Deaf Archives.

Chapter IV   A Pictorial History of Deaf Britain

Thomas Davidson

William Henry Hamilton Trood

Thomas Davidson (1842 – 1910)

Thomas Davidson became deaf at the age of four due to illness and was educated as a private pupil of Dr. Thomas Watson of the Old Kent Road Asylum. Upon the latter's death, he was educated at a hearing school in Chatham and thence at the Marlborough School of Art.

From the very first, he painted professionally for a living and achieved fame primarily for his paintings of Nelsonian and Roman events. Most of his paintings were elaborate, detailed, large-scale affairs, some of which found their way to city municipalities in Canada and Australia.

One of his paintings can be found hanging in the school canteen at the Royal School for Deaf Children, Margate.

He was a regular attendant at services for the deaf held at St. Saviour's Church, and was on the committee of the Royal Association for the Deaf and Dumb. He was also one of the first members of the British Deaf and Dumb Association when it was formed in 1890.

Thomas Davidson was also keen on debate, and was the first President of the newly formed Deaf and Dumb Debating Society that held regular debates and lectures in St. Saviour's Church Lecture Hall.

He died on 15 November 1910 whilst living in retirement at Walberswick, Suffolk, and is buried in St. Andrew's Church in the same plot of ground as his hearing wife Charlotte and painter son Allan Douglas Davidson (1873 – 1932).

William Henry Hamilton Trood (1859 – 1899)

Born in Taunton, Somerset, to a wealthy coal merchant, he became deaf at the age of 5 due to illness.

Of his education little is known but it seems likely that his family engaged a private tutor for him – he may have also have been a private fee-paying pupil at the West of England School for the Deaf at Exeter.

He started painting professionally from an early age, and was soon contributing regularly to publications such as *Punch, Illustrated London News* and *Graphic* newspaper. Many of his paintings were of dogs, generally in humorous and sentimental situations. He also contributed drawings of political satire, where politicians' faces were imposed on dogs.

William Trood was also an intrepid traveller, and once made a trip to Morocco, where the Sultan of Morocco presented him with a silver-inlaid Damascus sword.

He died, unexpectedly, after a short illness aged only 39 whilst staying at the Phoenix Hotel in Taunton.

One of his paintings was seen for sale at an auction in Crewkerne, Somerset, in 1988, where it was sold for £7,500.

Rupert Dent (1853-1910)

Rupert Dent was born deaf at Wolverhampton, and during his pre-school years, he had a governess provided by his wealthy father, a Miss Jane Bessmeres who later was to found the Wolverhampton and Shrewsbury Missions for Deaf people.

Dent was educated at the Manchester Institution for the Deaf & Dumb (later to become the Royal Residential Schools for the Deaf). Following this, he entered Wolverhampton School of Art where he was encouraged to develop his talent in animal painting. This talent was to provide him with a good living, with exhibitions all over the country and regular contributions to *Punch* magazine. Dent also exhibited regularly at the Royal Academy.

After many years living in Wolverhampton, he moved to Cheltenham in 1892 where he remained for the rest of his life. For many years in Cheltenham, he conducted a Sunday afternoon class for Deaf people from the area.

Rupert Dent died on 2 January 1910 after a brief and sudden attack of pneumonia.

William Frederick Mitchell (1845–1914)

Fred Mitchell was born deaf without speech at Calshot Castle, Hampshire, in 1845 and was educated at the Old Kent Road Institution in London.

He made his living as a lithographer and by painting pictures of ships for naval officers, although he was never given the credit that was due to him. He had an arrangement with Griffin's Bookshop in Portsmouth to take orders for his work, and the firm printed two volumes of *The Royal Navy in a Series of Illustrations*. The same firm framed and sold a lot of Mitchell's paintings.

Although Fred Mitchell led a fairly reclusive life on the Isle of Wight, he nonetheless took an active part in deaf community life. He was one of the first deaf people to join the British Deaf and Dumb Association in 1890.

He died in Ryde in 1914.

In 1987 Ashford Press printed a book by Conrad Dixon titled *Ships of the Victorian Navy*. All 48-colour plates in this book were by Fred Mitchell, but the artist was barely mentioned in the acknowledgements. Many of his paintings are held by the National Maritime Museum in Greenwich.

Rupert A. Dent

One of the Paintings by William Mitchell
Greenwich Maritime Museum

Chapter IV   A Pictorial History of Deaf Britain

Harry Ash

Alexander Bilibin

A Page from the Guide to Chirology
Designed, Written and Published by Harry Ash

Harry Ash 1863-1934

One of the greatest of all Deaf pioneers and artists who never fully received the recognition that was due to him was Harry Ash, who was born in Bridgewater, Somerset, and lost his hearing at 18 months of age through scarlet fever.

Educated at the Old Kent Road Asylum for the Deaf and Dumb and at Margate, Ash was an exceptional scholar with a passionate interest in foreign languages, starting with French five months before he left school, studying by candlelight after all the other children had gone to bed. He later studied German, Dutch and Spanish.

An exceptional designer and artist, he won a free scholarship to the School of Art in King's College, London where he studied figure drawing. Like Charles Shirreff before him, Ash harboured a dream of publishing a dictionary of signs but failed to get any financial backing for his idea. He did, however, design and publish a *Guide to Chirology* and a series of booklets called *Comic Graphics* which contained signs, gestures and written versions in English which he hoped would interest the general public in sign language and the manual alphabet.

Alexander Bilibin 1903-1971

Born in Russia, he became totally deaf at the age of 9 following a double mastoid operation. He was educated at the Ince Jones Oral School for Deaf Boys where from the outset he showed great promise in Art.

Following his deaf education, he spent four years at the Royal Academy Schools and also studied in Paris. It was whilst Bilibin was at the Royal Academy that he heard of a struggling deaf artist who had failed to get into the Academy, Alfred R. Thomson (see page 102). Bilibin went to meet him and despite the fact that Bilibin was oral and relied on lipreading and Thomson preferred to use sign language, they formed a friendship that was to last 53 years until Bilibin's death, despite Bilibin's temperamental nature, which sometimes resulted in rows between the two.

Alexander Bilibin's chief claim to fame was as a scenic artist in the film industry both in England and in Hollywood, and for his mural decorations in the old Cunard liner, the Queen Mary.

Bilibin died in 1971, three weeks after suffering his third heart attack. Few attended his funeral, but his great friend Thomson was one of those who attended.

War Artists

All branches of the armed services at various times made appointments of official War Artists, who were commissioned to paint battle scenes or portraits for the armed services. During the Second World War, there were two deaf artists - Alfred Reginald Thomson who was an official War Artist to the Royal Air Force, and Roland Vivian Pitchforth, employed by the Admiralty as official War Artist.

Alfred Reginald Thomson, R.A., (1894 – 1979)

A.R. Thomson was born in Bangalore, India, in 1894 and was educated at the Royal School for Deaf Children, Margate, in England before he went to study art at the London Art School, Kensington, and exhibited at the Royal Academy from 1920. He was elected A.R.A. in 1939.

The Royal Air Force always had two salaried artists at any one time, and one of these was a portraitist. In 1940, Thomson was considered as one of the portraitists, but his deafness was considered enough to disqualify him. The post went to Eric Kennington who however resigned in 1942 over criticism of the 'violence' of his portraits, and now without an explanation for the change of heart over his deafness, Thomson was appointed to succeed him.

Among the portraits that Thomson painted for the R.A.F. was one of Wing-Commander Leonard Cheshire, D.F.C. - later to be awarded the Victoria Cross and made Group Captain.

However, "Tommy" Thomson (as he was known) was much more than a War Artist. He painted portraits of numerous distinguished people, including the deaf jockey Lester Piggott, the boxer Tommy Farr, the King of Greece. In his twilight years, Thomson suffered ill health and died in hospital in the early hours of 27 October 1979 after collapsing at home.

Roland Vivian Pitchforth, R.A., R.W.S. (1894–1982)

Vivian Pitchforth was born in Wakefield with normal hearing and studied art at the Wakefield School of Art, thence the Leeds School of Art, leaving in 1915 to join the Royal Artillery with which he served in France until 1918.

He was demobilised from the Royal Artillery stone-deaf from the noise of the 60-pound guns he helped to fire and for the rest of his life, he relied on lipreading which he learnt at classes for deafened soldiers and sailors at the Royal School for Deaf Children, Margate.

After four years at the Royal College of Art, he started to paint professionally, mostly in watercolour.

He was official War Artist to the Admiralty during the Second World War, when he painted many dramatic scenes. He was also employed to make records of the work of the Civil Defence and the war industries.

He was a hard worker, and the Tate Gallery, Imperial War Museum and many other provincial galleries hold numerous works.

Chapter IV   A Pictorial History of Deaf Britain

Alfred Reginald Thomson at Work

Roland Vivian Pitchforth

Chapter IV   A Pictorial History of Deaf Britain

Joseph Gawen's Famous Sculpture *The Good Shepherd*

Bronze and Silver Sculpture by Kathleen Trousdell Shaw
At Cadmore End Parish Church, High Wycombe

Joseph Gawen (1825-1901?)

Joseph Gawen was the first of three well-known Deaf people who achieved fame in sculpture, although he was never given the credit he was due. For example, it is reliably accepted that it was Gawen who did most of the work in sculpting the statute of Nelson that stands on top of the column in Trafalgar Square, although the credit is attributed to Britain's most eminent sculptor, Edward Hodges Bailey, who was Gawen's employer.

Joseph Gawen was born in Brighton in October 1825. One of two Deaf brothers who attended the London Asylum for the Deaf and Dumb at Old Kent Road, he was apprenticed to Bailey after leaving the Asylum in 1844.

Gawen produced many sculptures, including a bust of the Prince of Wales and King Edward VII, but perhaps his most well-known masterpiece was the statute of the *Good Shepherd* which for many years stood outside St. Saviour's Centre for the Deaf in West London. This statute was rescued from its exposure to acid rain and pollutants in July 1998 by the British Deaf History Society, and moved to the inside of the Centre.

Kathleen Trousdell Shaw (1865 – 1958)

Kathleen Shaw was one of the few Deaf women who made an important mark in Deaf history in the late 19th and early 20th centuries. She grew up in a pleasant and comfortable home in Ireland and was 5 years old when her hearing began to fail. By the age of 17, she was totally deaf.

Her gift for sculpture was discovered when she was nine years old, still uneducated. She would spend hours watching a stonemason at work in the local churchyard. One day, he gave her a piece of stone and two chisels. With this stone, she made a remarkable copy of a Michelangelo and was sent, when ten years old, to the Dublin School of Art where she learnt drawing and sculpture.

Her greatest work, the bust of Archbishop Alexander, Primate of All Ireland, can still be seen today in Armagh Cathedral. Also in Armagh, she won a competition to design and sculpt a war memorial. This war memorial, a statute of a bugler, still stands in the market place in Armagh.

She became the first woman sculptor, and only the deaf woman, to be made a member of any Royal Academy in the British Isles when she was made a member of the Royal Hibernian Society in 1907.

After the 1914-18 war, she retired to the little village of Cadmore End, near High Wycombe, where she designed and made a gift to the village of a beautiful war memorial. This memorial, an octagonal font-cover of bronze surmounted by a silver figure of a mother and baby, can still be seen in the parish church.

In her last few years, she became totally blind and had to rely on the deafblind alphabet to communicate.

Dorothy Stanton Wise (c1880 – 1918?)

One other Deaf woman was also to achieve fame as a sculptress. Dorothy Stanton Wise was born deaf at Dover where she was educated at home by her mother, who had taken her to see the Rev. Thomas Arnold at Northampton for advice on her education.

She also attended a kindergarten school where she first demonstrated her talent for modelling with clay. When her kindergarten time was over, her parents engaged a modelling tutor to come in twice a week, and she was so good that at the age of 7 she was admitted to the Dover School of Art where she stayed until she was eighteen. Her parents then moved to London and admitted her as a free scholar to the sculpture studio in the Royal College of Art, where she stayed for four years and graduated an A.R.C.A.

Then she started to earn her living by designing and sculpting many items of distinction and merit, earning gold medals at exhibitions at the Royal Academy, Manchester Art Gallery and Liverpool's Walker Art Gallery. A number of her sculptures were also sold to Queen Alexandra.

One of her best-known works is a marble memorial to Bishop Prideaux, which can be seen today in Worcester cathedral.

Dorothy Stanton Wise discovered the deaf community in her late teens and was a strong supporter of the BDDA. She contributed regularly to the British Deaf Times, mostly about travel in France.

Dorothy Stanton Wise was never heard of again after 1918 when she was in her prime as a sculptress. No works of art are known to have been produced by her after that year. The most likely explanation is that she was one of the victims of the great influenza epidemic of 1918-9, but no trace can be found of any obituary for her.

Martin Dutton (1921 -)

From sculpture to a different form of artwork, woodcarving. Britain had for many years one of the best woodcarvers in Martin Dutton whose skill in woodcarving was to earn him countrywide recognition as a master craftsman. Born deaf, he was educated at the Yorkshire Residential School for the Deaf where he developed a love of woodcarving which led to him setting up his own business in 1950.

Martin Dutton was known as "The Lizard Man" because his signature and trademark was a lizard. Many of his carved figures were installed in a number of churches. Perhaps his best known work was a four-foot high figure of St. Blaise, the patron saint of woolcombers. This can be seen in the Roman Catholic Church at Bradford, Yorkshire.

For many years, he helped to run the British Deaf Association's Woodcarving Courses at their summer schools in York.

Chapter IV   A Pictorial History of Deaf Britain

Dorothy Stanton Wise

Martin Dutton

Chapter IV   A Pictorial History of Deaf Britain

Robert Menzies Scott (1891-1977) at work as a young man. He was born into a Deaf family and educated at Donaldson's School. Many of his paintings reflected life on Glasgow's Clydeside industrial scene.
Photo: Glasgow & West of Scotland Society

John Andrew Pearson of Leeds with some of his paintings exhibited at Deaf Expressions, Cambridge. A professional architectural illustrator, he was educated at Burwood Park School.
Photo: SHAPE Deaf Arts

John Wilson
A professional actor and SHAPE Deaf Arts Officer, responsible for the revival of interest in Deaf Art and Culture.
Photo: John Wilson

Deaf Art at the Millennium

It was to be nearly a century after the first-ever Exhibition of Deaf Art at Glasgow in 1895 that another public exhibition of paintings by Deaf artists was organised. In June 1993, the Julius Gottlieb Gallery at Carmel College in Oxfordshire exhibited the works of six Deaf artists.

For most of those 98 years, Deaf Art had been in the doldrums, with only the odd showing of any works by Deaf individuals such as A.R.Thomson, David Hockney and Vivian Pitchforth at exhibitions, but rarely was an exhibition devoted solely to the work of a Deaf artist or artists.

Two exceptions were in Scotland when exhibitions were organised to commemorate the work of local Deaf artists. Robert Menzies Scott had an exhibition in 1977 (the year of his death) at Hamilton Museum. A few years afterwards, Perth Art Gallery honoured their local Deaf artist, John Guthrie Spence Smith (1880-1951) with his own exhibition.

The revival of Deaf Art in the 1990s was due in no small measure to the efforts of an organisation called SHAPE, and its Deaf Arts officer, John Wilson. Following the success of the exhibition at the Julius Gottlieb Gallery, another exhibition was held in St. John's College, Cambridge, in October 1995. Called *Deaf Expressions*, it not only exhibited paintings by British Deaf artists, but also paintings and other works of art by Deaf artists from as far away as India and Sudan. Nearly 80 pieces of work were exhibited and over £2000 worth of work had been sold by the end of the first day.

Set up through a bequest to the Royal National Institute for Deaf People that was specifically arts-related, the charity SHAPE had as its objectives three main aims: to promote access to the arts, to promote arts and culture and to create opportunities for employment in the arts. This wide brief covered the theatre, film and other art-forms in addition to visual arts. SHAPE Deaf Arts has been responsible for a large number of national projects including drama, dance, creative signing, sign song, multimedia, plastic and visual arts for all ages of Deaf people. In 1997, a magazine called *Deaf Arts UK* was launched.

The formation of the British Deaf History Society in 1993 has also led to an increase in the awareness of the contribution made to society by British Deaf artists in history, with a number of paintings being pinpointed and catalogued. Unfortunately, the Deaf Community does not currently have the requisite funds to purchase any paintings that come up for sale for the preservation of British Deaf history. Several paintings were on offer in recent years. For example, a painting by William H. H. Trood called *"My Family"*, a fine picture of dogs and cats, came up for auction in Somerset in 1987 and was snapped up for £7,500.

Thanks to SHAPE, interest in Deaf Arts is in good shape to face the challenges of the Millennium. This interest is reflected not only in the increase of Deaf people participating in the arts, both as audiences for mainstream arts and as practitioners of Deaf Arts, but also in the growing number of prestigious arts organisations eager to make their work accessible to the Deaf community. At the Millennium, advances in information technology open up new potential for Deaf Art and Deaf artists on a global scale.

Chapter V   A Pictorial History of Deaf Britain

John Goodricke
*Reproduced by the kind permission of the
Royal Astronomical Society, London*

CHAPTER V

DEAF PEOPLE 1760-1900

The catalyst was the founding of Braidwood's Academy for the Deaf ant Dumb in 1760, the *first* school for deaf children in the world. Some will argue that the first school was in France, founded by the Abbé l'Epée, but it did not start as a school proper until 1763.

With this came some remarkable developments in the deaf world due to the birth of deaf education. In the late 18th century, these included the first Deaf Member of Parliament; the first (and only) Deaf painter to be given a royal appointment; the first Deaf person to be made a Fellow of the Royal Society, and the founding of the Royal Academy with a deaf man as its first president. As Britain moved into the 19th century, this produced the first Deaf barrister and many Deaf people of brilliant ability who were to sow the seeds of the present-day Deaf community. We also saw the growth of teaching as a profession for Deaf men and women. One fine product of deaf education was John Goodricke.

John Goodricke (1764 - 1786)

John Goodricke was born in Groningen, Netherlands, to an English diplomat and his Dutch wife on 17 September 1764 and became deaf in infancy due to a severe illness. In 1772, he was sent from the Netherlands to Edinburgh to be educated at Braidwood's Academy. His progress must have been satisfactory because in 1778 he was allowed to enter Warrington Academy, at that time a well-known school in Cheshire. It made no special provision for handicapped pupils. Goodricke may thus be said to have been one of the first, if not the first, successfully *integrated* pupils. At the Academy, he excelled in mathematics. He had for a teacher William Enfield, a mathematician of some renown whose hobby was astronomy. Through him, Goodricke started to study astronomy.

On leaving Warrington Academy, Goodricke returned to his family who had settled in York where there was already an accomplished astronomer, Edward Pigott. Goodricke was to form a close partnership with Pigott who had fine instruments and a useful network of scientific contacts. Pigott had yearned for companionship in astronomy and welcomed his new pupil eagerly. Even so, he was to complain in 1783 that 'there is not a soul here to converse with on astronomy' because he and Goodricke communicated almost entirely by pencilled notes. On 12 November 1782, Goodricke recorded the message that was to make him famous:

> *'This night I looked at Beta Persei and was much amazed to find its brightness altered - it now appears to be of about the 4th magnitude…'*

For his work, Goodricke was awarded the prestigious Copley medal and the Royal Society elected him to a fellowship. However, Goodricke died at York only two weeks later, supposedly due to a cold from exposure to the night air in astronomical observations. He was only 21 years old.

Francis Humberstone MacKenzie, Lord Seaforth (1754 - 1815)

Francis MacKenzie was born deaf, the second son of Major William MacKenzie, nephew of the 5th Earl of Seaforth. He was placed with Thomas Braidwood at his Academy in Edinburgh where he learnt to some extent to speak. However, for the major part of his life, Francis MacKenzie used sign language to communicate with his peers. He was a very fluent fingerspeller, and many of his associates such as Lord Melville and Lord Guildford acquired fluent fingerspelling skills. He was a highly intelligent and articulate man, given to writing numerous letters.

On 22 April 1782, he married Mary Proby, daughter of the Dean of Lichfield, who bore him 4 sons and 6 daughters.

In 1783, his elder brother Thomas, who had succeeded his second cousin Lord Seaforth in 1781 as Chief of the clan MacKenzie, died and Francis succeeded his brother as Chief of the clan and inherited the considerable Seaforth estates which were in a neglected state.

Because of his interest in his Scottish estate, MacKenzie stood in 1784 against all expectation for Parliament against Lord Macleod, the sitting member for Ross-shire, and was elected, it is said, with a number of fictitious votes.

He served as MP from 1784 to 1790 when he resigned because of his financial problems and gave his interest in the seat to a friend, William Adams.

On the outbreak of war with France, MacKenzie raised the 78th Regiment of Foot, Ross-shire Militia, with himself as Lieutenant-Colonel Commanding. In 1794, he added a second battalion. Although he rose to the rank of Lieutenant General of the Army by 1808, he never joined his, or any other regiment, on active service.

The impact of events in France on domestic politics drew him out of political retirement, and upon his friend Adams being offered a seat at Banbury, he stood again for Ross-shire and was handsomely re-elected. On his return to the House, he gave silent support to the government as a result of which the Seaforth peerage was revived, and he was created 6th Lord Seaforth.

He was appointed Governor of Barbados in 1800, and during his governorship up to 1806 he strove to improve the conditions of slaves. He was reported to have been an able and vigorous governor.

On his return to Britain in 1806, Lord Seaforth played no further significant part in national politics, and his later years were blighted by misfortune. His financial embarrassments caused him to sell the 'gift land' of his house, as well as much of his estates. In addition, the only survivor of his four sons died unmarried in 1814 and MacKenzie himself died a few months later, a physically and mentally broken man.

These last tragic events fulfilled the words of s seer, Kenneth Mackenzie, prior to his execution by the 3rd Lady Seaforth in the 1660s: -

'In the days of a deaf and dumb caberfeidh, the gift land would be sold and the male line of Seaforth will cease.'

Chapter V   A Pictorial History of Deaf Britain

**Francis Humberstone MacKenzie,
6th Lord Seaforth**
*Reproduced by the kind permission of the
Queens Own Highlanders Regiment Museum,
Fort George, Inverness*

Chapter V   A Pictorial History of Deaf Britain

John Philp Wood
The greatest of all Braidwoodian pupils with unequalled all-round skills and contributions to the Deaf community.

The grave of John Philp Wood
St. Cuthbert's Churchyard in the shadow of Edinburgh Castle.

John Philp Wood (1762 - 1838)

Another graduate of Braidwood's Academy who made a success of his life was John Philp Wood. Born in the parish of Cramond, a small village near Edinburgh, he became deaf at very early age through scarlet fever, an infectious disease prevalent in his days. Wood was then sent to the celebrated Thomas Braidwood's Academy for the Deaf and Dumb in Edinburgh, where he was taught under the combined system with a strong emphasis on reading, writing and manualism. Wood excelled in fingerspelling like many Deaf people of his time, but was also well-educated in reading and writing.

This education enabled him to obtain a post of clerk to the Accountant at the Scottish Excise Office in 1778, where he showed good aptitude for figures. After transfer to and working in the office of the Solicitor of Excise for six years, where he had responsibility to maintain and distribute auctioneers' bonds and also to register lawyers' opinions, he returned to his first department in 1797. After a period as assistant Accountant, he became a fully-fledged accountant and in 1802 was promoted to the post of Over Deputy for signing licences.

His work at the Excise Office was so respected that he was appointed Auditor of Excise in 1809 by the Prime Minister, Spencer Percival. Wood earned the tag of being "Honest" for his sincere and diligent auditing. Sir Walter Scott wrote of him in his *Journal* dated 27 June 1830: "*Honest John, my old friend, dined with us. I only regret I cannot understand him, as he has a very powerful and much more curious information.*"

Away from the Excise Office, Wood became interested in history and genealogy and in 1791 published a biography on John Law entitled *A Sketch of the Life of John Law of Lauriston, Comptroller General of the Finances of France.* There followed in 1794, *The Ancient and Modern State of the Parish of Cramond*, a book that credited Wood as Scotland's first ever person to write a parochial history. His interest in genealogy proved an useful asset when he was persuaded in 1813 to prepare the second edition of *The Peerage of Scotland*, which gained him recognition as Scotland's leading genealogist of his time.

After Braidwood's Academy had moved to Hackney in the outskirts of London in 1783, there were no schools for the Deaf in Scotland. In 1809 a meeting was held in Fortune's pub in Edinburgh to discuss the formation of a new public school for Deaf children. The outcome was that Wood was appointed one of the joint secretaries of the Edinburgh Institution for the Education of the Deaf and Dumb, established on 25 June 1810. However, pressure of work forced Wood to resign his post in 1817, but not before he made legal history when Robert Kinniburgh, the headmaster of the Edinburgh Institution, engaged him as a relay interpreter in the famous Jean Campbell case in Glasgow.

Wood kept up his connection with the Edinburgh Deaf community by being one of the first members of the Edinburgh Congregational Church for the Deaf and Dumb in 1830.
John Philp Wood died on 25 October 1838 at his home in South Charlotte Street. A few doors up the street, a baby was born who was to revolutionise the world of communication – Alexander Graham Bell.

Charlotte Bain (1785 - 1846)

The morning of Thursday 25 December 1806 dawned calm and fair, and boats from many little fishing villages along the Moray Firth prepared to go to sea. As the twenty-two men in the three boats from the village of Stotfield, near Lossiemouth, took their respective stations in the boats, a young girl came running down from the village to the shore in breathless haste. It was Charlotte Bain, a 21 year old uneducated deaf girl without speech.

She instantly jumped into the boat in which her father was seated and seizing him by the breasts of his coat, motioned him to return to the shore. The father, thinking it was some foolish notion she had taken to have him out of the boat, took no notice of her frantic signs, but she would not him go and dragged him with almost superhuman effort out of the boat. Her father feared for her reason and left the boat telling his fellow fishermen he would remain at home that day.

Charlotte then employed every sign that she knew to tell the other fishermen that none of them should put to sea on that day, to no avail. She then took her father's hat from his head, laid it upside down on the sand, rocked it backwards and forwards a few times, then upset it. The fishermen understood what she meant, that there could be a capsize if they put to sea, but they laughed at her, thinking she had mental hallucinations and put out to sea.

The men left early in the morning for the fishing grounds a few miles out from Stotfield, put out their lines and made a good haul. When they were returning home about noon, a fearful hurricane arose out of the southwest. Mountainous seas broke over their boats, and in spite of the desperate efforts of the men to row back to the Hythe at Stotfield, the gale carried the boats down the Firth to the open sea. Neither men nor boats were ever seen again. This terrifying storm raged with unabated fury for four hours until the wind veered to the north and gradually died away.

Stotfield was not the only village to suffer tragedy that day. All along the coast, other boats and men were lost but Stotfield was the only village to lose its entire fishing fleet, and the storm left 17 widows and 47 orphaned children.

When the extraordinary circumstances were known, Dummie Bain, as she was called, passed through the rest of her life as a seer. Young girls would come to her to have their fortunes read, to see what sort of husbands they would get, the number of children they would have and so forth, all of which circumstances she would signify by movements of her hands and fingers. With the general spread of schooling becoming available, her occupation as seer waned and Charlotte used her second sight in later years sparingly.

She died unmarried on 5 August 1846.

Chapter V   A Pictorial History of Deaf Britain

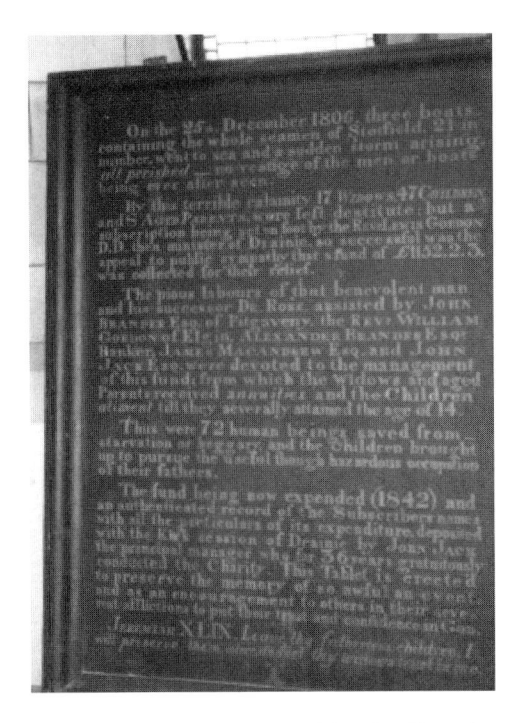

Fishing Disaster Memorial at St Geraldine's Church, Lossiemouth

Original fishermen's cottages at Lossiemouth
Charlotte Bain lived in a cottage like this.

Chapter V   A Pictorial History of Deaf Britain

William Spencer Cavendish, 6th Duke of Devonshire
Reproduced by permission of The Chatsworth Settlement Trustees

William Spencer Cavendish, 6th Duke of Devonshire (1790 - 1858)

William Spencer Cavendish, sixth Duke of Devonshire, was born in Paris on 21 May 1790. Called Hart by his family and always known by his successors as the Bachelor Duke, he inherited Chatsworth together with nearly 200,000 acres of land in England and Ireland, at the age of twenty one, when he succeeded his father in 1811. Though in opposition to the Government of the day, he was immediately appointed Lord-Lieutenant of Derbyshire.

He was educated at Harrow and Cambridge, and became deaf in early childhood, which caused him to become studious. He was said to have had a great sense of humour, which made him both funny and sad, an irresistible combination, which led him to be a great host at times. His embassy to the coronation of Tsar Nicholas in Moscow in 1825 (which cost him £50,000 more than the sum allowed by the government) was famous for its splendour and his entertainments in Derbyshire, London and Ireland were no less magnificent.

Princess Victoria came to stay at Chatsworth in 1832 and later when she was Queen in 1843. He gave many events taking immense trouble to make his guests enjoy themselves.

The Duke was unusual for a Cavendish in that he was not a politician, although he interested himself in Irish questions, keenly supported the Reform Bill of 1832 and was a willing champion of anyone he thought unjustly treated.

His life, his work and his pleasure was taken up with Chatsworth and the other houses, and with his friends. He devoted himself to an immense rebuilding and renovation programme at Chatsworth House, Derbyshire, where he loved to spend many hours in the library.

Today, Chatsworth is one of the biggest tourist attractions in the country. Much of this was due to the attention, money and detail lavished by the sixth Duke, along with work of his protégé, Sir Joseph Paxton.

Paxton was a young gardener at Chatsworth when, encouraged by the 6th Duke, he built a giant conservatory 300 feet long, 145 feet wide by 60 feet high which soon attracted the world's attention and led to Paxton being commissioned to build the Crystal Palace for the Exhibition of 1851. (The conservatory at Chatsworth was sadly demolished after World War 1 but many of Paxton's improvements still remain to be seen.)

The 6th Duke never married and died in 1858 a rather disappointed and unhappy man.

The connection of deafness with the Dukes of Devonshire persists to this day: the 11th Duke is Patron of the National Deaf Children's Society and also of the Royal School for the Deaf, Derby. It is through the generosity of the 11th Duke that the Duke's Barn Countryside Centre, a marvellous study and conference centre on the Chatsworth estate, was presented to the school in 1986.

The Deaf Landed Gentry

Northamptonshire is unique that it had at the same time, two Deaf people who were born into the landed gentry.

Ambrose Isted (1797 - 1881)

In the parish church in the village of Ecton, a few miles from Althorp where Princess Diana is buried, there is a large vault dedicated to the Isted family. This is the burial place of Ambrose Isted, who was born deaf and dumb and was baptised on 22 February 1797 in Ecton. His parents were Samuel Isted (1750-1827) and Barbara, the eldest daughter of Thomas Percy, Bishop of Dromore. The wealthy family originated from Framfield, Sussex, and settled at the Manor of Ecton (later Ecton Hall) during the early eighteenth century.

At the age of eight, Ambrose Isted was sent to Dromore, Ireland, where he received his early tuition from his grandfather before being admitted to the London Asylum for the Deaf and Dumb as a private fee-paying pupil. He received a good all round education which was to stand him in good stead in later life.

He thoroughly enjoyed hunting and all kinds of sport. Every year for sixty years, Ambrose rode ten miles north to Pytchley for the Meet of the famous Pytchley Hunt. He wore the traditional red coat with the white collar, the Pytchley trademark, and was always well-mounted. In his old age, he was forced to give up his beloved hunting and instead he assumed the horn for his local hunt as the master of the Pytchley Harriers. Ambrose Isted was able to establish for himself a distinguished position in Northamptonshire, earning the nickname *"The Deaf Squire"*. He is unique as the only Deaf Master of a English Hunt.

He exhibited a keen interest in both the affairs of his old school and the Royal Association in Aid of the Deaf and Dumb, often attending its meetings and was a ready donor for its funds. He died on May 13 1881.

George Percy Patrick, Lord Carberry (1810 - 1890)

One of the few aristocrats to feel an affinity with his fellow Deaf was George Percy Patrick, later Lord Carberry of Laxton Hall, Northamptonshire. Born Deaf in Co. Wexford, Ireland, Lord Carberry never spoke in his life. He was educated privately at home in Northamptonshire in his early years, then sent to France at the age of 10 to the Paris Institution for the Deaf and Dumb.

His Irish birth and French education gave him a lifelong interest in the welfare of Deaf people both in Ireland and in Europe, using his family wealth to support many schools for deaf children and organisations for deaf adults. He became associated with St. Saviour's Church for the Deaf, contributing £110 to its building fund and a further £200 to enable the trustees to complete the chaplain's residence.

When the National Deaf and Dumb Society, the forerunner to the British Deaf and Dumb Association, was formed in 1879, Lord Carberry gave financial support to the organisation, and was elected its first President.

Chapter V A Pictorial History of Deaf Britain

Ambrose Isted

George Percy Patrick, Lord Carberry

Chapter V   A Pictorial History of Deaf Britain

John William Lowe

John William Lowe (1804 - 1876)

The law as a profession is regarded as a difficult one for *hearing* people, and not many manage to become solicitors; still fewer get called before the Bar to become barristers. For people deprived of hearing, the law is regarded as a forbidden or impossible profession. All the more remarkable then that in 1829, a born-deaf person with no speech was called to the Bar and become a barrister.

John William Lowe was born in Russell Square, London, on 24 September 1804 to a wealthy solicitor, William Lowe, and his wife, Eliza. When he was six years old, he became a private pupil of Dr. Joseph Watson at the Asylum for the Deaf and Dumb Poor. His father being a man of means, Lowe remained under Dr. Watson's care for twelve years, receiving the best of attention because of his undoubted abilities and studious nature. By the time he left the Old Kent Road school, he had absorbed the classics and learnt French. He was also proficient in mathematics and in the sciences at university level.

Although Lowe under Dr. Watson had also learnt enough speech to make himself understood by members of his family, he was to say that his usual method of communicating with his family was by his fingers, and with strangers, by writing.

John Lowe' mental attainments at the age of 18 were so great that his father saw nothing incongruous in advising him to take up the law as a profession. Through influential friends, he was made a member of the Society of the Middle Temple in 1820 and placed in the office of two eminent solicitors, a Mr. Justice Patterson and a Sir Nicholas Tindal, who later became the Lord Chief justice of England and Wales.

Lowe was quick to learn the various practices of the law profession, and decided upon conveyancing, transferring property from one person to another by purchase, lease or deed, as that branch of the law where his deafness was less of a handicap. He did so well by the end of 1829 that he took the oath as a barrister of the Middle Temple – a most unprecedented event which created a sensation in the profession.

By Frances Jellicoe, he had four children and the three who survived infancy quickly learnt sign language in order to communicate with their father.

In his leisure hours, Lowe was a linguist and by the time he was 34 years old, he could read and write in French (modern and old Norman), Latin, Greek (ancient and modern), German, Italian, Spanish, Portuguese, Dutch and Danish. His chief means of learning a vocabulary was to read a foreign-language translation of the New Testament side by side with the English version. In his 35th year, he commenced the study of Hebrew and the Psalms became his favourite reading in that language.

Lowe continued his career until 1871 when he fell victim to a pulmonary disease, which prevented him from joining the services for the deaf at the new St. Saviour's Church. He died on 3 February 1876.

John Kitto (1804 - 1854)

Born in Plymouth, Devon, to a poor stonemason, also called John, and his wife Elizabeth, John Kitto was a sickly lad who cared for nothing but books. He was educated at four Plymouth schools, all not even on a regular basis; he only attended when his grandmother could get together the few pence required to pay his fee. This was all the education that he had.

At the age of 12, Kitto was taken on by his father to assist him in his trade. It was shortly afterwards when he was working for his father slating a new roof that he lost his footing in the act of stepping off a ladder and fell thirty-five feet to the ground.

In his book *Lost Senses,* Kitto relates his feelings and impressions when awakening from the coma caused by his fall and how, when he demanded that people around his bed speak to him, someone wrote on a slate, 'YOU ARE DEAF'. Kitto never heard sound again.

Unfit to work, he was left to spend his time as he pleased and he devoted himself to reading, selling scraps of old iron and painting childrens' books and shop labels to raise the few pence needed to buy books.

In November 1819 the poverty of Kitto's family finally forced them to send him to the workhouse, where he was set to learn shoe making. After two years, he was judged to have learnt sufficient skills and was apprenticed to a Plymouth shoemaker who treated him so badly that he was re-admitted to the workhouse. He was then employed as a sub-librarian in Plymouth. This suited Kitto as he could get as many books to read as he wished. After a year of this, he worked for an Exeter dentist, a Mr. Groves, as a dental technician. Mr. Groves had aspirations to become a missionary and was instrumental in getting Kitto a place in the Missionary College in Islington, London, where he learnt printing with a view to being of some service in some foreign missionary institution. In 1827 he was sent to Malta but because of his declining health, he returned to England in 1829.

Shortly afterwards, his former employer Mr. Groves desired a tutor for his children when he went on a missionary tour of the Middle East and selected Kitto for the position. This gave the opportunity for Kitto to acquire knowledge of customs and scenery which he put to good use on his return to England in 1833 by writing articles in the *Penny Magazine* under the title, 'The Deaf Traveller'.

Charles Knight, the editor of the *Penny Magazine,* suggested to Kitto that he prepare an illustrated bible. Kitto did with such enthusiasm that *The Pictorial Bible* was ready in less than two years. This book established Kitto as a writer and he wrote a number of books based on the Scripture, including the work which is still regarded as the best of its kind, *Cyclopaedia of Biblical Literature.*

John Kitto was made Doctorate of Divinity by the University of Giessen in 1844 and in 1845 became a Fellow of the Society of Antiquaries.

His health, never very good, began to fail in 1851. In August 1854, he proceeded to Germany to try out the mineral waters there, but died on 25 November 1854 at Cannstadt, near Stuttgart, survived by his wife, whom he had married in 1833, and seven children.

John Kitto

Chapter V   A Pictorial History of Deaf Britain

Harriet Martineau

Helen Marion Burnside

Deaf Women Writers

The 19th century produced two great women writers who were deaf and achieved great fame in their particular fields of writing, Harriet Martineau and Helen Marion Burnside.

Harriet Martineau (1802 - 1876)

One of the literary giants of the period 1850 – 1880 , Harriet Martineau was referred to by Charles Dickens in one of his books as 'the little deaf woman of Norwich'. Her deafness became evident at the age of 12 while she was attending a school run by a Reverend Perry, when she found that she could not hear very well if she sat too far from the teacher. By the time she was 16, it had worsened as to become very noticeable and inconvenient to herself.

In the solitude resulting from her deafness, Miss Martineau turned to journalism and literary writing. She became a prolific contributor to magazines and newspapers and began to have books and novels published. Her reputation was established with the nine-volume *Illustrations of Political Economy,* and she received a good income from her magazine contributions which enabled her to go to America in 1834.

In America, she showed that her sympathies lay with those who favoured the abolition of slavery. Always a forthright woman, she incurred the wrath of the anti-abolitionists and her life was threatened. On her return to England in 1837, she published an account of her travels followed by two best-selling novels, *Deerbrook* and *Life in a Sick Room.* Earlier, she had written *Letter to the Deaf* in which she gave advice to deaf people based on her experiences.

Harriet Martineau suffered from a heart defect which caused her ill-health in her later years and she died in Birmingham in 1876.

Helen Marion Burnside (1844 - 1920)

Helen Marion Burnside was born at Bromley Hall, Middlesex. For a large part of her life, she lived and worked with Miss Rosa Nouchette Carey, the novelist in Surrey.
She lost her hearing completely at the age of 10 due to a childhood illness. Until then, her ambition was to become a composer. This, of course, she had to give up, but, a few years afterwards, she commenced writing poetry. A small volume of these verses was published in 1864, one or two of which were set to music. This suggested the writing of other lyrics and poems for magazines. From then onwards, a great many verses were published, mostly as Christmas Card verses and about 150 of her songs were set to music. Helen Burnside became better known as the "Christmas Card-Laureate", writing Christmas poems for nearly thirty-seven years at the rate of something like 200 a year.

A poor lip-reader, she came to use the manual alphabet frequently, making sure that her many friends learnt this method to communicate with her.

Alexandra, Queen Consort (1844 - 1925)

There has never been a British monarch, or before the union of England and Scotland, an English or Scottish monarch, who was Deaf.

The nearest Britain came to having a Deaf monarch was in the case of Prince Albert Victor, elder son of the Prince and Princess of Wales, later King Edward VII and Queen Alexandra. Prince Albert had inherited the hereditary disease, otosclerosis, from his mother who had herself inherited it from her own mother, Queen Louise of Denmark. However, Prince Albert Victor died of thyroid even before his father became King.

Born on 1 December 1844, Queen Alexandra is probably Britain's best known Deaf Royal. She was so beautiful that the Prince of Wales - who was then the most eligible bachelor in the world - fell in love with her photograph before he even met her.

When Alexandra and the Prince of Wales finally met, the meetings they had were brief and chaperoned. It seemed that the fact she was deaf was withheld from the Prince who was determined to rush into marriage with this fabulous beauty.

The marriage took place at St. George's Chapel in Windsor Castle on 10 March 1863, and the young Danish Princess overwhelmed her new mother-in-law, Queen Victoria, with her beauty. The Queen was, however, heard to lament, "Alas! She (the Princess) is deaf and everybody observes it, which is a sad misfortune."

The Prince of Wales, who was notorious for his liking for loose women, grew to bitterly regret rushing into the marriage. Alexandra never had a formal education and found she had very little in common with her husband, despite having four children by him. The Prince often poked fun at her deafness and was impatient in her company.

Queen Victoria and the Princess of Wales became very close. As Alexandra never learnt to lip-read and refused to use an ear trumpet, it is likely they communicated in fingerspelling. Queen Victoria was fluent in fingerspelling (she comforted a dying Deaf woman in the Isle of Wight for several hours a time and was also able to communicate with other Deaf people such as William Agnew) and probably taught Alexandra the British manual alphabet.

With her fingerspelling skills, Alexandra would sometimes attend St. Saviour's Church for the Deaf in Oxford Street, London, where she enjoyed the services.

During her period as Queen Consort and after the King's death as the Queen Dowager, Alexandra would sometimes purchase a number of works of Deaf art and sculpture, especially if the work of art was of herself. A number of Deaf artists and sculptors therefore enjoyed her patronage. The Queen particularly favoured the young Deaf sculptress, Dorothy Stanton Wise.

Queen Alexandra died in 1925 at the age of 81.

Chapter V   A Pictorial History of Deaf Britain

Queen Alexandra

Chapter V   A Pictorial History of Deaf Britain

Reverend Richard Aslett Pearce

Samuel Bright Lucas

Reverend Richard Aslett Pearce (1854 - 1928)

Born In Southampton, he was educated as a private pupil at the Brighton Institution for the Deaf and Dumb by the sign and manual system, along with his Deaf brother and sister, Walter Seaward Pearce and Fanny Pearce.

He stayed at the Brighton Institution for 12 years, obtaining a high class education. On leaving the Institution at the age of 18, he entered his father's attorney offices as a secretary. In his leisure time, he became interested in church work through the influence of a Reverend Mansfield Owen who had a cousin who was Pearce's boyhood Deaf friend. Together with another clergyman, the Rev. Owen encouraged the young man to seek out as many local deaf people as possible and bring them to church services.

In 1879 Pearce together with the Owen cousins, and the Rev. Samuel Smith of St. Saviour's Church for the Deaf in London established the Winchester Diocesan Adult Deaf and Dumb Mission. This interested the Bishop of Winchester in work amongst the deaf and soon afterwards Pearce commenced studying for Holy Orders.

He passed the Bishop's examination and was ordained a Deacon in the Church of England in an interesting ceremony at the Parish Church of Farnham, Surrey, in 1885. The ordination was conferred upon him by the special approval of the Archbishop of Canterbury.

Richard Aslett Pearce was the first born-deaf man to be ordained in England, and he continued to do pastoral work throughout Hampshire until his death in 1928. As his diocese included the Isle of Wright, he would often have occasion to hold signed conversations with Queen Victoria who was acquainted with some Deaf people near her favourite retreat at Osborne.

Samuel Bright Lucas (1840 - 1919)

Samuel Bright Lucas was born in London in 1840. Losing his hearing in infancy, he received his education partly under a private tutor and partly at Bristol under Dr. Webster.

In 1868 he married Miss Jessie Oliver, by whom he had two sons. A member of the National Liberal Club, he travelled widely in Norway, Sweden, Germany and Europe and was extremely well read. A keen billiards player and salmon fisherman, he achieved some distinction as a water-colour artist, exhibiting in the Royal Academy.

What distinguished Samuel Bright Lucas from others was his interest in the welfare of the deaf and dumb in London. For many years, he was the Secretary of the Royal Association in Aid of Deaf and Dumb. He was forthright in expressing his opinions and in the defence of the RADD. More than any other person, it was Samuel Bright Lucas who was directly responsible for the collapse of the National Deaf and Dumb Society, seeing it as a rival to his beloved Royal Association. He was less successful in confronting the newly formed British Deaf and Dumb Association a few years later, but continued to serve the RADD until his death in 1919 after a short illness.

Mighty Deaf Pens of the 19th Century

The 19th century produced many Deaf people who were excellent writers. Two of them were born within two years of each other.

Alexander Fairley Strathern (1844 - 1890)

He was born in West George Street, Glasgow, the son of the Sheriff of Glasgow. He lost his hearing at an early age and was for some time a day scholar at the Glasgow Institution under the late Duncan Anderson. Prior to that, he had been at an ordinary day school.

After leaving school, he was apprenticed as a wood-engraver, but never took to that trade kindly, and later learnt the printing trade. Although he was involved to some extent in the Deaf community, particularly in Glasgow, he was probably best known throughout the country by his connection with the *Deaf and Dumb Magazine*, which he edited and published for some time after the late Rev. Samuel Smith gave it up.

Frederick Lawrence Tavaré (1846 - 1930)

F. L. Tavaré was born at Cheetham in Manchester on 13 December 1846, the son of an art teacher. His deafness was discovered when he was aged 2, and he was sent to the Manchester Institution in October 1854 as a pupil and boarder. He remained there until December 1861 and studied drawing.

On leaving school, he won certificates in freehand and modern drawing from the Science and Art department of the Committee of Council on Education examination. When his father died on June 17 1868, Frederick and his younger brother, Charles, succeeded to his connection as teacher of drawing and maintained it until 13 December 1872.

Although Frederick L. Tavaré was best known for his pictures and sketches taken from quaint, tumbledown, timber-fronted relics of Old Manchester that were doomed to destruction, he was quite an authority on the antiquities and annals of his native city and county. He contributed many articles to *the Manchester Weekly News* and the *Manchester City News*. The editor of The Dictionary of National Biography applied to Mr. Tavaré for assistance in the compilation on the brief of Charles Swain, and duly acknowledged the source of his information.

Before these two newspaper and magazine publishers flourished, however, there was an unique autobiography written by a former pupil of the Edinburgh Institution for the Deaf and Dumb. **Alexander Atkinson (1806 - 1879)**, in writing *The Memoirs of My Youth* (published in 1865), became the first born-deaf person to write out his autobiography, which is a classic in terms of detailing his experiences as a schoolchild in Edinburgh and as a young man in Newcastle-upon-Tyne.

Eclipsing them all, however, was a literary giant of the late nineteenth and early twentieth-centuries, whose research and persistence to detail made an enormous contribution to Deaf History, Abraham Farrar.

Chapter V A Pictorial History of Deaf Britain

Alexander Fairley Strathern

Frederick Lawrence Tavaré

Chapter V   A Pictorial History of Deaf Britain

Abraham Farrar, F.G.S.

Abraham Farrar, F.G.S. (1861 - 1944)

One of the most remarkable of deaf men who was an oralist but who respected those that used sign language was Abraham Farrar. Born in Leeds, he became deaf at the age of 3 due to scarlet fever. His father had an estate near Leeds which yielded a considerable income, and which later helped Farrar to pursue his academic quest.

Farrar was the first pupil to be educated by the Rev. Thomas Arnold, whose Private Oral School at Northampton's reputation was established with the success of teaching Farrar.

Abraham Farrar was a child prodigy who passed both the London University and Cambridge University examinations by the time he was 17, and could no doubt have gone on towards a degree had he been inclined to do so. His father, however, preferred that Farrar went in for a professional career, and consequently he was articled to a firm of architects and surveyors in Northampton, becoming a Fellow of the Geographical Society.

On his father's death, Farrar abandoned his professional career, content to live off the income from his father's estate which he managed admirably, and instead concentrated on what was to be his lifetime's consuming interest – the compilation of literature on deafness.

Abraham Farrar was the first real researcher into the history of teaching the deaf and he unearthed many previously unknown items of literature about the deaf and was largely responsible for building up Oxley's Library of the Deaf. This Library was largely fragmented after Oxley's death and many rare articles and books disappeared, although some were housed at Manchester University.

His researches in Spain on deaf characters in the early days of deaf education by monks were particularly revealing.

Farrar was always scrupulously fair in his writings on deaf history, neither favouring use of sign language or oralism, constantly giving credit where this was due to either method. Even so, Abraham Farrar was regarded by oralists as the greatest triumph for the oral method of teaching the deaf. In the days of continued controversy between oral and manual methods of deaf education, he was a bone of contention between the two camps. Francis Maginn was once driven to address a BDDA Congress that *'Oral' pupils could not be kept from signing. Even Mr. Farrar spelt on his fingers very well'.*

That much was true. When he had to, Farrar would respect another Deaf person's mode of communication and use the manual alphabet. This was something those glorying in his success always conveniently overlooked. Abraham Farrar never forgot that when it really came to the crunch, during the hearings by the Royal Commission of 1889 into the use of sign language and manualism in schools, the Oralists contemptuously brushed aside his counsel that the Oral method would not suit every Deaf person.

Heroic Swimmers

The 19th century produced two men of exceptional swimming ability, which few would ever be able to emulate.

Alexander Ferguson (1841 - 1889)

Alexander Ferguson was born deaf in Dundee and was sent to the Edinburgh Institution for the Deaf and Dumb. After leaving the institution, he obtained employment as a stonemason in Dundee Docks.

What distinguished Alexander Ferguson from the rest of his fellow men was his exception ability as a swimmer. Starting as a boy of 10, he rescued a large number of people from drowning in various parts of Scotland and also in England. For some of these rescues he was awarded medals, including a silver medal from the Royal Humane Society. The deed that earned him this medal involved the rescue of a soldier who fell overboard from the paddle-steamer, *Juno*, as it was entering Inverness harbour. The soldier was sucked underneath the paddlewheel, which was still in motion. Ferguson, standing on the quay, saw this happen and dived in fully clothed and at great risk to himself, dragged the soldier out of the paddlewheel and hauled him unconscious to the quay where other people saved his life.

However, some of his more publicised swimming feats were done for cash and include swims that the majority of exceptional swimmers would baulk at. For example, he swam across the Firth of Clyde on four occasions and across the Firth of Forth on one occasion. Perhaps his greatest and most dangerous feat was to swim across part of the stormy Pentland Firth at the top of Scotland from John O'Groats to the island of Stroma.

Alexander Ferguson died in 1889 of pneumonia after making one swim too many.

James John Weeble (1878 - 1961)

On 25 July 1898, an Edwin Bailey was bathing on the beach in rough seas at Porthtowan, Cornwall, when he was caught by a strong current and swept out to sea.

One other man, a Henry W. Harris, a railway official, went to his rescue and succeeded in reaching the drowning swimmer, but got into difficulties himself and could not bring the other to the shore. Both men were in serious danger of drowning.

The men's difficulties were spotted by James John Weeble, a Deaf man from Redruth, and ex-pupil of the Royal West of England School for the Deaf, Exeter. At very considerable risk to himself, he swam out fully clothed and after a tremendous struggle, succeeded in dragging both men back to the beach.

James J. Weeble was awarded the Royal Human Society's Bronze Medal on 15 August 1898 for this gallant rescue.

James J. Weeble died at Plymouth aged 83 on 4 April 1961.

Alexander Ferguson

James John Weeble

Chapter VI   A Pictorial History of Deaf Britain

Interior of Edinburgh Congregational Church for the Deaf
The oldest Deaf Church in the World.

St. Saviour's Church, London, 1840s
The oldest Deaf centre in Britain

CHAPTER VI

MISSIONS AND CENTRES FOR DEAF PEOPLE

The first organised meetings of Deaf adults began to be held in the early 19th century, first in Glasgow, then in Edinburgh, London, Manchester and Leeds. The early meetings were largely prayer meetings and associated with church activities. However, they formed the roots of the present-day adult deaf organisational network.

In 1822, John Anderson, the former Headmaster of the Glasgow Institution for the Deaf and Dumb, was teaching privately from his house in St. Andrew's Square when he was approached by several ex-pupils desiring a place to meet and maintain contact with each other. He started holding prayer meetings on Sunday evenings, which also developed into a limited form of social gathering. When he left to take up the post of Headmaster at the new Liverpool Institution in 1824, a short time elapsed without any Sunday prayer meetings before another teacher from the Glasgow Institution, a J. Ferguson, revived them. These prayer meetings took place on Sunday afternoons in a private medical lecture room in North Portland Street during the latter part of 1825, and continued until 1827 when Mr. Ferguson became an ordained minister of the Church of England and left the city.

After his departure, an interval of many years elapsed without any regular meetings. Only the rare occasional meeting took place, usually conducted by a deaf person.

Meanwhile in Edinburgh, the Congregational Church for the Deaf and Dumb had been set up in 1830. This is still in existence today. This was followed by a group in London that was later to become the Royal Association in the aid of Deaf and Dumb (RAD) in 1840.

By 1844, deaf adults in Glasgow were beginning to feel the absence of a regular meeting place acutely and a group of deaf people met to appoint a Deaf man called William Ure as their representative. He approached the then Headmaster of the Glasgow Institution, Duncan Anderson, for assistance in procuring premises to establish a meeting place where they could hold prayers and social gatherings.

What was later to become the Glasgow Mission to the Deaf and Dumb was established in a hall in the Andersonian University. Regular meetings were held there, with periods also spent in Balfour's School in North Portland Street (1848-1850). An off-shoot also began meeting in 1857-1858 in the Young Men's Christian Association premises in Frederick Street as the Glasgow Deaf Mutual Improvement Society, a group of religious Glasgow deaf church members who strongly disapproved of drinking.

This study of early history of missions for deaf adults shows that whilst Glasgow can lay claim to having had the earliest adult deaf group, Edinburgh's Deaf Society has the longest continuous existence of any adult deaf organisation anywhere in the world (*See Walter Geikie, page 93*).

Early History: The first Missions in England- London and Manchester

Just as the first deaf schools started in Scotland, so did the first adult deaf organisations. However, it was in England that adult deaf organisations took off. The first was in London where many former pupils of the Old Kent Road Asylum found that their need to meet and socialise was lacking. A group of them agreed to meet together for prayer at a small meeting room in Fetter Lane. This became known to some interested people who took a house in Red Lion Square where some destitute men and women were lodged and taught trades.

From these small beginnings, the Association for the Deaf and Dumb (later to become the RAD) took its roots. By 1851, this Deaf Mission had become more of a social than religious place of support to Deaf people and therefore it reorganised itself in 1854 by sending the deaf inmates back to their families and appointing in 1855 Samuel Smith, a teacher at the Yorkshire Institution, as a lay-missioner. Samuel Smith took the view that the spiritual needs of deaf people could only be properly provided for if they had their own church and an ordained minister. With the support of his committee, Smith studied for Holy Orders, becoming ordained in 1861 and got busy fundraising.

In 1870, the foundation stone of St. Saviour's Church for the Deaf and Dumb was laid by H.R.H. the Prince of Wales in Oxford Street and formally opened in 1873 with several members of the Royal Family in the congregation.

In Manchester, the beginnings of the adult deaf movement can be traced back to James Herriot, a Deaf man from Edinburgh who had a good education at the Edinburgh Institution. Born on 1 September 1815, James Herriot moved to Manchester in 1843 in search of new prospects. He was shocked at the difference between the Deaf communities of Manchester and Edinburgh. Whereas in Edinburgh, there were well-educated Deaf men of the calibre of Burns and Geikie, in Manchester those of his own age were inferior in literacy skills and older ones were completely uneducated. In 1846, Herriot obtained free use of the library next to the Presbyterian Church on St. Peter's Square, where for the next two years the first Deaf association in Manchester operated. In 1849, this officially became the Manchester and Salford Adult Deaf and Dumb Benevolent Association, which was in existence for over 100 years, for much of that period at Quay Street (the present site of Granada television) before it merged with the Manchester Deaf and Dumb Society in 1950. This Society had been formed in 1854 by the committee of the Manchester Institution as a rival to the Manchester and Salford Adult Deaf and Dumb Benevolent Association.

In 1878, the Manchester Adult Institute for the Deaf and Dumb opened as the first ever building specifically erected as a social meeting place, as opposed to a church, in the world. This building still stands, although Manchester Deaf Centre (as the merged bodies are now known) occupies University-owned premises in the Oxford Street precinct about half a mile down the road from the old institute.

James Herriot died in 1880.

Chapter VI   A Pictorial History of Deaf Britain

Manchester Adult Deaf and Dumb Institute
The first purpose built social centre for Deaf people in the World

James Herriot

**The founders of the Aberdeen Adult Deaf Mute
Improvement Association 1879**
J.T.Lyon (Deaf); C.McHardy (Deaf); J.McHardy (Deaf); A.Pender (Missioner)
Photo: R.Cormack

The Growth of Deaf Missions

In Leeds, a clergyman named the Reverend Edward Jackson found that youths that had left the Yorkshire Institution at Doncaster were roaming the streets at a loose end causing mischief. In 1850, through his own efforts, he got together a group of people interested in the spiritual care of blind people as well as deaf people and formed the Leeds United Institution for the Blind, the Deaf and the Dumb. It was not until 1875, however, that the foundation stone of their first centre was laid. This association of societies continues to the present day in the present building at Centenary House, North Street, Leeds.

In Dundee, the then headmaster of the Dundee School for the Deaf - a Deaf man named Alexander Drysdale – took the lead to establish an adult deaf mission in 1853 at the request of former pupils from his school.

This inspired Deaf men in other parts of the country to do the same for their local Deaf people. These included George Healey (Liverpool, 1864), W. A. Griffiths (Birmingham, 1867), J. Davis (Stoke-on-Trent, 1868), J. Rowlands, (Cardiff, 1869). In Aberdeen, three young Deaf men got together with a Mr. A. Pender to form the Aberdeen Adult Deaf-Mute Improvement Society, with Pender as their first missioner.

The development of the Adult Deaf and Dumb Institute at Liverpool was a particularly inspiring one that started with a visit to London by a young George Healey. There, he learnt of the work being carried out at St. Saviour's Church by the Reverend Smith and what was happening in other parts of the country. Back in Liverpool, he led the formation of an Adult Deaf Society and obtained a lay-preacher's licence from the Bishop of Liverpool to conduct services for local Deaf people, which took place in the school. He carried on being associated with the institute until his death in 1927, having seen the society develop from humble beginnings in a schoolroom to a grand institute built in 1887.

Interested persons, mainly clergymen or Institution headmasters, formed other missions and adult deaf societies. This was the case in Belfast, where the Headmaster of the Ulster Institution, the Reverend Kinghan, formed the Kinghan Mission. The same happened in Sheffield in 1863, when the efforts of the Headmaster of the Yorkshire Institution resulted in the formation of a local association. In Nottingham (1868) and Southampton (1879), clergymen who had learnt of the work of the Reverend Samuel Smith formed local associations. The clergymen at Southampton appointed a Richard Pearce as the first missioner. In due course, he was ordained as a priest and became the first born-Deaf person to do so.

The Reverend Smith was not always interested in local issues. A meeting called the Leicester Deaf and Dumb Association was held in September 1874 when the Reverend addressed a gathering of 8 Deaf men and took the collection back to St. Saviour's for the benefit of the London Deaf! It was not until 1897 that the Leicester Mission was officially formed!

Glasgow: 1890s

The 1890s were probably the most remarkable decade in British Deaf history – no other decade with the possible exception of the 1980s saw the social status of Deaf people held so high in public esteem. This was especially true in Scotland and in particular Glasgow, which may justly claim to have been the Deaf 'capital' during this era. In this decade, Glasgow held a Grand Bazaar and the first ever exhibition of deaf art; it also built its new deaf centre, had a flourishing soccer team and staged the first soccer international between Scotland and England.

Glasgow also had a weekly deaf column in the *Glasgow Evening Times*, written by a variety of people. Through their own efforts, Deaf people were in the forefront of Glasgow society.

Despite the trend in deaf education from sign language to oralism, the social standing of deaf people who relied on fingerspelling and sign language was given a tremendous boost by the dignity and bearing of people like William Agnew. He took tremendous pride that he was on 'fingerspelling terms' with Queen Victoria. All these people were firm supporters of sign language – William Agnew in particular used to bombard the *Glasgow Evening Times* and the *London Times* with letters denouncing the spread of the 'German Method' in out schools.

The social standing of deaf people may also have in no small way been aided by the Princess of Wales (later Queen Alexandra) who was stone deaf and who used fingerspelling as well as lip-reading to communicate.

The year 1890 was also a very significant year in deaf history for it saw the birth of the British Deaf and Dumb Association.

Since the re-formation of the Glasgow Mission for the Deaf and Dumb in the 1850s, the mission had been based at premises in Renfield Street from 1870 onwards. Now, in 1890, it was obvious the premises had become inadequate to cater for the social, pastoral and spiritual activities of the Deaf citizens of Glasgow, and that a better and bigger building was needed.

The deaf of Glasgow were at the time extremely fortunate to have in William Agnew a most intelligent and capable man. He was an artist in his leisure time and through his hobby had come into contact with Queen Victoria. He also enjoyed a friendship with Lord and Lady Blythswood (Glasgow Deaf and Dumb F.C. in the 1890s were renamed Blythswood Athletic). Although he could not speak and relied entirely on sign language, he was a forceful personality and moved about amongst the rich merchants of Glasgow.

He took it upon himself to promote the idea of having a noble building for an Institute in Glasgow and in this venture, two brothers named James and Edwin Docharty ably supported him. Sons of a famous Scottish painter, they were themselves able painters. An added advantage that the Deaf people of Glasgow had over any other Deaf community in the country was that they had a regular 'Deaf and Dumb Notes' column every week in the *Glasgow Evening Times,* the largest selling Scottish evening paper. This meant that fundraising news and any other news about Deaf people was in the forefront of everyone's attention.

Leading Members of the Glasgow Mission for the Adult Deaf and Dumb 1894
Photo: Glasgow and West of Scotland Society for the Deaf

Chapter VI A Pictorial History of Deaf Britain

Ceremony of Laying the Foundation Stone Glasgow, February 1894
Photo: Glasgow & West of Scotland Society for the Deaf

William Agnew
Director of the Glasgow Adult Deaf & Dumb Mission
Photo: Glasgow & West of Scotland Society for the Deaf

Glasgow: The Grand Bazaar and Opening Ceremony

In a short period of time, the Deaf people of Glasgow had raised through their efforts the entire costs of the proposed building. This included a handsome contribution from Queen Victoria herself. However, they needed money to purchase a prime site in the centre of Glasgow.

In order to raise the sum required of £5000, they organised a Grand Bazaar, which was held in St. Andrew's Hall and formally opened by the Duchess of Montrose. Thanks to William Agnew's connections amongst Glasgow's high society, the Bazaar was extremely successful and raised more than enough to purchase a prime site on the corner of West Regent Street and West Campbell Street.

An exhibition of paintings and works of art by deaf artists in Britain followed – the first of its kind to be held. All artists living in Scotland, along with many of the better known artists from England like Thomas Davidson, Rupert Dent and William Trood all sent paintings. Many were sold to raise further funds to furnish the new institute.

This was held at St. Andrew's Hall between 19 and 21 of November 1891 and was opened once again by the Duchess of Montrose. Ironically, her son was later to become totally deaf and become President of the RNID.

The Bazaar totally exceeded all expectations and was a rousing success, raising in excess of £6,000 when the Building Committee had only dared to hope to raise at the most optimistic a sum of £5,000.

Never a person to let anything grow under his feet, Agnew arranged for ceremonies for every possible occasion. The laying of the foundation stone was greeted with great fanfare and a sense of occasion, and the official opening of the institute was a most elaborate affair in which beautifully designed invitations were sent out to many dignitaries.

William Agnew (1846 - 1914)

William Agnew was born deaf in Glasgow and at an early age was sent to be educated at the Glasgow Institution for the Deaf and Dumb, where he proved to be a remarkable scholar. Throughout his life, Agnew could not speak and relied entirely on sign language and fingerspelling, but was a highly articulate man – he penned a great number of articles in Scottish and national newspapers giving his views on the introduction of oralism into British schools.

A man of immense dignity and bearing, he was also a talented amateur artist in his leisure time outside his employment as a writer with the Glasgow law firm of Moncrief, Barr, Paterson and Company. His artistic fame rested primarily on the now long-lost series of paintings he did of Queen Victoria and Elizabeth Tuffield, nee Groves.

For his work in connection with the new building, William Agnew was made a director of the Institute, a position he retained until his death after a long illness in 1914.

The Early 20th Century

The early 1900s saw a boom in the opening of new centres and missions for Deaf people as more and more schools came into existence and churned out Deaf people with some form of education.

Perhaps, one of the most important developments in that period was the formation of the National Deaf Club in the autumn of 1906. The title was then, as it still is now, largely a misnomer born out of optimism for a nation-wide club membership of deaf people. It is true the club attracted a few members from the provinces, but its membership has been confined mostly to London.

Originally formed as the Friends' Club for the Oral Deaf who desired to have the opportunity of socialising with their own type, it changed to its present title in September 1908 when it opened its membership to deaf people of whatever school, not just oralist. It was the first deaf club in the country to levy an annual subscription charge for membership. The club's membership tended to attract deaf people of a certain social standing, such as wealthy businessman A.J. Wilson, and the type of activities pursued tended to reflect the social strata – chess, table-cricket, tennis and badminton.

Notwithstanding the type of membership, the formation of the National Deaf Club was an important development for deaf people. From it came what we see in the Deaf community today, a sense of belonging to a body that was acceptable in social terms.

Elsewhere, the early years of the 20th century saw the passing of many of the old stalwart deaf missioners, who were being replaced by hearing missioners. The Milan Congress of 1880, having successfully removed deaf people from teaching in deaf schools, was now seeing the process being carried a little further by quite unintentionally closing the doors on the employment of deaf people as missioners.

The doors never quite closed properly, however. Here and there, Deaf people were still being appointed but they were almost a dying breed. Edwin Docharty at Blackburn, David Fyfe at Warrington, Alex McDonald at Stockport, Algernon Barnett at Northampton and Harry Rowland at Cambridge were some of the few Deaf people who were appointed as missioners.

Apart from these few Deaf missioners, the clergy retained a powerful grip on the affairs of deaf people and the age of paternalism was at a high. Most of the clergy were involved in the Guild of St. John of Beverley, which regarded working with Deaf people as its vocation. It was not uncommon to find deaf people being referred to as 'our poor brethren' and British deaf magazines of the time had over 95% of their pages filled with information of the doings of missioners and other hearing people who were 'interested in working with the deaf'.

Chapter VI   A Pictorial History of Deaf Britain

Lawn Tennis with the National Deaf Club
This club attracted Deaf people of a certain social strata.
Photo: The Hallett Collection

David Fyfe (1883 – 1967)
Missioner at Warrington for 30 years
Photo: Warrington Society for the Deaf

Edwin Docharty (1869 – 1931)
After working for the *Glasgow Weekly Mail* be became Missioner for the East Lancashire Deaf and Dumb Society.
Photo: Glasgow & West of Scotland Society

Chapter VI   A Pictorial History of Deaf Britain

Two Photographs showing war time bomb damage at Southampton's Fairbairn Centre for the Deaf

Photos: Hampshire, Isle of Wight and Channel Islands Association for the Deaf

Deaf Missions and Centres in the War Years, 1939 - 45

The imposition of strict blackout regulations at the start of the Second World War severely disrupted adult deaf club activities at the beginning of the war; many were forced to cancel long-arranged social events and rearrange social club hours. One casualty of the war was the British Deaf & Dumb Association's plans to celebrate its Jubilee year in 1940.

There were moments of black humour as well regarding the safety of deaf people in wartime conditions. For example, a paragraph heading in the London *Evening Standard* reported as follows: -

HOW THE DEAF WILL BE WARNED OF AIR RAIDS....
WARDEN PULLS STRING – OFF COME BEDCLOTHES.

At Warrington, a deaf man decided to pay a visit to a relative he had not seen for some time and set off to cycle there. Unfortunately, due to all road signposts being removed, he soon lost his way and had to ask someone for directions. Due to his speech-impediment, he was mistaken for a German spy and was arrested and spent some uncomfortable hours in custody before being released.

In Manchester, a deaf tramp who roamed the country for 9 years was arrested as a spy because he had 55 Ordnance Survey maps in his possession, as well as two compasses and twenty crisp £1 notes.

A number of deaf people, including children, lost their lives during air raids by German warplanes on the British mainland. This included a family of eight when a bomb scored a direct hit on their air-raid shelter.

However, deaf people were in danger at any time during the blackouts. At least seven were killed by buses and trams operating in blackout conditions and many were injured. One deaf electrician from Gillingham, Kent, a Thomas Pearce, was sent to do a job in Southport, Lancashire. Whilst there in unfamiliar surroundings, he failed to see a sentry in the dark and was shot dead after the sentry challenged him three times.

Although a number of deaf people, especially in London, Coventry and Southampton lost their homes, deaf institutes, churches and schools seem to have received more damage.

Deaf centres that were destroyed by enemy action included Southampton, Coventry, Clapham St. Bedes, Great Yarmouth, Manchester's Roman Catholic Centre and the premises of the National Deaf Club. Centres that received considerable damage included Norwich and Birmingham. In Bristol the square in which the deaf centre stood was reduced to rubble except for the deaf centre, which remained standing largely undamaged except for blown windows. The Centre later took the opportunity to build a new centre on the bombed site. In Manchester, the Church of All Saints was blasted to rubble, but the Deaf Institute on the opposite side of the road remained unscathed.

Perhaps the greatest amount of damage done to deaf centres in a short span of time occurred in the Baedaker Raids of May 1942 in South West England.

Deaf Missions & Centres: The Baedaker Raids – May 1942

In May 1942, South West of England suffered an intensive bombing campaign by the German Luftwaffe that really had little to do with the War. The air raids were commonly known as the Baedaker raids, after a publishing house that produced travel guides.

The Germans made a sudden switch from bombing major cities, industrial and military targets and bombed minor cities and towns that did not have anything remotely there connected with any major war effort. There were 6 of these places that might be called tourist towns, like Torquay, Exeter, Bath, Weymouth etc, - the very towns, which had travel guides published by this firm. The firm itself was a casualty of the raids and never published again.

There was first a minor raid on Exeter on a Thursday night, followed the next night by a much larger raid, which caused great damage to parts of the town. Amongst the buildings damaged was the church hall where the deaf of Exeter met and where the Missioner had his offices.

Then the Germans left Exeter alone for one full week, during which they bombed, amongst other towns, Bath, Weymouth and Torquay. The Deaf Institute in Bath was totally destroyed and all records were lost. Torquay Deaf Club suffered some damage, but nothing that could not be easily repaired.

In Weymouth, one of the causalities was the Toc H building, which amongst other things was home to the local Deaf club. This building was totally destroyed and the Deaf people of Weymouth were without a club for some months.

One week after the first raid on Exeter, the Germans returned in force and devastated the centre of Exeter. Already previously damaged, the Deaf centre was reduced to rubble.

Another casualty of this bombing raid was the Royal West of England School for the Deaf at Exeter. At that time, the school seemed a safe haven, not only for the children of the area the school served, but also for the 52 children and staff of the Anerley School for the Deaf, London, who had been evacuated there on 14 September 1939. Blasts from high explosives caused substantial damage to all buildings of the school and no room escaped damage. Fortunately, with all the children sleeping on the ground floor instead of in the bedrooms, there were no serious casualties. Within four days, all the children had returned home and the school was closed for two months to enable repairs to be carried out.

There were no human casualties in any of the deaf centres, although a few deaf families were made homeless when their homes were hit. Deaf people in Exeter moved into another building near the centre of the town, but not for very long. In early 1943, four Heinkel 111s made a low-level sneak raid on the town in broad daylight. The raid took less than five minutes, but the damage suffered by Exeter was greater than it had suffered in the Baedaker raids, causing greater loss of life with over 250 people killed. One of the buildings totally flattened was the new Deaf centre, so for the second time within the space of one year, Deaf people in Exeter had to find new club premises.

Bomb Devastation in Kings Square, Bristol

This was opposite the old premises of Bristol Deaf Centre and later became the site of the new Deaf Centre.

Photo: Bristol Deaf Centre

The Royal West of England School for the Deaf, Exeter

The consequences could have been serious for Deaf children if the bomb that went through the roof was more powerful. Children from this school and also evacuees from Anerley School for the Deaf, London, were sleeping on the ground floor at the time of the air raid.

Harry Macdonald of Truro, A.R.P. Warden
Photo: Melinda Napier

One of the BDDA's Mobile Units given to the Red Cross
Photo: Deaf Quarterly News

Deaf Club Members assist the War Effort

As in World War 1, deaf persons were not permitted to serve in the armed forces, yet there were thousands of able-bodied deaf men and women who could be used to serve their country in a civilian capacity.

This resource was fully realised by the Home Office who recommended that Deaf men should be recruited as Air Raid Wardens (A.R.P's) and fire-watchers. Many deaf men did in fact serve in these capacities, and also as stretcher-bearers in air-raid conditions.

They did immensely valuable work. In many localities, the largest group of able-bodied fully fit men were mainly Deaf members of Deaf centres. In Wigan, for example, the majority of the Deaf men members were fully-qualified Air Raid Wardens. In Hull, 12 of the Deaf Men were trained in casualty and decontamination work for the local Civil Defence. In Leeds, 14 men were employed full-time on Air Raid work and the cellars of their Institute were converted into a sturdy air-raid shelter.

At the end of the War, it was found that over 50 men from Manchester Institute for the Deaf were entitled to the Defence Service Medal for their work with the Civil Defence and this could be repeated throughout the country. Many never got to receive their medals though.

One Deaf person who did much sterling work in the front-line city of Southampton was Herbert C. Street, an Air Raid Warden and a sergeant in the Home guard. Southampton, being a principal port, was subjected to repeated bombing raids and Herbert proved himself to have an uncanny ability to locate approaching aircraft before most of his fellow wardens. He was always in the thick of rescue work and he was later awarded the British Empire Medal for 'admirable services rendered to Civil Defence'. Another A.R.P Warden was Harry Macdonald of Truro.

A desperate shortage of labour caused by many workers in industry being called up enabled hundreds of deaf men and women to get employment. In Swansea, Deaf men were taken on to work in the docks. A deaf woman, Mary Swain of Oldham, was awarded the BEM for her wartime work in a tank factory.

In deaf clubs and institutes throughout the country, there were also much fund-raising and knitting for the armed services. One deaf centre contributed over 700 knitted pairs of woollen socks. Deaf women in Wakefield, Birmingham and Belfast produced hundreds of knitted pullovers and other woollen articles.

Leeds adopted the destroyer *H.M.S. Leeds* as its mascot and contributed to the comforts of the sailors. Many other institutes adopted a variety of the armed services funds as their mascot and held 'gift sales', 'bring and buy' events and so on to raise money for their special fund.

The British Deaf and Dumb Association selected the British Red Cross Society to raise funds for, and raised enough to purchase and equip two mobile physiotherapy units.

The Spurs Club in London raised a magnificent sum of £760 in three years for a variety of armed services' benevolent funds.

The Post War Years

In the aftermath of the Second World War, many institutes and centres struggled to repair their bomb-damaged premises, or find new ones, like Bath. Social life for Deaf people slowly began to pick up with the resumption of inter-institute sports matches and club outings. In many centres, VE Day was greatly celebrated with special church services and parties.

The immediate post-war years were still the Age of the Missioners. Even that supposedly Deaf organisation, the British Deaf and Dumb Association, reserved its main grants for the benefit of those who wished to train as missioners! The Association also gave large grants to the Birmingham and Reading institutes for the provision of chapels.

A Bill that went through Parliament in 1947 strengthened the grip that missioners had on their deaf clients. Hailed by many missioners and welfare officers as well as the BDDA as 'just what was needed for deaf people', the National Assistance Act became law in 1948. It made a number of provisions regulating the type of assistance the State could or should provide for various classes of the British public.

Under the terms of the Act, local councils and societies for the deaf were required to register schemes for the promotion of the welfare of, and provision of services for, deaf people. For the first time, deaf persons were to be part of a register that would entitle them to seek assistance.

The Act also empowered councils, societies and other suitably recognised voluntary organisations to appoint welfare officers for deaf people. They were to assist in the overcoming of disabilities, to give such advice and guidance as might be appropriate, and encourage participation in the activities of social centres and clubs for deaf people. Also empowered by the Act were the provision of practical assistance, religious services and recreational facilities in social centres for deaf people. The scope of the Act was extremely broad, empowering a wide range of leisure facilities for the benefit of Deaf people, from outings and children's parties to the provision of social centres, holiday homes and homes for Deaf people.

The theory behind the implementation of the Act was well intended but paternalistic. It gave a lot of power to missioners and the new breed of 'welfare officers'. The result saw Deaf people in the 1950s and 1960s in the position of being cosseted and having everything possible being done for them, at the price of their independence, with no say in any decision-making. Many services given by missions, deaf centres or voluntary societies were provided on a 'take it or leave it' basis, irrespective of whether these were what Deaf people actually wanted.

With hindsight, it was one of the worst Acts of Parliament implemented on behalf of Deaf people and it was to take along time to eradicate the yoke of second-class citizenship it placed on the Deaf community.

Chapter VI   A Pictorial History of Deaf Britain

Children's Party 1955
These occasions were typical of the Missioner era.
Deaf people were treated as "Our poor deaf brethren", as a
result of the National Assistance Act, 1948.
Photo: Diane Warburton

A Typical Day Out, early 1950s
Photo: Hampshire, I.O.W and Channel Islands Association for the Deaf

Chapter VI   A Pictorial History of Deaf Britain

Leicester Mission for the Deaf
Opened on 18 July 1961.

Vale Royal Deaf Centre
This is one of a few new or rebuilt Deaf centres made possible with
Lottery grants.
Photo: Author's Collection

Deaf Centres at the beginning of the 21st Century

The last half of the 20th century saw many changes in the infrastructure of centres, institutes and social clubs for Deaf people. The words 'institute', 'for the Deaf' or 'the Deaf and Dumb' were deemed to be Victorian and disliked. As Deaf centres or societies adapted to changes in the wider society, many modernised their thinking on what they called themselves. For instance, the old Manchester Adult Deaf and Dumb Institute became simply Manchester Deaf Centre when it relocated.

Not all societies or Deaf centres changed their names. Of the major organisations, Birmingham Institute for the Deaf, Leicester and County Mission for the Deaf, and the Hull & East Yorkshire Institute for the Deaf still retain old-style titles. Others have adapted catchy phrases or slogans, such as Deaf Connections (Glasgow), Deaf Direct (Worcester), Deafness Support Network (Cheshire) and Deafway (Preston).

Many of the buildings themselves also changed. Some outgrew their usefulness whilst others were demolished because of inner-city modernisation programmes that included the building of new ring roads. The latter affected Leicester's Causeway Lane premises and Coventry's Hill Street headquarters, both of which had to come down. Consequently, both these cities took the opportunity to plan and build magnificent new centres for local Deaf people incorporating all modern amenities and recreation rooms as well as a small chapel at each centre. Coventry's Henry Fry Centre for Deaf People holds the distinction of being the first Deaf centre in Britain to obtain a bar licence in 1967.

Glasgow was one place where the Deaf community outgrew its premises. It sold the old institute built through the efforts of William Agnew and moved into a brand-new state of the art building in Norfolk Street, which included facilities such as a gymnasium, sauna and modern offices.

Some centres missed marvellous opportunities for re-development. The London centre of St. John of Beverley at Green Lanes suffered a serious fire in 1960. Only the church and one small lounge escaped unscathed. It was decided simply to repair the damage caused by the fire, instead of completely re-developing the centre. The same centre suffered another arson attack in August 2000. Whether they now take the opportunity to completely re-develop this time remains to be seen.

Other centres, such as Nottingham, found themselves a listed building for preservation purposes but through great internal innovation completely refurbished their centre.

Funding from the National Lottery in the 1990s enabled some centres to re-develop and create new facilities to face the 21st century with confidence. These included Sunderland, Pontypridd and Vale Royal in Northwich.

Only time will tell what the future will be for Deaf centres in the 21st century. Some with old and unsuitable premises such as Whitehaven in Cumbria face closure. Others, such as Edinburgh, face the dilemma of deciding whether to sell up and re-locate.

Chapter VII   A Pictorial History of Deaf Britain

James Paul (1848-1918)
Regarded by some Deaf people as the true founder of the BDA.
Original founder of the National Deaf and Dumb Society.

CHAPTER VII

DEAF ORGANISATIONS

History

The first organisations for deaf people were mainly confined to selected localities, where adult deaf missions had been formed, such as the Edinburgh Deaf and Dumb Benevolent Society. By the mid-1870s, there were organisations for adult deaf people in principal towns and cities such as Glasgow, London, Manchester, Leeds, Cardiff, Belfast, Dundee, Liverpool, Aberdeen, Birmingham and Stoke-on-Trent.

In some smaller towns or cities, such as Halifax, Bolton, Sheffield, Bradford, Greenock and Paisley, the local societies formed were offshoots of the original societies formed at Manchester, Leeds or Glasgow that had become too unwieldy to manage. In London, it was found that Deaf people in the south and east of the city had difficulty getting to regular services and gatherings at St. Saviour's Church so two branches were opened at Deptford and West Ham.

One very significant adult deaf organisation had its beginnings in Kilmarnock in 1874 when a Deaf man named James Paul opened a small mission for the benefit of local deaf people.

James Paul was a visionary. He foresaw the need for all the diverse adult deaf organisations to come together as a national organisation. He contacted a few like-minded people, such as George Healey at Liverpool and proposed the formation of the National Deaf and Dumb Society.

In 1879, one year before the fateful international congress at Milan, the Society held its first meeting, with James Paul as its first Secretary. Unfortunately, its existence was short-lived. Perhaps the focus of its aims was wrong in that it sought to support the formation of, and existence of, adult deaf and dumb missions when maybe it should have been to support the continued provision of sign language and deaf teachers in education. Perhaps, in 1879, no one foresaw the grievous impact the Congress at Milan would have on Deaf education and the future of Deaf people.

Be as that may, the National Deaf and Dumb Society was torn asunder by internal dissension, led mainly by people associated with the Association for the Deaf and Dumb in London such as Samuel Bright Lucas and Thomas Davidson. As a result, it folded in 1884 but not before it had inaugurated two important undertakings, the Stockton-on-Tees Mission for the Adult Deaf and Dumb, and the Ayrshire Mission.

By its very existence, however, the National Deaf and Dumb Society had laid the ground for the foundation of the British Deaf and Dumb Association. Notwithstanding the fact that the proposal for the existence of a national Deaf and Dumb organisation was penned by Francis Maginn in a deaf magazine article, many of the same people who helped to set up and run the NDDS were also involved in the setting up of the BDDA. Many Deaf historians regard James Paul as the true founder of the national Deaf movement.

Great Men of the Early British Deaf Movement

The early struggles of the nationalist Deaf movement could not have been achieved without the drive, vision and determination of a small group of Deaf men. In particular, there were four giants to whom the Deaf community still is greatly indebted.

James Paul (1848 – 1918)

James Paul was born at Cardross, Dumbartonshire, and lost his hearing in infancy through illness. From the age of 8 to 15, he was educated at the Glasgow Institution for the Deaf and Dumb where he was said to be *'one of the brightest of a clever band of scholars'*.

His first job was as an apprentice bookbinder, but this did not satisfy his ambitions and he began to take a leading part in the affairs of the Deaf. His forcefulness, intelligence and personality soon established him as a national leader.

As early as 1872, he was proposing the formation of a national body for deaf people, but it took long and persistent efforts on his part before the National Deaf and Dumb Society was founded in 1879, though it did not last long. When the BDDA was formed in 1890, James Paul became involved as its first Treasurer.

He married a Jane McCaig in June 1879 and by her had a son and daughter. He remained as Missioner to the Ayrshire Mission until his death in 1918.

George Frederick Healey (1843 – 1927)

George Healey was a remarkable man who devoted his whole adult life to the cause of Deaf people. He was born in Gateacre, Liverpool, and lost his hearing at the age of three months as a result of brain fever following a fall from the arms of his nurse, although his deafness was not discovered until he was two years old.

At the age of 8 he was sent to the private school for the deaf at Rugby run by Mr. Bingham, formerly headmaster of the West of England Institution at Exeter. When this school transferred to Southgate, he was educated privately at home.

After his education, he was apprenticed to his father's coach-building premises, graduating after three years to an office position, which he retained until his father retired in 1890.

From its inception in April 1864, George Healey was Honorary Secretary of the Liverpool Society for over 50 years and was present at the first meeting of the British Deaf and Dumb Association in Leeds in 1890. He was later elected honorary treasurer - a position he was to retain for an incredible quarter of a century, earning himself the title of 'The Grand Old Man'.

He was active in deaf work right up to his death in 1927.

Chapter VII *A Pictorial History of Deaf Britain*

George Frederick Healey
"The Grand Old Man of the Deaf Movement"

Chapter VII   A Pictorial History of Deaf Britain

Francis Maginn
He was influential in helping to set up the
British Deaf and Dumb Association

Charles Gorham
Editor of the Deaf and Dumb Times
and first secretary of the BDDA

Francis Maginn (1862 – 1917)

Francis Maginn was not, as many people say, the *founder* of the British Deaf Association. This does not, however, diminish the significance of his contribution to the founding of that organisation.

He was born in Johnsgrove, Co. Cork, Ireland, the son of the rector and Rural Dean of Castletown Roche, and lost his hearing through scarlet fever at the age of five.

At the age of 9, he was sent to the London Institution where he excelled himself so much that when the school's Margate branch was opened in 1875, the headmaster, Dr. Elliott, appointed him one of the first pupil-teachers, promoting him three years later to a junior teachership.

In 1883, Maginn quitted teaching and spent a year studying at home before going to Gallaudet College, Washington, U.S.A. (the first British deaf student to do so) in 1884. However, the death of his father in 1887 intervened and Maginn returned home before he could complete his course. It so happened that the Missions to the Adult Deaf and Dumb of Ireland were seeking a missionary and Maginn applied for the position. It was largely due to his powers as an organiser that the Belfast mission achieved the success that it gained.

Maginn was a firm believer in the national deaf movement and became one of the first vice-presidents of the BDDA when it was founded in 1890.

Intervening in a dispute between two deaf people, Francis Maginn was stuck a severe blow on his chest, from which he never fully recovered and this ultimately led to his early death in 1917.

Charles Gorham

It is not known where and when Charles Gorham was born or educated but he seems to have been an exceptionally clever man and talented sportsman, helping to found Nottingham Deaf football and cricket clubs. Later he moved to Leeds where he started up *The Deaf and Dumb Times,* which he edited and published for two years from 1889-1891 until it was taken over by *The Deaf Chronicle.*

It was as Editor of *The Deaf and Dumb Times* that Gorham made his greatest contribution to the Deaf community. He was a great motivator and took up the issue of a need for a national Deaf organisation. He used the pages of his magazine to advocate this need, reporting on international conferences such as the Paris Congress in 1889 that showed what strengths Deaf people could gain as a collective body.

It was Gorham who was largely responsible for the first draft constitution of the newly formed British Deaf and Dumb Association, paying out of his own pocket for the services of a solicitor to help with the draft. Although this draft constitution was subjected to a few amendments at the inaugural Congress of the BDDA, it remained as the framework of the organisation until 1970. One of the amendments that Gorham disagreed with (like Maginn) was the use of the word 'Dumb' in the title. Although he was appointed the first Honorary Secretary he resigned after one year and faded into obscurity. His date of death is unknown.

The formation of the British Deaf and Dumb Association

The British Deaf Association, or the BDA as it is now known, is – after the Royal Association for the Deaf, an organisation for deaf people, rather than of deaf people – Britain's oldest national deaf organisation. It owes its roots to the inspiration of James Paul of Kilmarnock who with several others launched the short-lived National Deaf and Dumb Society (NDDS) in 1879.

Internal bickering and strife was the cause of the demise of the NDDS after an existence of seven short years.

There were enough strong-minded and far-sighted deaf people about, the most prominent of whom were George Healey of Liverpool and William Agnew who felt strongly about the need for a national organisation of deaf people. Of particular importance was the need to provide a Deaf voice to counter the growing emphasis on oral education. The catalyst came with the publication of an article in *The Deaf and Dumb Times* in January 1890 by Francis Maginn of Belfast.

Strongly influenced by his association with Edward Miner Gallaudet of the college of that name in Washington, D.C., USA, where he had spent some years studying, Maginn wrote under the title 'The Proposed National Association of the Deaf':

"... to place the deaf before the public in their true light and proper position, as useful members of the community at large, the formation of an Association on American lines is most desirable."

Invitations to all deaf societies and missions were sent, inviting them to a National Deaf Conference to be held at the Lecture Hall of St. Saviour's Church in London on 16-18 January 1890. This conference unanimously passed a resolution:

"In the opinion of this Conference it is advisable that a National Society should be formed, the chief objects of which will be the elevation, education, and social status of the deaf and dumb in the United Kingdom."

The conference also passed a motion which set up a steering committee composed of six deaf men and six hearing men under the chairmanship of the Reverend W. Blomefield Sleight, headmaster of the Brighton Institution for the Deaf. The Deaf representatives included Healey and Agnew, as well as Maginn.

The steering committee only needed to meet twice, during which they agreed on the proposed constitution, the venue for the first Congress and the title of the new association. The constitution had been drawn up by a firm of solicitors in Leeds, which was also chosen as the inaugural venue of the new association.

In spite of the advice of Maginn, who followed the recommendations of the Royal Commission on the Education of the Deaf and the Dumb and the Blind, and also the American delegation at an international conference in Paris the previous year, the steering committee agreed on the name The British Deaf and Dumb Association. In ignoring the advice of Maginn and the Americans, the steering committee thus condemned the BDDA to seventy years of mediocrity. It was not until 1971 that the words 'and Dumb' were dropped from the Association's title.

Chapter VII *A Pictorial History of Deaf Britain*

BRITISH DEAF & DUMB ASSOCIATION CONGRESS SWANSEA 1893

The third Congress at Swansea
Photograph: Church of the Holy Name Mission to the Deaf Swansea

Chapter VII   A Pictorial History of Deaf Britain

Above: The BDDA Congress Dinner, Royal Venetian Chamber, Holborn, London 1903
Photograph: British Deaf Association
Below: BDDA Congress Garden Party, Botanical Gardens, Birmingham 1922
Photograph: Birmingham Institute for the Deaf

The British Deaf and Dumb Association: 1890-1970

There was initially a disagreement on that section of the draft constitution dealing with admission to membership. A second, and final, meeting of the steering committee took place the day before the Congress opened to sort this out and resulted in a clause which allowed hearing people taking an active interest in the welfare of, or education of, the deaf and dumb to be eligible for membership.

The first officials consisted of a President, Vice Presidents, Secretary and Treasurer; not until later was the position of Chairman created. The first President was the Reverend William Blomefield Sleight, but the first secretary was Charles Gorham of Leeds, a deaf man who was then the editor of the *Deaf and Dumb Times*. He only held the post for one year before it passed to James Muir who held it until 1905. James Paul was appointed the BDDA's first treasurer.

The Presidency has always remained the province of a hearing person, so did the Chairmanship until 1983, but the secretary was always a deaf person until 1961 when Allan Brindle Hayhurst was appointed.

The clause in the constitution that enabled hearing people to be elected to be the Association's Executive Council led to a situation where Deaf candidates standing for election had to wear the label 'Deaf' in the voting. It also came to be dominated by missioners and welfare officers, which left the BDDA a strangely ineffective force for all its national importance. Considerable criticism of the organisation in the 1920s and 1930s appeared in deaf magazines and the BDDA was especially fortunate in having as secretaries at the time William McDougall and, from 1934, Leslie Edwards, Deaf men of strong character, who could hold the association together during those turbulent times.

The first Congress passed only one resolution. However, that resolution was to be the mainstay of the association's existence ever since. It read:

> *"That this Congress of the British Deaf and Dumb Association, held in Leeds, indignantly protests against the imputation of the Right Hon, Earl Granville, in his recent speech in London, that the finger and sign language was barbarous. We consider such a mode of exchanging our ideas as most natural and indispensable, and that the Combined System of education is by far preferable to the so-called Pure Oral. We are confident that the Combined System is absolutely necessary for the welfare of the deaf and dumb."*

The BDDA, and latterly the BDA, never wavered in its resolution that sign language was the best method of education. Now, at the beginning of the 21st century, the possibility exists that British Sign Language could receive official status. This achievement would give all those founder members pride and satisfaction.

British Deaf and Dumb Association: Secretaries of Stature

In its early years, the fledgling BDDA was – despite the domination of missioners - fortunate to have at its helm Deaf men of stature who were to hold it together and see it through some difficult times. Apart from that Grand Old Man of the British Deaf movement, George Healey, who was to be treasurer for 30 years, there were two men who held the Secretaryship of the association for a total of 46 years between them.

William McDougall (1865 - 1950)

William McDougall was born in Tillicoulty, Scotland, and became deaf through illness when aged 5. He was educated at Donaldson's School for the Deaf, continuing after school life as a pupil-teacher. Leaving temporarily, he went into partnership with his brother in a woollen mill, but returned to Donaldson's after a few years. He was the only deaf member of the teaching staff.

In 1904 he was offered, and accepted, the post of Missioner at Carlisle which he was to retain until his retirement in 1935.

He became Secretary of the BDDA in 1906, a post he was also to hold until his retirement, a term of 29 years during part of which the post of Treasurer was joined to the Secretaryship.

It was during his time at the helm that the BDDA experienced a tremendous growth in membership largely due to McDougall's unflagging efforts on its behalf.

Leslie Edwards (1885 - 1951)

Leslie Edwards was a rare breed in those years when deaf people were at their lowest ebb. He strode the world like a giant on his own terms, his influence for good equally immense among Deaf and hearing people.

As well as being Missioner to the Deaf at Leicester, he was also a lay preacher of some renown and an able cricketer who led Leicester Deaf Cricket Club to their first ever championship in 1927.

Appointed to the Secretary-Treasurership of the BDDA on the retirement of William McDougall in 1935, he was to hold the position throughout the difficult war years and was just beginning to see the development of the post-war BDDA when he met his untimely death in October 1951.

He was to be succeeded by the Rev. Mark Frame who was to hold the position for ten years before resigning.

Chapter VII   A Pictorial History of Deaf Britain

William McDougall
Secretary of the BDDA 1906-1935
Photograph: Deaf Quarterly News

Leslie Edwards
Secretary of the BDDA 1935 – 1951
Photograph: The Deaf News

Chapter VII   A Pictorial History of Deaf Britain

BDDA Congress Participants, Manchester 1909
Photo: Manchester Deaf Centre

BDDA Congress Participants, Birmingham 1922
Photo: The Hallett Collection

The BDDA Congresses & Summer Schools

The single most important achievement of the BDDA was to wield together a social, recreational and educational infrastructure for the adult Deaf that withstood all the assaults made upon the signing Deaf community by oral educationalists and others who wished to see the demise of British Sign Language.

The focal point of the BDDA's activities has been its Congresses, starting with Leeds in 1890. Up to 1913, they were held every two years before the First World War put a stop to activities until 1920, but from 1922 onwards the Congresses were held every three years except during the Second World War.

Perhaps the most important Congresses were Leeds in 1890 as the first, Cardiff in 1947 which saw the popularity of the BDDA start to grow dramatically, Plymouth in 1962 when a new Constitution was adopted and Bournemouth in 1971 which saw the title altered to the British Deaf Association.

The Congresses have been held as follows:

1890 :	Leeds	1920 :	Glasgow	1965 :	Llandudno
1891 :	Glasgow	1922 :	Birmingham	1968 :	Scarborough
1893 :	Swansea	1925 :	Southampton	1971 :	Bournemouth
1895 :	Dublin	1928 :	Belfast	1974 :	Ayr
1897 :	London	1931 :	Leicester	1977 :	Eastbourne
1899 :	Liverpool	1934 :	Torquay	1980 :	Scarborough
1901 :	Kilmarnock	1937 :	Isle of Man	1983 :	Torquay
1903 ;	London	1947 :	Cardiff	1986 :	Rothesay
1905 :	Windermere	1950 :	Aberdeen	1989 :	Swansea
1907 :	Edinburgh	1953 :	Brighton	1992 :	Blackpool
1909 :	Manchester	1956 :	Blackpool	1995 :	Scarborough
1911 :	Aberdeen	1959 :	Edinburgh	1998 :	Glasgow
1913 :	Bradford	1962 :	Plymouth		

The Congresses of the 1950-90s were usually of weeklong duration. The 1990 Centenary Year programme, held in Brighton, was also a special occasion as was the Millennium Celebration programme, held in Belfast.

Apart from the Congresses, one of the main activities of the BDDA was its Summer Schools, which were held every year from 1948 to the 1980s. These Summer Schools catered for all ages and encompassed many activities, from woodcarving courses held in York to Mountain Venture and pony-trekking courses. They were extremely popular and provided occasion for Deaf people all over Britain to come together and learn new activities as well as make friends.

The Summer Schools changed nature in the late 1980s and were continued into the 1990s as part of the BDA's Youth programme.

The British Deaf Association 1970-2000

The last three decades of the 20th century saw many changes within the British Deaf Association. The first landmark came in 1971 when the Congress at Bournemouth voted to drop the words 'and Dumb' from the Association's title, thus ending over 80 years of controversy.

Back in 1961, Allan Brindle Hayhurst had become the first non-deaf person to be secretary of the association ending a tradition which went back to Charles Gorham in 1890, a move seen by some deaf people as further loss of control and destiny of their organisation.

However, Hayhurst was to bring to the BDDA a degree of professionalism it had hitherto not known. Under his leadership, the BDA was to grow into an organisation that started to employ professional staff with a corresponding increase in activities, coupled with the acquisition of offices in Carlisle. Inevitably, there was a financial cost that the BDA was never able to overcome satisfactorily.

One casualty of the BDA's financial crisis was what many people regard as its biggest mistake, the sale of Fulford Grange and its fine estate, the site of the Ernest Ayliffe Home for Elderly Deaf People. It is not difficult to imagine the alternative uses to which this could have been put, to the benefit of the Association and Deaf people.

At the Torquay Congress in 1983, the BDA made a break with nearly a century of tradition when Jock McDonald Young, a Deaf man from Glasgow, was elected Chairman. He was the first Deaf person to hold the post. The chairmanship has since remained in Deaf hands with first Murray Holmes, then Austin Reeves succeeding him.

Also in 1983 the British Deaf Association was honoured when Princess Diana, H.R.H. the Princess of Wales, consented to become Patron of the Association, and a Royal Visit was made to Carlisle in 1984 to cement the patronage. Over the years to follow, Princess Diana was to give much support to the BDA, and to Deaf people in general, visiting several events. One of the most memorable occasions was the BDA's Centenary celebrations at Brighton.

Throughout the 1980s and 1990s, new emphasis in government funding opportunities led the BDA to initiate a number of projects and schemes, mainly in the area of sign language, advocacy, youth services, media services and health promotion and new offices in Crewe and in London. Together with a new initiative supported by the Scottish and Welsh Offices that saw other offices set up in Glasgow and Cardiff, the focus of the BDA switched to that of provision of certain statutory services whilst at the same time retaining traditional values.

Unfortunately, the impetus could not be kept up. The views of the professional staff employed (both Deaf and hearing) did not meet with favour with those of the elected Executive as to the direction the BDA should take. Allied with the perennial financial problems that constantly beset the Association, there could be only one result. In February 1996, it was resolved to issue redundancy notices to almost half of the current staff, including all managers, as well as work towards the closure of the Carlisle and Crewe offices at the earliest possible opportunity.

Chapter VII   A Pictorial History of Deaf Britain

Princess Diana visiting the BDA Centenary Congress at Brighton, 1990
Photo: Author's collection

Relaxing evening at the Brighton Centenary Congress, 1990
Photo: Author's collection

Congress with an International flavour, Blackpool, 1992
This congress was held jointly with the European Union of the Deaf
Photo: Author's collection

Bobby Bailey shows off his Reebok Deaf Person of the Year Award, Blackpool 1992
Photo: Author's collection

BDA Carlisle Office
Photo: Author's collection

BDA Crewe Office
Photo: Author's collection

Chapter VII   A Pictorial History of Deaf Britain

Left: Michael Quinlan of the London Deaf Video Project receiving a cheque from Carlton TV. The Project paid for itself through numerous grants, fees and donations like this one.
Photo: British Deaf Association

Sign Language Services' Interpreting Agency staff discussing a booking. The BDA's unit set the ground for future development of Communication Support Units across the country.
Photo: British Deaf Association

The Health Promotion Staff in 1992
At that time, there were two offices, one in the FACTS Centre, North London, and the other at the Crewe headquarters. Later two other offices were set up in Cardiff & Prestwich.
Photo: Author's collection

Health Promotion Roadshow van outside Heathlands School, St. Albans in 1993. A total of 11 schools were visited in 1993 and 1994 as part of a Safer Sex campaign.
Photo: Author's collection

BDA Service Departments

One of the problems that beset the BDA in the late 1980s and early 1990s was the enormous success of several service departments, which led to some conflict between the elected Executive committee and the professionals linked with these departments. The view of the Executive was that the BDA had never previously been a *service-led* organisation and that such services were contrary to the ethos of the BDA. The views of the professionals were that such services were meeting a demonstrated need by members of the Deaf community.

Notwithstanding the fact that most service departments brought in a significant cash injection to the BDA, and were more or less paying their way, these services were costly to run. The additional support needed to service these departments, i.e. in Finance and Administration, was also financially crippling for the BDA.

These departments were the Sign Language Services department, which operated the Interpreting Agency, the Health Promotion and Advocacy Services departments. Another section of the BDA, the London Deaf Video Project, operated by Information Services, was also doing a superb job in the dissemination of information.

All these departments were innovative service leaders. The Interpreting Agency opened the way for future developments in local communication support units to be later set up by the RNID and some local Deaf societies, and was also heavily involved in the provision of expert sign language advice to government departments.

Advocacy Services had a vital role in the provision of personal advocacy for Deaf individuals. In community advocacy, it empowered Deaf people to influence the services provided by local authorities.

The London Deaf Video Project, as the name implies, produced a range of information videos in BSL for the Deaf community, a lot of them under contract from the government's Central Information Office. This service enabled Deaf people to have better access to public information. For example, in 1992 the unit advised the Department of Health on its video about the Community Care Act.

Perhaps the department that caused most annoyance and grievance to the Executive committee, though not the general Deaf population, was Health Promotion. Starting out originally as a small project under the name Aids Ahead to promote awareness about HIV and AIDS, it grew rapidly over a short time into a service that was providing health information and healthcare support across a range of health issues under contract with various health authorities. It was also operating from offices in a HIV Centre in north London, Prestwich Hospital in north Manchester, an office in Cardiff and its headquarters in Crewe. It was also running a large volunteer service and providing training for Deaf people in HIV, Drugs and Sexual Health counselling and befriending, leading the way to future certificate in counselling courses being established. It was also innovative in securing statutory authority funding for the provision of certain services.

By late 1995, with support department costs spiralling out of control and funding periods coming to an end, the Executive Committee decided these services had to be drastically pruned.

The British Deaf Association at the Beginning of the 21st Century

The BDA today is a much smaller, streamlined organisation than it was at the beginning of the 1990s, concentrated in one main office in London, with smaller one-roomed offices in Cardiff, Belfast, Scotland and Warrington. The much-beloved Carlisle office has now been sold off, the Crewe office closed. Many of the old departments that provided a range of services to Deaf people throughout Britain have now either been disbanded or restructured with different aims and objectives more in keeping with the association's ethos and financial resources.

Amongst the departments that were lost were the Sign Language Services' Interpreting Agency and the Health Promotion department. Also lost was the Advocacy department, which had provided such sterling value over the years with advice to Deaf people. This was replaced, briefly supported by Lottery funding by Deaf Dial, but when the period of funding expired, Deaf Dial was in its turn also discontinued.

Another profound change was the position of Patron.

Diana, Princess of Wales, who had been the BDA's Patron since 1983 was tragically killed in Paris in August 1997. Only the previous year, she had made a decision to cut back on her public duties, withdrawing as Patron of many charities. During her thirteen years with the BDA, she was an enthusiastic supporter of Sign Language, capturing headlines in 1992 by launching the Sign Language Dictionary with a presentation in BSL.

Ironically, only a few weeks before her tragic death, Prince Andrew, HRH the Duke of York, had agreed to become the BDA's new Patron.

The old term "secretary" had been discontinued with the change of title to "Chief Executive" to reflect modern trend. With the appointment of Jeff McWhinney as Chief Executive in April 1995, the BDA had broken with a 34-year period when the principal paid officer of the association was a hearing person.

Jeff McWhinney

Jeff McWhinney was born in Belfast on 9 May 1960 to Deaf parents and attended the Jordanstown Schools for the Deaf before going to Mary Hare Grammar School in 1972. His first job (after an abortive period of training as an electronic engineer) as a trainee insurance broker with an insurance firm in Belfast in 1980. In 1984 Jeff moved to London after obtaining employment as a Development Officer with the Breakthrough Trust. Following this he worked for the London Boroughs Disability Resource Team and Wandsworth Economic Development and Grants Office. Prior to his appointment as Chief Executive of the BDA, he was Director of the Greenwich Association of Disabled People.

A keen soccer player, he represented Ireland in a number of Deaf internationals the first one being against Switzerland in the early 1980s. On his move to London Jeff played for the successful Surbiton Deaf football team. He was also a presenter in a number of TV programmes – ITV's *Sign a Story* series, Channel 4's *Sign Wheel* series and occasionally for the BBC's *SEE HEAR!*

He is married with 2 children.

Chapter VII   *A Pictorial History of Deaf Britain*

Jeff McWhinney
First Deaf Chief Executive, 1995-
British Deaf Association

Chapter VII   A Pictorial History of Deaf Britain

Leo Bonn
Photo: Royal National Institute for Deaf People

Doug Alker
First Deaf Chief Executive, Royal National Institute for Deaf People

Royal National Institute for Deaf People

The RNID, as the Institute is known, was originally founded in 1911 with the cumbersome title of National Bureau for Promoting the General Welfare of the Deaf. This title, however, still ably expresses the aims of the RNID.

The founder of the Bureau was a Mr. Leo Bonn, a wealthy merchant banker who was himself deaf and had become interested in the cause of deaf people after visiting the famous teacher Mary Hare and a deaf school in Stoke. His family bank provided the early financial backing needed to establish the Bureau, which met for the first time in the dining room of his home at Upper Brooke Street, London. By 1924, the Bureau was able to recruit a small staff. The same year it was decided to restructure the organisation as National Institute for the Deaf.

In 1928, the 'Counties Association for the Deaf' came into begin; these have now been reconstructed as the Regional Associations.

In the period 1929-36, the RNID began to establish homes and hostels for the deaf and to inaugurate lip-reading classes, which led to the establishment of the City Lit Centre for the Deaf in London.

In 1936 the institute was established at 105 Gower Street and began to develop its technical department, where it concentrated on technical and scientific research into assistive devices for the benefit of deaf and hard-of-hearing people. The word 'Royal' was included in the title in the Institute's Jubilee Year in 1961 by the approval of the Queen.

Later the RNID's departments included the Library (the largest specialist library on deafness in the U.K.), research, community services, information services as well as research into technical, scientific and environmental aids.

An important area of the RNID's work was the development of its residential services. It maintains a number of hostels, homes and rehabilitation centres throughout the country, one of which, Poolemead in Bath, is the best of its kind to be found anywhere.

In 1986, the RNID reorganised its services into six directorates: Community Services; Advocacy and Information; Residential Services and Employment; Financial and Administration; Fundraising; Communication Services. In doing so, a vigorous equal opportunities policy was pursued, including that of Director of Community Services.

Doug Alker was the first deaf person ever to be appointed at director level in the RNID or for that matter, the BDA. In 1990, his post was restructured as Research and Development. In January 1995, he became the first-ever Deaf Chief Executive of the RNID following a campaign by Deaf people anxious to see the appointment of a Deaf person to the post and also that of the BDA, which was also vacant at the time.

Born in Wigan, Lancashire, in 1942, Doug Alker was educated at Mary Hare Grammar School and for about 20 years afterwards, he was employed by ICI in Blackburn before joining the RNID. In his spare time, he was well-respected in Deaf and hearing circles as a magician and as a fully qualified Football Association coach.

The RNID at the Millennium

By the early 1990s, it was obvious that the RNID was outgrowing its headquarters at Gower Street, where it had been for over half a century. The Library, the RNID's oldest department was the first to go. It was relocated to the Institute of Laryngology and Otology in Gray's Inn Road, London – a move bemoaned by many Deaf people, especially historians, as a particularly bad one, resulting as it did in the deterioration of a priceless piece of Deaf heritage through lack of care and pilferage.

The main headquarters departments relocated to new offices in Featherstone Street, where the organisation continued to go from strength to strength, increasing its services to deaf, deafened and hard-of-hearing people. Much of this increase took place outside London, with the consolidation of four main English regional offices plus one each in Cardiff, Belfast and Glasgow. Allied to the development of these offices were the growth of Communication Services Units and Employment Services projects.

One significant development late in the 20th century that made a considerable impact on deaf people's lives was the national telephone relay service, set up with help from British Telecom. RNID Typetalk, as the service was called, revolutionised the way Deaf, deafened and hard-of-hearing people used telecommunications. Based in Liverpool in three separate buildings, it is in operation 24 hours a day and 365 days a year bridging the gap in telecommunications between deaf and hearing people.

At the end of the 20th century, the RNID was an organisation bigger than all other deaf organisations combined, with staff in 23 different locations. In addition, the RNID were maintaining 20 residential units for various groups and ages of deaf and hard-of-hearing people. Some were rehabilitation units; others were elderly people's homes. Some specialised in services for deaf-blind people.

Its organisational clout meant that the RNID was in a better position to campaign for many Deaf rights than the weak BDA itself and reap the financial rewards for doing so.

In 1997, Doug Alker, the first Deaf Chief Executive, was replaced in a controversial manner by a deafened man, James Strachan, in what was described as a *coup d'é-tat* by the oralist lobby within the RNID. A former investment banker and director of Merrill Lynch, the world's largest investment bank, James Strachan had worked with the RNID since 1976 and had been a member of their Finance Committee, creating a new fundraising and marketing strategy.

Under Strachan's leadership, the RNID launched a manifesto that would take them into the new millennium, in three priority areas - hearing aids, education and subtitling. This included campaigning to ensure that digital hearing aids became standard on the National Health Service, building foundations to give deaf children the best possible education and ensuring equal access through subtitling to television, video, DVD and cinema. There were also campaigns to improve the law and attitudes towards hearing loss and disability, to create Typetalk access and to increase statutory obligations to provide sign language interpreters in health, social services and education.

Chapter VII   A Pictorial History of Deaf Britain

James Strachan
Chief Executive, Royal National Institute for Deaf People at the Millennium

Chapter VII   A Pictorial History of Deaf Britain

Sue Daniels
The first deaf person to become Chief Executive of the
National Deaf Children's Society.
A qualified teacher, she was previously a
lecturer at the City Lit Centre for Deaf People in London

The National Deaf Children's Society

Founded in 1944 by a group of parents concerned at the implications posed by the 1944 Education Act, it was originally known as the Deaf Children's Society. The word 'National' was not added to the title until 1958. Its primary objective at the time it was founded was to campaign to improve deaf education and to sort out problems experienced by parents in bringing up deaf children.

Though its primary objectives still remain, the NDCS (as it is known) offers a wide range of educational, welfare, technical and information services to parents of deaf children and professionals working with deaf children, and has about 135 regional branches throughout the United Kingdom.

In the appointment of a deaf woman, Susan Daniels, as its Director in 1992, the NDCS broke new ground at a time when the other leading organisations were still led by hearing Chief Executives.

The NDCS was in a perilous state at that time. Like the BDA, it's desire to provide services was outstripping available resources and in order to move forward, the Society had first to take a step back and do some restructuring, which involved some redundancies. Part of taking a good look at itself also involved the creation of a Vision and Values Statement that clearly set out the purpose for the existence of the organisation. This included declaring the belief that the challenge of deafness could be a rewarding experience.

With this statement as the basis, the NDCS approached the Millennium confidently, boosted by a string of National Lottery grants, which gave impetus to the development of new services, including the opening of a new office in Wales.

British Association of Teachers of the Deaf

The association had its origins in three teacher training colleges. These were:

'Association for the Oral Institution of the Deaf and Dumb' based at Fitzroy Square, London. Founded in 1872

'Society for Training Teachers of the Deaf and for the Diffusion of the German System', based at the training college at Ealing, founded in 1877

'College of Teachers of the Deaf and Dumb', founded in 1885.

A fourth body, the National Association of Teachers of the Deaf (N.A.T.D.), was formed in 1895.

The first two training colleges also had schools for deaf children attached to them and teachers' certificates were awarded to students who taught on the oral system to the exclusion of any other method. The third, the C.T.D.D., awarded certificates to students using any mode of communication.

These qualifications were not recognised by the Board of Education until 1909 when all joined together to produce one diploma, at the insistence of the N.A.T.D. Even then, the Scottish Department of Education still refused to recognise the diplomas.

All these bodies have now amalgamated or reformed themselves to become the British Association of Teachers of the Deaf (B.A.T.O.D.)

Hearing Concern

Social clubs for the Hard of Hearing had existed as far back as 1918 with one at Edinburgh. However, such clubs were mostly confined to large provincial centres and London.

In 1945, a Madeleine de Soyres, a French Canadian living in Welwyn garden City, conceived the idea of a county organisation for people like herself who were Hard of Hearing and so the Hertfordshire League for the Hard of Hearing was formed, followed shortly by the Middlesex and Surrey League.

As more Leagues and Clubs began to form, in 1946 Miss de Soyres proposed the formation of a national body, and after a stormy inaugural meeting held at the National Institute for the Deaf in Gower Street, the British Association of the Hard of Hearing was formed in 1947.

BAHOH, as the association was known, had several objectives, the main being to foster the social and cultural activities of the Hard of Hearing and to promote their interests.

BAHOH changed its name to Hearing Concern in the early 1990s and maintains a full time office at 7 Armstrong Street, London.

Council for Advancement of Communication with Deaf People

In 1980, the BDA approached the Department of Health and Social Security for funding to establish a Communication Skills project, which aimed to set standards of competence in sign language amongst learners and to create a register of interpreters.

By 1982, the project had developed to such an extent that it needed to stand on its own feet, thus the Council for Advancement of Communication with Deaf People was born. This cumbersome title has usually been abbreviated to CACDP.

In 1987, CACDP expanded into Northern Ireland and appointed John Carberry as its development officer for that country.

CACDP is now an awarding body in sign language and other human aids to communication recognised by the Qualifications Curriculum Authority. It has developed a progressive structure of training and examinations in communication skills that are a stimulus to learning and a measure of ability. Its qualifications have gained national recognition.

Set up at a time when there was growing concern that Sign Language skills were declining and a shortage of interpreters who themselves had no formal qualifications or training, CACDP's initial development focused on Sign Language and Sign Language interpreting. It has since broadened out into many other areas of training linked with deafness. It has established curricula, examinations and qualifications in Lipspeaking, Communication Skills with Deafblind People, Deaf Awareness, Deafblind Awareness and Speech to Text Reporting and Note-taking. A new qualification for the Millennium was the Certificate in Electronic Note-taking for Deaf People. It has also supported the development of training for Communication Support Workers (or Educational Interpreters)

Chapter VII   A Pictorial History of Deaf Britain

A Sign Language Class at Coventry College
Photo: CACDP

Two BSL Students discuss the merits of some of the material on sale at the CACDP Sign Fair
Photo: CACDP

Chapter VII   A Pictorial History of Deaf Britain

A Breakthrough Family Activity in the 1970s
Photo: The Breakthrough Deaf-Hearing Integration

David Hyslop, OBE.
President, Breakthrough Deaf-Hearing Integration

Breakthrough Deaf-Hearing Integration

Breakthrough was first registered in 1970 by a group of deaf adults who were, at the time, dissatised with the available outlets for deaf people and concerned at the isolation of the deaf individual from the rest of society. In reality, an informal association known as 'The Group' had existed for some ten years, meeting locally and organising a larger get-together every Easter.

A focal point was concern at the lack of a deaf contribution to society, to show what deaf people could do. For a variety of reasons, these opportunities did not seem to exist within the BDA or the RNID, nor was there free integration and communication between deaf and hearing people, an avowed aim of Breakthrough.

The main activity in the late 1960s and early 1970s was an annual Family Weekend at Thorpeness, Norfolk, where deaf and hearing families and friends came together to live together for a weekend. This manner of living together made everyone aware of the problems of communication between deaf and hearing persons. Later, Breakthrough obtained a farm in Swindon, called Roughmoor, which they turned into an activity centre. It was well used and immensely popular with all sections of the deaf community, especially schools. Unfortunately, societal changes and a rapid building programme in Swindon Town made the farm unviable and it was closed in the 1980s.

From these humble but determined beginnings, Breakthrough developed into a well-respected organisation in the deaf world, with headquarters at Selly Oak in Birmingham. One early contribution that Breakthrough made to the Deaf Community was through its development and expertise in telecommunications technology, particularly in vistels, one of the earliest forms of textphones. Most recently it has installed a network of 17 videophones.

Breakthrough works to improve the lives of deaf and hearing people through a wide variety of social activities, information services, especially through Mobile Advisory Services, and the provision of specialist training programmes ranging from basic skills through to management for deaf people along with awareness workshops and communication courses for hearing people.

One of Breakthrough's early members, David Hyslop, is now chairman and President. In the 1996 New Year's Honours List he was awarded the OBE for his services to the Deaf community. He presides over an organisation that now operates from four regional bases and more than 60% of the staff are deaf.

Sense, the National Deafblind and Rubella Association

One of the most important organisations in the Deaf World today is Sense, the National Deafblind and Rubella Association, which was set up as The Rubella Group in 1955. It became a charity in 1961. This was a time when specific educational provision for deafblind children was virtually non-existent and rubella epidemics were particularly bad. There was one special unit at the Royal National Institute for the Blind's Condover Hall School in Shropshire with just five places (later expanded to 15). Some deafblind children were placed in Deaf schools or visually impaired children but most of these placements failed. Although the children were well cared for, much of their special needs could not be met. It has to be remembered that the majority of schools were still pursuing an oralist tradition and the use of sign language was anathema to many teachers. They could not be seen to be using the deafblind alphabet with some children and still be punishing other deaf children for signing! Few therefore reached their potential, and many were condemned to spend their adult lives in mental hospitals as uneducable.

After years of campaigning, there were two breakthroughs in 1970. In that year, rubella immunisation of all schoolgirls and young women began and the Education Act 1970 paved the way for special units in residential deaf schools to be set up to provide for children with dual sensory loss.

By 1974, most of the beneficiaries of the charity had grown up, and there was demonstrably a need for a service for young adults and older deafblind people, therefore the word 'children' was dropped from the charity's title.

Two other breakthroughs came in the early 1980s. The first came in the form of the Education Act of 1981, which introduced the concept of 'special needs'. These were to be assessed and documented in a 'statement of needs' which specified the type of provision required for each child. However, it was still deemed appropriate that deafblind children were placed in schools for children with severe learning difficulties and it was not until 1989 that local education authorities and special schools were obliged to consider the specific needs of children with dual sensory loss.

The second breakthrough was when the Magpie Appeal in 1982 enabled the opening of the Family Centre in Ealing, which was able to provide weekday schooling for children, staffed by qualified teachers, and weekend training courses for parents, teachers and other professionals. The following year, 1983, the charity adopted the name Sense.

From then onwards, progress has been rapid. Following the closure of the Royal School for Deaf Children in Birmingham, Sense became the sole trustees and was able to develop further education and residential facilities for young people. Group homes were set up for deafblind people of all ages including in 1999, Boston Lodge, the first care home specifically for older deafblind people. Holiday programmes expanded to 120 people taking them each year, supported by volunteers, and services for people with Usher Syndrome were set up.

Today, under the title Sense International, it is regarded as a world leader in deafblind provision, with staff in four countries.

SENSE Campaigns

A group of Deafblind people outside the Houses of Parliament during a lobby for equal rights.

Chapter VII   A Pictorial History of Deaf Britain

A Deaf Broadcasting Council lobby in the early 1970s

Reclamation & Restoration of Gawen's *"The Good Shepherd"*
Volunteers of the British Deaf History Society at work.

Deaf Broadcasting Council

In 1979, a small organisation for the deaf, the National Union of the Deaf, launched an initiative and assisted in the production *Signs of Life* for the BBC" Open Door series of programmes, and as a result, there was convened the Deaf Broadcasting Campaign. Its original aim was to press for a weekly news programme using sign language, subtitles and voice.

Within a short period of time, however, the DBC (as it is known) had expanded its role and objectives into other areas of television to such an extent that it became a highly respected umbrella consumer organisation representing most national deaf and hard of Hearing organisations.

While it is impossible to pinpoint the exact impact the DBC has had on television media and authorities, it has undoubtedly been responsible for improving the quality of deaf people's lives to the extent that a positive attitude has been created amongst deaf viewers. They now feel they have the right to demand and expect from television an equivalent service to that which the general public accepts as the norm.

The DBC could not have achieved what it has without the considerable sacrifices made by its Secretary, Austin Reeves, a deaf man from Coventry. At the Rothesay Congress of the BDA in 1986, the BDA made one of its most popular choices when it awarded Austin their Medal of Honour for services to deaf television.

The Deaf Broadcasting Campaign changed the last word of their title to Council in 1988 to reflect their increased status. During the 1990s, it has been heavily involved in high level consultations in an attempt to secure Deaf people's rights to services provided by satellite and digital television. All the work is still done on a voluntary basis, and owes much to the dedicated efforts of its current secretary, Ruth Myers.

British Deaf History Society

Founded in 1993 to promote and advance the interest in the discovery, research and preservation of the histories of Deaf people, their communities, culture and language, the BDHS has made some remarkable achievements in its short life span. It is run entirely by volunteers and has been responsible for establishing a number of memorial plaques to Deaf people, acquiring a number of historical records and preserving items of national importance to the Deaf community.

It has a Research and Publications department that produces the *Deaf History Journal*, which has achieved international acclaim for the content of its historical articles. Through this department, the Society has also published a series of books, which place on written record rare and useful historical information for future generations of Deaf people and historians.

The British Deaf Sports Council

The British Deaf Sports Council (BDSC) was born out of a need to set up a national Deaf sports association to represent British interests in World Games for the Deaf, which had since 1924 been organised by the CISS (International Committee for Deaf Sport).

When France staged the first Games in Paris in 1924, the Federation of London Deaf Clubs had assumed this responsibility. It assumed the same responsibility for the next Games in 1928, but certain members felt that it was really a responsibility for a national body to assume but it was not until 1930 that efforts to set up the national body proved successful. In Manchester that year, the British Deaf Amateur Sports Association (BDASA) was formed.

One of the first, and perhaps the biggest, hurdles this fledging organisation had to face was that of staging the World Games in Britain in 1935. Some 298 competitors from 14 countries took part in these Games, which were held in venues such as the White City, Arsenal's Highbury Stadium and the Empire Pool.

In 1974, the title was changed to the current BDSC and in 1982, it was agreed that the BDA would employ a Sport and Leisure Officer whose remit was to administer the BDSC together with maintaining a leisure service for the BDA. This agreement did not prove to be very workable, and in 1989, the links with the BDA were severed and the BDSC has since gone its way alone, with the former BDA Sport and Leisure Officer now employed by the BDSC as the Executive Director.

The achievements of the BDSC are quite remarkable, given that all top officials with the exception of the Executive Director and Personal Assistant, were all volunteers and much of the success of the British World Games teams has been largely due to these dedicated volunteers.

Hearing Dogs for the Deaf

The idea of training hearing dogs to assist deaf people was first introduced to the UK back in 1982. The first dog 'Favour', a tan and white crossbred dog, was selected from the National Canine Defence League and the idea of training dogs to assist deaf people became a reality.

The aims of the Charity were to improve the lives of deaf people through the training and placement of specially trained dogs. The majority of hearing dogs were selected from rescue centres, giving an extra appeal to the Charity, which offered safe and loving homes to otherwise unwanted dogs.

The first training centre was set up in Chinnor, Oxfordshire, but now this has relocated to Lewknor and a third training centre will shortly open (2001).

The dogs vary from the largest, scruffiest mongrel to the smallest pedigree, all easily recognisable be their distinctive golden yellow jacket. Once trained hearing dogs are issued with a certificate by the Department of Health and Environment, which allows deaf people with hearing dogs access to public places.

Chapter VII   A Pictorial History of Deaf Britain

Roland Haythornthwaite, MBE
Executive Director, British Deaf Sports Council 1989-2000
(Administrator since 1974)
Photo: R.Haythornthwaite

A Hearing dog with it's owner out shopping
Photo: Hearing Dogs for Deaf people

Chapter VII   A Pictorial History of Deaf Britain

National Union of the Deaf members at a demo outside the Department of Education & Science building, London
Photo: Raymond Lee

Jack Straw at the FDP Conference 1997
Photo: British Deaf News

National Union of the Deaf

The National Union of the Deaf (NUD) is no longer active but it deserves its place in history for its achievements during its short life span. It came into being in 1976 when a number of like-minded Deaf people got together to express their frustration and concern over the ineffectiveness of the two major organisations for Deaf people, the BDA and the RNID, in pursuing policies that they believed should form the core of any campaign for Deaf rights.

The NUD attracted activists like Raymond Lee, Paddy Ladd and Maggie Woolley. To give the organisation some status in the eyes of grassroots Deaf people, they approached the doyen of Deaf literature Arthur F. Dimmock who gave his enthusiastic support for their aims. Another well respected figure who gave his support was Stan Woodhouse who was later to receive the M.B.E for his services to the Deaf community. He agreed to become President of the NUD.

The NUD saw itself chiefly as a campaigning group, taking on board issues such as Deaf Education and Deaf Employment.

One of their first campaigns was to lobby for a television programme for Deaf people that used BSL as it's main communication. They succeeded in persuading the BBC's Community Unit through its Open Door series to make a television programme for Deaf people called *Signs of Life*. This was the first television programme to feature Deaf presenters using sign language. This was to lead to a regular weekly programme called *SEE HEAR!*

Another of their notable successes was the organisation in conjunction with the Deaf Tribune Group of an Alternative Congress during the International Congress on the Education of the Deaf, held in Manchester in July 1985. They also organised a demonstration outside the offices of the Department of Education and Science in London.

Although many people saw the tiny NUD as "rebellious mavericks", the success of its campaigns forced a change of thinking within the BDA and the RNID and both started to embrace its policies during the 1980s and 1990s which led to a natural demise of the organisation.

The Federation of Deaf People

In the late 1990s the BDA once again reverted to being an organisation that seemed to lose sight of the important issues facing the Deaf community. With the loss of so many dedicated professionals, both Deaf and hearing, who had the real interests of Deaf people at heart it became weak and lacking in dynamic leadership. Similarly the RNID became with the departure of Doug Alker an organisation that appeared 'really not interested in the Deaf'.

This led in 1997 to the formation of The Federation of Deaf People (FDP), set up because some people felt too many Deaf people were not taking action to highlight their very real political concerns. Their first conference at Blackburn in November 1997 attracted speakers such as the Home Secretary, Jack Straw and the American professor Harlan Lane.

Despite its success in organising the BSL Marches, only time will tell if the FDP will grow into an organisation of significance in the Deaf community.

> **Dumbe Mans Friend.** 85
>
> Sir *Miles Fleetwood* hath two handsome Gentlewomen to his daughters, both borne *deafe* and *dumbe*.
>
> *De La Barre* the rich Dutch Merchant, who lived at Eeling in Middlesex, had two daughters born *deafe* and *dumb*, they were both married: A Friend of mine who was once in their companies at Brainford (their Husbands also being there;) told me he did much admire at their dexterity of perception; for by the least motion of their Husbands countenance or hand, they presently conceived of their meaning.
>
> Master *Freeman* of London Skinner, had two daughters both *deafe* and *dumbe*.
>
> One Master *Diet* a Parson in Staffordshire, hath a Brother and Sister both *deaf* and *dumbe*.
>
> One *Thomas King* Farmer of Langley, in the County of Essex, had by one woman a sonne and three daughters, all *deafe* and *dumbe*.
>
> One in Osmaston, within a mile of Darby, had foure sonnes and all of them were borne *deafe* and *dumbe*.
>
> One *John Gardiner* of Thaxted in Essex, hath a sonne and daughter both *deafe*

Extract from Bulwer's *Philocophus* (1648)
George Freeman, the Master Freeman mentioned here was
Framlingham Gaudy's Art tutor in Sir Peter Lely's
Art School.

CHAPTER VIII
SOCIAL LIFE AND EVENTS

History

Little is known about the social life of Deaf people before the start of Deaf Education and the formation of adult deaf organisations. However, enough early accounts of Deaf people mentioned in print show that before the growth of our transport system, the social lives of Deaf people usually revolved around their families or their local villages and towns.

Richard Carew's *Survey of Cornwall* in 1595 mentions Edward Bone having a friend named John Kempe, who lived 8 miles away from him. From Bulwer's *Philocophus*, published in 1648, we learn about a number of Deaf people, some of whose fathers were baronets and prominent persons with positions in government. It is likely that they exchanged information about their deaf children, perhaps even arranged for them to meet.

Family records of John "Dumb" Dyott show that he left Lichfield after the Civil War in 1647 and married a Deaf girl named Katherine in London. For this to happen, there had to be some form of socialisation of Deaf people in London itself.

We know from Samuel Pepy's diaries that a minister in the government of 1666, Sir George Downing, was able to converse in sign language with an unknown Deaf boy. Downing had spent his childhood in the Kent Weald. From this area, emigrants had gone to America and settled in Martha's Vineyard where for many years until the end of the 19th century a form of British Sign Language existed. From this, we can infer that in the Kent Weald in the early 1600s, Deaf people socialised, intermarried, had both Deaf and hearing relatives who all knew how to converse in sign language.

From the Gawdy papers in the British Library, we know that when Framlingham Gaudy was seriously ill with smallpox in 1661, the family were looking for a nurse <u>*who could sign*</u> to take care of him. This infers knowledge of the existence of other signing Deaf and hearing people in London. This may, in part, also be due to his tutor's knowledge of his Deaf daughter's acquaintances

We learn from Daniel Defoe's *Life and Times of Duncan Campbell*, published in 1720, that Campbell was in contact with other Deaf people in London.

From the memoirs of an actress called Mrs. Siddons, we learn that during her time in Bath, she modelled for Deaf painters Richard Crosse, Charles Shirreff and Sampson Towgood Roche who were all resident in Bath at the same period. Human nature being what it is, she may have told each one of them about the other two painters. Perhaps they even met and socialised. Or was it the other way round – perhaps the first Deaf painter to paint Mrs. Siddons introduced <u>*her*</u> to the others, which implies they were acquainted!

In Scotland, Sir Thomas Lauder's biographical notes of Walter Geikie state that Geikie socialised with other Deaf people in Edinburgh before the formation of the Edinburgh Congregational Church for the Deaf and Dumb in 1830.

But we are still in the dark as to the extent of socialisation that went on before the start of organised adult Deaf activities.

Deaf Social Life in the 19th Century

The adult Deaf community, as we know it today, effectively became a cohesive being in the early 19th century with the formation of adult institutes, deaf churches, sports clubs all contributing to a sense of identity shared by many. This was a step forward from the small, fragmented gatherings of Deaf people of earlier centuries.

The first adult Deaf gatherings were mainly for the purpose of holding prayer meetings. Some of the oldest Deaf organisations started out in this way, in Glasgow, Edinburgh, London and with James Herriott in Manchester. These also probably provided opportunities for socialisation in a limited form.

As these gatherings grew in number, the purpose became more of socialisation rather than purely religious meetings. Soirees and lectures became popular in the 1870's and 1880's. For instance, Aberdeen held a programme of regular weekly or fortnightly lectures from 1879 to 1893, following the example set by Liverpool who had held regular Saturday evening lectures from 1870. Liverpool also held the first Christmas party in 1869, which took the form of a tea party.

In London, the artist Thomas Davidson founded a Deaf and Dumb Debating Society, which held monthly sessions in the Lecture Hall of St. Saviour's Church, Oxford Street.

Drama was also a favourite activity amongst Deaf people in the 19th century, with many Deaf institutes and missions including dramatic performances in their social programmes.

With the formation of the Manchester Adult Deaf and Dumb Institute as a social meeting place in 1878, the growth in deaf social life extended into sport, with the formation of a number of adult Deaf sports clubs, particularly soccer and cricket. Inter-institute sports matches started to commence, and were keenly contested (and watched) by Deaf people. Over 3000 deaf people made the train trip to Glasgow for the first Deaf football international match in 1891, and a party of 30 people accompanied the Leeds Deaf football team to their match in the same city in 1895.

In Glasgow and in Edinburgh, a favourite activity amongst Deaf adults lay in the arts. Each city formed an Artists club or group where aspiring painters met to learn from each other how to draw and paint.

With better transport facilities becoming available, Deaf people also began to travel to visit others in different parts of the country, or go on outings as a club or group. Riverboat trips, such as the day out by Deaf people in Northwich and Chester in 1883, were particularly enjoyed.

Day outings into the country were also popular, either by train or horse wagon, especially by Deaf people living in cities or large towns. Manchester Adult Deaf and Dumb Institute, for example, arranged regular days out to the countryside in Cheshire or Derbyshire throughout the 1880s and 1890s.

Some of these activities included visits to public houses and inns and the resultant drinking sessions were frowned upon by others who broke away to form their own temperance societies, which were very much the vogue in those days.

Chapter VIII   A Pictorial History of Deaf Britain

A Day Out, 1890s
Photo: Manchester Deaf Centre

Glasgow Deaf Mutual Improvement Temperance Society. 1864
A society set up to combat excessive drinking among
Deaf people and to preach abstinence from alcohol.
This is one of the oldest known photographs in Deaf History
Photo: Glasgow & West of Scotland Deaf Society

Chapter VIII   A Pictorial History of Deaf Britain

**Clapham St. Bede's Club Outing
1908**
Photo: The Hallett Collection

**Stoke-on-Trent Members charabanc
outing, 1910**
Photo: Staffordshire Society for the Deaf

Oxford & Reading Deaf Club Members Outing to Radley College, 1919
Photo: Ronald Lee

Southampton Deaf Club Members Outing, 1914
Photo: Hampshire, I.O.W. & Channel Islands Association for the Deaf

Deaf Social Life: Early 20th Century

Three events, the two world wars and the Great Depression blighted life for Deaf people in the early 20th century. During this period, the after-effects of the Milan Congress of 1880 were also beginning to bite with a vengeance, with Deaf people leaving school poorly educated and without many prospects in life.

Due to the introduction of the National Insurance and Workmen's Compensation Acts, many employers were reluctant to employ deaf people resulting in great unemployment. Briefly during World War I, there was some prosperity as munitions factories and other war-driven employers clamoured for their services to fill the desperate shortage of labour caused by many other men going to war.

After cessation of hostilities, however, the optimism of having a 'Land fit for Heroes to Live in' turned sour with rising unemployment and widespread poverty. And Deaf people suffered along with the rest. In many ways, their lot was made much worse because of poor education standards and very few Deaf men or women of ability came through to lead the rest.

One bright light in the depression of those years was the advent of motor coaches, which enabled many Deaf institutes to organise outings and charabanc trips. Another form of transport, the bicycle, proved a boon in allowing many Deaf people to escape the deprivations of their existence.

By the 1930s, morale amongst Deaf people was at an all-time low. Largely judged incapable of managing their own affairs, Deaf people generally had their social events organised for them, rather than by them, mainly by hearing missioners.

By then, most large towns had their deaf institute or centre. Sports events and social outings were commonplace and it was in the final decade before the second World War that Deaf Britain's sports infrastructure was established with the formation of the British Deaf Amateur Sports Association.

In London, the choice of participation in deaf events had hitherto rested with either the church-based institutes under the aegis of the Royal Association for the Deaf and Dumb, or the upper-class independent National Deaf Club which was very sports-minded. Although originally set up for the oral deaf, it was now so full of upper class sporty-type Deaf people that oral-deaf people were feeling isolated from social activities once more. This led to the formation of the Spurs Club by a Cecilia Pollock.

It took the onset of the second war to raise the status of Deaf people once again, with many giving excellent service in the Civil Defence, and obtaining employment as replacements for men called into the armed forces.

Sadly, this second period of prosperity did not last very long after the war ended and Deaf people were back in the hands of the missioners and welfare officers as second-class citizens once again.

However, the seeds for the demise of the influence of missioners and welfare officers were sown in the first ten years after the war with the founding of two schools for academically bright children, Mary Hare Grammar School and Burwood Park School. Both were to provide future generations of Deaf leaders.

The Deaf Scout and Girl Guide Movement

One activity that was extremely popular with young Deaf people in the early part of the 20th century was the Scout and Girl Guide movement. Although Deaf schools in Britain traditionally had a long involvement in the Scout and Girl Guide movement, scouting was not confined to schoolboys and schoolgirls. Between the wars, many deaf centres also had their Senior Scout and Rover troops.

The British Deaf Scout movement was born in 1910 when the Headmaster of the Royal Cross School, Preston, Mr. J.G. Shaw, was on a motor tour of Yorkshire during his July holiday and got into severe difficulties at Skipton when his can ran off the road. Luckily for him, there were scouts camping nearby and they got his car back on the road.

Impressed by the Boy Scouts he had encountered, Mr. Shaw resolved to start a troop at his school. When the pupils returned to school after the summer holidays in August 1910, the Royal Cross School Troop was formed, followed shortly afterwards by the Royal Cross School Guides Troop.

The movement in Preston was so successful that in 1911, the school organised a jamboree for the Scouts and Guides of the district and a total of 420 Scouts and Guides from all parts of Preston and district took part. The Chief Scout, General Baden-Powell, attended the rally. It was the biggest event the school ever organised.

The first adult Scout troop formed was the 1st Duke of Grafton's Own (Clapham St. Bede's) which was formed in 1913, and within a few years there were also Scouts and Guides established in London at West Ham, Green Lanes (St. John of Beverley's), North Clapham and Stoke Newington. Other Scout and Guide troops were established at Leicester, Newcastle-upon-Tyne, Liverpool and Coventry. In Scotland, Glasgow produced the first Deaf Senior Scout, George Scott, who took part in a Grand Rally of Senior Scouts at Ibrox Park, which was inspected by the Duke of Windsor in 1931.

Most Scout and Guide troops did not survive the Second World War. Most disbanded in the late 1940s or early 1950s. After this, only the schools continued to have Scout troops.

Some schools, like the Northern Counties School for the Deaf in Newcastle, had a Cadet Corps movement before they changed to scouting. This school's Cadet Corps scored a unique achievement when they participated in the Royal Tournament at Olympia in 1927 and carried off the Lady West Trophy against fierce competition from other, *hearing*, Cadet Corps.

Today, in the new millennium, the Scout and Guide movement is almost non-existent amongst Deaf people throughout Britain, perhaps due to competition from other leisure interests, In its heyday, the movement was responsible for giving hundreds of young men and girls great fulfilment and sense of purpose. Some of these young men became Queen's Scouts. Two of them, Andrew Ford of Exeter, and Glen Harris of Coventry, were presented before the Queen and the Duke of Edinburgh at Windsor Castle.

Chapter VIII   *A Pictorial History of Deaf Britain*

1st Duke of Grafton's Own (London) Scout Troop, making breakfast at Camp
Photo: The Hallett Collection

Stoke-on-Trent Deaf Scout Troop preparing for Camp
Photo: Staffordshire Society for the Deaf

A Deaf Girl Guide Troop from West Ham
Photo: The Hallett Collection

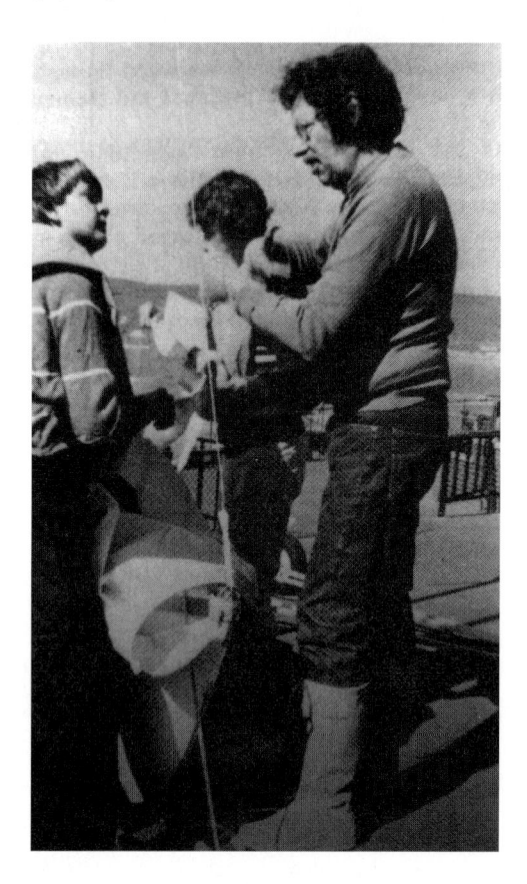

Chapter VIII   A Pictorial History of Deaf Britain

Sailing Lessons on one of the BDA's Summer Schools
Photograph: British Deaf News

One of the BDA's Summer Schools at Coleg Harlech, Wales
Photograph: British Deaf Association

The BDDA Summer Schools

Much thought had previously been given to the desirability of higher or continued education for deaf people: schemes had been discussed many times, but never carried out and the intervention of the War did not help.

The main problem was that for deaf people, there was no opportunity in the then present structure of education for them to acquire any form of higher or continued education, and in 1948, the BDDA grasped the initiative to establish one-week-long Summer Schools for deaf people.

The first was held in Edinburgh in the summer of 1948 when only a few attended, but the summer of 1951 saw the BDDA's summer school really take off at Ruskin College, Oxford. Activities included lectures as well as outings to Windsor Castle and the new Mary Hare Grammar School. It proved to be enormously popular.

In succeeding years the Summer School was held in various venues, with Coleg Harlech at Merioneth, Wales being a popular venue. It was held there three times during the 1950s. Other venues included the University of St. Andrews and St. Luke's College, Exeter.

From this small beginning, the British Deaf and Dumb Association's Summer Schools became so popular that in 1959 their activities were extended to include Mountain Venture courses. Later, these activities were extended further still pony-trekking and sailing. In 1963, for the first time, the Summer School went 'across the water' to Ballycastle in Northern Ireland.

Leisure activities were not, of course, confined to the BDDA's Further Education Service. Many centres for the deaf had their own sports and leisure activities. For example, in 1951 Croydon club members went on an outing to Margate, a visit to the school being included.

The BDA's Summer Schools continued to be held in the 1970s but were now part of their Further Education and Youth Service programme. In these years, the accent was often on courses such as flower arrangement, floral picture making, woodcarving as well as the traditional adventure and physical sports courses. New activities such as water-skiing, archery, canoeing and fencing were popular. Some courses were designed to help deaf people to be aware of procedures, hence accountancy, current affairs, police work, fire prevention; committee procedures courses were also arranged.

Summer Schools declined in the 1980s with the growth of other leisure activities and were mainly held for young Deaf people. In 1986, for instance, the Summer School consisted of one week only at Hereford College for the Blind. Activities included day outings to the Ironbridge Gorge Museum in Coalbrookdale and the Museum of Cider in Hereford.

With the BDA's main focus in the 1990s being its Youth Activities, Summer Schools were usually held at Atlantic College in Wales for young Deaf people, but by the end of the decade, financial restraints meant that even these activities were being cut back. After 50 years wonderful service to the Deaf Community, the Summer Schools ceased to exist.

The Growth of Leisure Activities

One reason for the decline and demise of the BDA's Summer Schools is the growth in alternative leisure pursuits. One of the oldest Deaf organisations devoted to leisure pursuits is the Deaf Mountaineering Club. The DMC, as the club is called, was founded in 1960 by a small group of Deaf people who wanted to continue to enjoy rock-climbing after they were introduced to the sport by the BDA at its first Mountain Venture course in Keswick in October 1959. It soon grew in membership, attracting members from all over Britain and Northern Ireland.

During the 1960s rock-climbing was the most popular activity of the members, but from the 1970s onwards mountain and hill-walking, ridge walking and rock-scrambling gradually took over from rock-climbing as the main activity of members. Nowadays there is very little rock-climbing done.

Another leisure-related organisation with a long history that enjoys popularity with many Deaf people and their families is the Deaf Caravan and Camping Club. Formed in 1974, it organises rallies throughout the year on a monthly basis in England, Wales and Scotland. It celebrated its 25th anniversary in style in Cornwall during the last British Eclipse.

One activity that was popular in the 1970s, 1980s and early 1990s were the BDA Gala Weekends, which were usually held in a holiday camp, comprising of fun and games for participants. At the peak of their popularity, these weekends would attract upwards of a thousand Deaf people and their families.

One of the biggest Deaf-related events in the calendar that is still immensely popular is the annual Blackpool Rally. Taking place usually on the first or second weekend in September when the seafront illuminations are on, this rally attracts well over two thousand fun-seeking young Deaf people from all over the country. The infamous "Deaf Riot" in 1987 when a number of arrests were made following a clash between over 200 Deaf revellers and 70 police officers helped to give this rally some notoriety. Improved community relations between the police and Deaf people since then has kept this event largely trouble-free.

Apart from the BDA's annual conferences or triennial congresses, which are well attended for their social activities as much as for their business element, other Deaf-related annual events have come into prominence in the annual calendar. These include the National Deaf Children's Society's two-day Technology events, held annually in June in the Midlands, and the CACDP's Sign Fair, held annually in the Spring. Both events attract over a thousand people and are of importance in keeping different groups of Deaf people in contact with each other.

A 1990s desire for leisure pursuits with a bit of a challenge have led to the organisation of events such as yachting, water skiing, motor rallying. The latter was very popular, drawing forty teams for the first Deaf UK Auto Challenge in 1994, which included off-road driving in mountainous terrain in Wales. This led to other auto challenges being organised in Europe. Growing interest in yachting led to Royal Yacht Association foundation training cruises being organised for Deaf people off the South Coast of England.

Chapter VIII   A Pictorial History of Deaf Britain

Deaf Mountaineering Club Activities
In the 1960s rock-climbing was popular with DMC members. In the left photograph, Margaret Whitehouse of Leeds leads a climb in Borrowdale in the Lake District.
Photo: Irene Hall

A one-week Meet is held every year in the Scottish Highlands. In this 1994 photograph, members are walking up from Loch Quoich near Invergarry.
Photo: Irene Hall

Deaf Caravan and Camping Club Rally in 1994
Photo: British Deaf News

Chapter VIII   *A Pictorial History of Deaf Britain*

Changing Times
Differences in social and leisure activities pursued by Deaf people in the 1920s and 1990s

Deaf Social Life at the Millennium

If the Deaf pioneers of the 1880-1890s could step into a time capsule and be transported to the beginning of the 21st century, they would be astonished at the social changes that have affected and improved the lot of Deaf people.

In 1880-1890, Deaf people with a love of the theatrical had to go to Deaf Missions to partake in soirees and other drama presentations. In 2000, they have a pick of interpreted theatrical productions to go to and enjoy.

In 1880-1890, Deaf people had to endure 11 hours of a smoky and uncomfortable train journey from Manchester to Glasgow to take part in a Deaf football match. In 2000, 22 Deaf people celebrated the Millennium in Tenerife, and the BDA organised a challenging visit to Mexico!

In 1880-1890, Deaf people would have to walk, cycle, or otherwise travel miles just to pass a message to another. In 2000, most would simply click onto the Internet and send a email message, or use a mobile phone to send a text message.

In 1880-1890, a Deaf person depended on lectures given in Deaf Missions such as "Sights of America" (8 December 1884, Aberdeen Adult Deaf Mute Mission) to gain a taste of foreign travel. In 2000, the same Deaf person can learn as much from subtitled television programmes, or better still, do what a group of 25 British Asian Deaf people did, go to a Congress in America.

It is not just modern advances such as the Internet or modern technology, enlightened laws such as the Disability Discrimination Act, or the easy availability of modern travel that has changed Deaf people's lives. Many other factors have also influenced these changes, including better living standards and increased leisure time. Advances in education in the social sense have also contributed to these changes by increasing Deaf people's awareness of what is going on in the world and wanting access to it. Television programmes such as *"Who Wants to be a Millionaire!"* are forced through the Disability Discrimination Act to provide access for Deaf people wishing to try and enter the programme.

Social attitudes have also changed.

Whereas in 1880-1890, the Deaf Mission or Institute may have been the focal point of many Deaf people's daily lives, it now has to compete with other attractions that have a Deaf following. These attractions range from activity pursuits such as sailing, fell-walking, camping and caravanning, or challenging pursuits such as scuba diving, water-skiing, piloting aeroplanes, motor cycling. There are clubs for Deaf people in all of these activities.

Other Deaf people may simply prefer to go out and meet in pubs. Many Deaf people in London and other large cities have regular pub evenings where they gather and enjoy themselves.

Easy availability of modern travel has also increased the numbers of Deaf people who like to holiday together, leading to the setting up of several holiday companies specialising in this field, such as Funnel Tours, which have a regular clientele for their overseas travel programmes.

Chapter IX   A Pictorial History of Deaf Britain

Glasgow Deaf and Dumb F.C. 25th Anniversary 1896
Photo: Glasgow and West of Scotland Society for the Deaf

Manchester Deaf and Dumb Athletic Club 1874
(This was a rugby team)
Photo: Royal Schools for the Deaf Manchester

CHAPTER IX

DEAF SPORT

History

Since before the earliest recorded history, sport has played a central role in both the social and cultural life of all civilised societies. Within Deaf sport the relationships formed between all those who are involved played a deeper sociological role, enabling deaf people to maintain contact with each other as well as helping to form a cohesive and strong sense of community.

Deaf sport pre-dates the formation of national deaf organisations, and is largely responsible for providing many participants with a sense of Deaf identity that they may have lacked previous to their involvement with Deaf sport.

Although it is difficult to trace with absolute certainty, it is likely that Deaf sport owes its origins to the first schools for deaf children. For example, school records show that pupils in both the Glasgow Institution for the Deaf and Dumb at Langside and the Manchester Institution for the Deaf and Dumb were taking part in sports activities in the 1860s. The Yorkshire Institution for the Deaf and Dumb at Doncaster had introduced gymnastics, soccer and cricket to the schoolchildren by the early 1870s. These sports activities had originally been introduced for the purpose of building up pupils' strengths as many of the children who attended the schools were poor and physically deficient.

There is no dispute, however, who founded the first adult deaf sports club. This honour belongs to Glasgow, which founded Glasgow Deaf and Dumb Football Club in 1871. Its first matches were played against hearing teams. It was not until 1888 that they started to play against other Deaf teams. It is the oldest Deaf sports club in the world still in existence.

Also in 1871, an adult rugby club comprising of school staff and older pupils was formed by the Manchester Institution but the first proper adult deaf sports club was not formed until 1876 as the Manchester Deaf and Dumb Sports Club. The same year, Derby Deaf and Dumb Cricket and Football Club was also formed. These two adult sports clubs were formed directly as a result of close links with the schools in those cities. A similar situation took place in Liverpool with the formation of Liverpool Deaf and Dumb Cricket and Football Club in 1878.

Deaf Sport was responsible for starting off one professional football club, when the Yorkshire Institution played a football match against a hearing team, which later became Doncaster Rovers Football Club. The school even gave them their first kit.

The *first organised* inter-club sports match was a cricket match between Derby and Sheffield in 1882, which was won by Derby by one run.

The *first organised tournament or competition* was in Scotland by the newly formed Scottish Deaf Football Association in 1889. Edinburgh beat Glasgow in the final 3-1 in front of 2000 spectators at Falkirk.

Even before organised Deaf sport, however, there were some outstanding Deaf individuals whose prowess at their particular sport made them famous. One was even heavyweight boxing champion of the world!

James Burke (1809 – 1845)

A brutal business, prize fighting was fought under rules which enabled men to inflict terrible injuries on each other. Fights were fought to a finish when a man was downed and had been battered into insensibility. It might therefore be expected that many contests would provide fatalities, but this was not the case.

All the more tragic therefore that one of the earliest deaths in boxing, possibly the most controversial, resulted from a fight in which a deaf boxer took part.

James 'Deaf' Burke or the 'Deaf Un' as he was generally known was born in Westminster, London, on 8 December 1809, and became orphaned in early childhood. He became a gutter urchin who haunted the London waterfront.

One day, to escape heavy rain he wandered into a tavern called the 'Spotted Dog', which was kept by Joe Parrish, a veteran fighter. Impressed with the young lad, then aged 16, he began to teach him the science of the ring. Although he could not read or write, Burke learnt fast, but it was not until he was nearly 19, when Burke had his first fight.

This was against an Irish man named Ned Murphy. They fought 50 rounds, only to have the fight stopped because of darkness. Burke went on to win 3 out of 4 fights in less than a year, and in 1828 was matched with William Fitzmaurice at Harpenden, which went 106 rounds and lasted 3 hours.

Before his fight with Fitzmaurice took place, Burke achieved fame in entirely different circumstances. He became a hero when he rescued a number of people from a blazing house fire.

Burke's most famous fight, which made him World Champion, was with an Irishman called Simon Byrne in 1833. Byrne was not a particularly big man, standing only 5 feet 9 inches and weighing 13 stone, but Deaf Burke was even smaller at 5 feet 8 ? inches, and 12 stone 7 lbs. It was a hard, bloody fight lasting 3 hours and 16 minutes (this time still stands as a world record for a championship fight), before Burke knocked out Byrne with a tremendous punch, thus becoming recognised champion.

Byrne was carried away from the ring unconscious and died three days later without coming out of his coma. The deaf boxer and all those connected with the fight were arrested and charged with manslaughter. However, conflicting opinions of several doctors gained their acquittal.

However, the tragedy upset Burke and he became convinced people regarded him as a murderer, so he sailed across to the United States, where he had several fights which almost cost him his life due to crowd troubles. He was the first person to bring Prize Ring fighting to America.

Disillusioned with the fight scene in the States, Burke returned to England in 1837 to face William 'Bold Bendigo' Thompson. Burke was not in the best of condition and had lost his fighting spirit because of his problems in America. In the 10th round, he was ruled out for a foul and lost his world championship.

After 1840, Burke never fought again, becoming a stage actor advertising his magnificent physique, but excessive drinking and many women took their toll and he died penniless of tuberculosis in a lane off Waterloo Road in 1845.

Chapter IX   A Pictorial History of Deaf Britain

James Burke
Heavyweight Champion of the World

Chapter IX   A Pictorial History of Deaf Britain

Two Professional Boxers of the 1940s
Above: Peter Livingstone of Aberdeen
Below: Pat Cubis of St. Albans

Other Boxers

James Burke was not the only Deaf boxing champion that Britain has produced. In Aberdeen, a Deaf man named Harry Byres reigned supreme as Scottish featherweight champion from 1924 to 1930 before losing his title in Dundee to Jimmy McMillan.

Byres was a popular fighter on the Scottish boxing scene. Inevitably, he was nicknamed 'Deaf Burke' by Scottish fight fans. Byres might have become British featherweight champion if he had not narrowly been beaten on points over 20 rounds by the then champion, Johnny Curley. Byres in fact had Curley down on the canvas several times, but could not find the punch needed to finish the champion off.

Aberdeen also had another Deaf man who was a professional boxer in the late 1930s and early 1940s. The British Boxing Board of Control was not formed until 1929, and introduced professional boxing licences shortly afterwards. Peter Livingstone (1920-1986) was the first Deaf person in Britain to hold a professional boxing licence, number 27749, Registration no. B9131, issued on 13.3.1940. Peter Livingstone was a journeyman boxer who never quite achieved the fame of his Aberdeen predecessor.

Other Deaf men who became boxers and were granted licences by the British Boxing Board of Control were welterweight Pat Cubis of St. Albans, middleweight George Fordham of Edmonton, London. Both Cubis and Fordham fought around the same time in the late 1940s. Pat Cubis had quite a good record, without actually becoming a champion. Out of 92 professional fights, he won 74, drew 5 and lost 13. However, he never made much money out of boxing and fought more for the love of the sport than for money.

In 1981, another Deaf man, David Caves, joined the professional ranks.

Wrestling

It is not only in boxing that the Deaf community have produced champions in the ring. Wrestler Harry Kendall from London reigned supreme as undefeated British amateur wrestling champion with several titles and two bronze medals from the Commonwealth Games. When Kendall turned professional, he teamed up with another Deaf wrestler, Mike Eagers, to form a tag team called The Silent Ones.

Britain also had another excellent Deaf tag team in wrestling, Jim Lomas and Alan Kilby, who were known as the Maxwell Boys during the 1980s, after the name of their school in Sheffield, the Maud Maxwell School for the Deaf. Incidentally, Mike Eagers was also a former pupil of the same school.

The Rise and Decline of Deaf Sports Activities

The first cricket and football matches between different deaf institutes or clubs were watched by large crowds. About 500 spectators watched Derby beat Sheffield by just one run in the first thrilling cricket match in 1882, whilst over 2000 fans packed into Falkirk's Bainsford football ground to watch Edinburgh beat Glasgow in the Scottish Deaf Football Association Cup Competition in 1889.

These events whetted the appetites of Deaf sports fans for more organised events and it was not long before the first international sports match was played.

This was a football match between Scotland and England in 1891. In reality, all the players were drawn from northern English Deaf football clubs, as London at that time had no Deaf football teams except in schools. The novelty of a first international sports match proved attractive to many Deaf people starved of popular pastimes, and special excursion trains were put on to transport supporters to Glasgow from Manchester, Nottingham and Yorkshire. Many were willing to put up with a slow eleven hour journey and they were rewarded by excellent weather conditions on 28 March 1891 when the match finally got under way at Ibrox Park, Glasgow, the home of Glasgow Rangers FC, in front of a crowd exceeding 3000. The result was a 3-3 draw between the two teams.

The expense of long distance travel at a time of poor wages and low employment, however, meant that never again would any domestic Deaf sports event attract crowds of such numbers and the football internationals fell into disuse after three years, as did Scotland's Deaf Football Cup competition.

Leeds Deaf and Dumb FC made an exception in 1895 when they travelled to Glasgow for the celebrations linked with the opening of Glasgow's new Mission. They came away severely thrashed 6-0.

The majority of Deaf football and cricket matches were played in local hearing leagues. Many clubs did extremely well in their local leagues. Manchester Deaf FC, for instance, won the local league championship in 1905-6 and Leicester Deaf Cricket Club were their local league's Division I champions in 1927.

Full-size Deaf football and cricket teams (and also the women's netball and hockey teams that had brief periods when they flourished) have always had periods of growth and decline. The main reason for this is that Deaf sport is not guaranteed a regular supply of new members due to fluctuations in the sizes of various local Deaf communities.

Most regular inter-club contact came through flourishing indoor sports leagues. Even these leagues, however, also suffered periods of decline.

Cricket, as a Deaf sport, was mostly played for its social side, and until league and cup competitions were started in the 1950s, few inter-club matches were played other than as friendlies. Deaf cricket teams were sent to Denmark in 1981 and Barbados & St. Vincent in 1983 where they played hearing opposition, but an unique event took place in December 1995 when the first Deaf World Cricket Cup was played in Melbourne, Australia. Six countries took part, and Britain narrowly lost to Australia in the final.

Top: **Leeds Deaf and Dumb F.C. at Glasgow, 1895**
Middle: **Glasgow Ladies Deaf and Dumb Hockey Team 1922**
Photos: Glasgow and West of Scotland Society for the Deaf
Bottom: **England Batting against Australia in a Deaf Cricket World Cup 1999**
Photo: British Deaf Sports Council

Chapter IX   A Pictorial History of Deaf Britain

Great Britain Football Team 1928
Photo: Glasgow & West of Scotland Society for the Deaf

'England' as Great Britain in Stockholm, 1939
What happened to the Scots, the Welsh and the Irish?
Photo: Betty Shrine

World Games for the Deaf – The Pre War Years

The modern Olympic games were reconstituted in 1896 at Athens and proved highly successful in forging sporting links between nations. Naturally, the deaf world wanted to have the same opportunities.

In 1924 the French took the initiative and organised an International Games for the Deaf and Dumb, which was attended by deaf sportsmen from a number of mainly European nations. A team from Great Britain was organised under the auspices of the British Deaf and Dumb Association and took part in athletics, swimming, diving, shooting, tennis and football competitions.

Britain won the tennis doubles cup, the swimming relay race cup and took prizes in diving and shooting (medals were not given until after the war). In football, Great Britain beat Belgium 4-1 in the final to win the cup.

The Games were to be held every four years, and up to the start of the Second World War, Britain were to reign supreme at football in every Games except 1931 in Nuremberg in Germany when they lost the trophy in farcical circumstances. Drawn against Czechoslovakia in the first round, the same team that had been beaten in the final three years previously, the score was 0-0 at final whistle, so it was decreed that extra time be played.

Within two minutes of the start of extra time, the Czechs scored from a goalmouth scramble and the referee terminated the game. However, following a meeting at 2am in the morning, the Games committee decided that full extra time had to be played first thing in the morning. Alas nobody thought to tell the British team. Thus, Czechoslovakia, Holland and France (who had also drawn and had their game similarly stopped when France scored first) were on the pitch a few hours later when the British teams were still in their beds. As a result, Czechoslovakia was awarded the match only to be beaten by Germany who won the cup by beating Austria 4-1 in the final.

The 4th International Games were held in London in 1935, the only time that Britain has ever hosted the Games. One feature of these Games was that England saw, perhaps for the only time, the marching of the German jackboots, the Nazi salute and the flag with the swastika on public display.

The last International Games for the Deaf held before the Second World War was in Stockholm, Sweden in August 1939. It was notable for the hair-raising return of the British team and their supporters from Stockholm over the period 2–4 September. Whilst they were travelling, the Second World war broke out and their ship was stopped by a warship, which advised them to make a detour to avoid German ships. Instead of arriving at Harwich, the ship went to Aberdeen.

The Games in the pre-war years were notable for the British in that not only were they generally undisputed football champions in every Games bar one, they were also a force to be reckoned with in Lawn Tennis. They were the Men's and Ladies' Doubles, and Mixed Doubles champions at several Games, and were losing finalists in several others.

The World Games for the Deaf – 1949 to 1985

After a lapse of ten years due the Second World War the international Games restarted at Copenhagen under a new title, the Olympiad. This was the last Games at which trophies were given instead of medals. Great Britain once again displayed their prowess at Lawn Tennis, winning the Men's Singles and Men's Doubles tennis trophies. They also won the 96 km. Road Cycling trophy.

The football team had a tougher time, playing Holland at 9am one morning, then Denmark at 6pm the same evening. They won both games 5-1 and 7-0. The next day, Italy were the opponent in the semi-final, which went to extra time before Great Britain emerged 2-1 victors. The final against Belgium went to extra time was again played before Britain emerged winners 6-4. This was the last Games final Britain was to win until 40 years later at Christchurch, New Zealand, in 1989.

British tennis continued to dominate the next three Games held in Brussels (1953), Milan (1957) and Helsinki (1961). However, never again were the British to win any more Lawn Tennis finals

The 1950s-1970s Games were notable for the brilliant British efforts in Cycling, securing gold medals in Brussels (1953) when Nobby Clarke retained the title he won in 1949, Washington, D.C. (1965) when two golds and one silver were won by Malcolm Johnson. The Washington Games were the last to have the title "Olympiad". The International Olympic Committee decreed that the word "Olympics" could not be used outside of the Olympic Games proper, so the title was changed to the World Games for the Deaf, which is retained to this day.

Malcolm Johnson was also the hero in Belgrade (1969) with two gold medals. If he had not had a fall and a puncture in his third race, he might have completed a hat trick of medals. At Malmo, Sweden, in 1973, British blushes were spared once again by the brilliance of the same man who won two golds and one silver.

The next Games at Bucharest, Romania, in 1977 saw the smallest British participation since they commenced in Paris in 1924; there were just four swimmers and two officials. Lack of funds, disinterest, failure to meet qualifying standards all meant that, for the first time since 1924, Britain had no tennis, athletic or football competitors. No medals were won.

Britain also performed poorly in Cologne in 1981. These Games were due to be held in Tehran, Iran, but due to civil disturbances and the likelihood of war conditions in that country, they were switched at the last moment to Cologne.

However, it was at Los Angeles in 1985 that Britain had its best Games for decades when five golds, eleven silvers and ten bronzes were won. The introduction of badminton as a sport saw a strong British entry. This resulted in three golds, four silvers and three bronzes. In fact, the Men's Singles, Men's Doubles and Mixed Doubles were All-British finals, and the bronzes was also taken in the Mixed Doubles, making a clean sweep. On the athletics track, Britain got its first athletics' gold medals since 1957 when Tim Butler won both the 5,000 and 10,000 metres.

Malcolm Johnson winning the Gold, Washington DC, 1965
Photo: British Deaf News

Medal Winners at Athletics, Los Angeles, 1985
Photo: British Deaf Sports Council

Candy Perkins with one of her Gold Medals, Copenhagen, 1997
Photo: British Deaf Sports Council

The British Swimming Team, Christchurch, New Zealand, 1989
Photo: British Deaf Sports Council

The World Games for the Deaf – 1989 to 1997

The 16th Games at Christchurch, New Zealand, in 1989 were, without doubt, the costliest sports venture ever undertaken by British Deaf sport. The 42 competitors who went halfway round the world to represent Britain in Christchurch did their country proud by winning twelve gold medals, eight silvers and six bronzes, the best tally ever by a British World games for the Deaf squad. The British swimming team were magnificent, particularly the men, who beat USA – previously unbeaten over the past 20 years – in two relay races. Martin Lee of Fife got a hat trick of gold medals, the first British Deaf sportsman to achieve this in one World Games. In total, the swimming team came back with six gold medals, five silver medals and two bronze medals, a brilliant effort for a team of just 11 swimmers, who included two twins.

There were heroes as well in badminton, where the team achieved two gold medals, two silver medals and three bronzes and in athletics and football. For the first time since 1949 at Copenhagen, Great Britain's footballers won the final and the gold medal when they beat Ireland.

In contrast, the next World Games held in 1993 in Sofia, Bulgaria, were disappointing although Martin Lee won another gold medal in the 100m Men's breaststroke. These Games were blighted by poor facilities in many areas.

The last World Games of the 20th Century were held in Copenhagen in 1997, the second time they had been held in that city, the first being in 1949. These Games were notable for the performance of Candy Perkins in the athletics, winning the 800m and the 1500m. Britain's third gold medal of these games was won at badminton in the Ladies Doubles.

Winter Games for the Deaf

The modern Olympic Games movement is not confined to 'summer' sports like athletics, swimming and the like, but also has a separate Winter Games for skiing and other winter sports such as ice skating and ice hockey.

The first deaf International Winter Games took place after the Second World War, but Great Britain did not enter a team until nine Winter games had been held. Following the increase in popularity of skiing due to exposure on television, a team of three was entered in the 10th Winter Games at Madonna di Campiglio, Italy, in 1983. The team did not win any medals.

It was a different story in Norway in 1987. Crawford Carrick Anderson, a 16-year-old from Glasgow, exceeded all expectations to obtain Great Britain's first ever Winter Games medal when he took the silver in the Giant Slalom. This young boy also took bronzes in the Slalom and the Parallel Slalom – a very creditable performance for someone in his first ever Games.

No medals were won at the next Winter Games in Banff, Canada, when Anderson was injured and could not compete, but he returned to the team in Finland, 1995, to secure more medals.

Britain did not enter a team in the 1999 Winter Games at Davos, Switzerland.

Deaf Professionals in Sport

Apart from those in the fight game mentioned earlier in this chapter, there have been Deaf professional sportsmen in other sports. This has happened mainly in football. Examples were Billy Nesbitt, who won a Championship and FA Cup medal with Burnley in 1911-1923 and Jimmy McLean who played for Cardiff City in the 1920s. In Scotland, Alex Fraser (a former pupil of Aberdeen School for the Deaf) played for Kilmarnock in the late 1940s and went on to become the first Deaf person to become a professional referee. In the Stockport County team between 1955-8, there was Raymond Drake, probably the last profoundly Deaf player to play in the English Football League. He played a total of 203 games, scoring 238 goals – a remarkable feat by any standard.

However, perhaps the best-known Deaf footballer was Cliff Bastin of Arsenal.

Cliff Bastin (1912 - 1991)

Cliff Bastin was signed by Arsenal in 1929, and was the youngest player to appear in a FA Cup Final when he played against Huddersfield in the 1931 final. This was also the year Arsenal did the double, winning the League Championship.

In his career with Arsenal, Bastin scored a record number of 176 goals, which stood for many years until it was surpassed by Ian Wright. He also won 23 cup and championship medals, and represented England 26 times.

The noted British Deaf historian, Arthur F. Dimmock, recalled watching Bastin play for Arsenal in partnership with the legendary Alex James and noted that the pair of them used a form of sign language to communicate on the field.

Lester Piggott (1935 -)

In a different sport, Britain had someone who has arguably been one of the world's best ever jockeys in Lester Piggott.

His deafness was discovered at the age of 5, and had possibly been present since birth. Even at age 5, he was lipreading so well that his parents were shocked to discover he was deaf and he never lost his lipreading skills, even after attending the East Anglian School for the Deaf at Gorleston for a short period.

He was, and remained so as an adult, extremely shy and awkward in company of other people. He grew up on his father's stables where there were always horses around him and never lost his affinity with them, as he showed on more than one occasion on the world's racetracks.

He was on good terms with the Royal Family, many of whose horses he rode to victory at Epsom, Goodwood or Ascot and was awarded the M.B.E. for services to racing.

His life was shattered when, in 1986, he was convicted of income tax fraud and sentenced to three years imprisonment. He was deeply hurt when the Queen stripped him of his M.B.E. because of his conviction.

Chapter IX   A Pictorial History of Deaf Britain

Cliff Bastin, Arsenal FC, 1929
Photo: British Deaf History Society

Lester Piggott
Photo: Author's collection

Chapter IX   A Pictorial History of Deaf Britain

Sarah Jane Cooke
Photo: Author's Collection

Paul Hebblethwaite
Photo: British Deaf News

Ian Williams
Photo: British Deaf News

Craig Gardiner
Photo: British Deaf News

Other Sporting Achievements

Whilst they may not have reached the professional ranks, there were other Deaf people whose dedication in their own sporting arenas saw them raise to the top of their particular fields, showing that deafness is no barrier or disability in their sports. These have included little known sports such as trampolining, women's cricket, pony and carriage riding, Taekwon-Do, and another martial arts event, Tang Soo Do.

In the early 1980s Mike Hawthorne, a former pupil of Woodford School for the Deaf in London, was selected to represent Great Britain in trampolining. He is the first (and only) known Deaf person ever to represent his country at international level in this sport. Mike also participated in gymnastic events and in 1987, won the British Veterans Championships, the first Deaf person to do so.

A Deaf girl named Erica Cox from Redditch in Worcestershire, who also had additional disabilities, won several honours and competed in the National Riding and Driving Championships, coming second in the pony and carriage event, which was later made popular through the participation of Prince Philip.

Sarah Jane Cooke, a former pupil of Hamilton Lodge School for Deaf Children at Brighton, became an excellent player in Women's Cricket, and after being selected to tour Denmark with the England Women's junior squad, went on to play cricket at Test level for England.

Two young Deaf people took up martial arts and did so well that they became champions in their respective sports. Ian Williams of Coventry won three gold medals in the English Championship, the British Championship and the British Taekwon-Do Championship, whilst Paul Adams became the first Deaf person to become European Champion in the Under-14 group whilst representing Great Britain in the Tang Soo Do sport. A pupil at the Heathlands School for the Deaf in St. Albans, he had reached Black Belt standard when aged only 12.

Deaf Scotsman Craig Gardiner of East Kilbride won the 1995 West of Scotland under-78kg Open Judo Championship after being Scottish Junior Champion five times.

In a Games with a difference, Keith Gardner of Airdrie, Scotland, who also had cerebral palsy as well as profound deafness, represented Great Britain in the 1992 and 1996 Paralympic Games, winning silver medals in both Games. In Barcelona (1992) he got his silver in the Indian Club event and in Atlanta (1996) in the javelin event.

A sportsman with a difference is Paul Hebblethwaite, whose hobby and sport of sailing was to see him achieve some distinction as a sailor, leading to a place in one of the BT Global Challenge round-the-world yacht races. He secured a place as a crewmember of *Time and Tide*, one of the boats competing in the race. The yacht completed the round-the-world race and although unplaced, the crew earned praise from other competitors for their sportsmanship and determination.

In another sport, Crawford Carrick Anderson (the same person who won Britain's first Winter Games medals) competes regularly in professional Mountain Bike Downhill events.

Chapter X   A Pictorial History of Deaf Britain

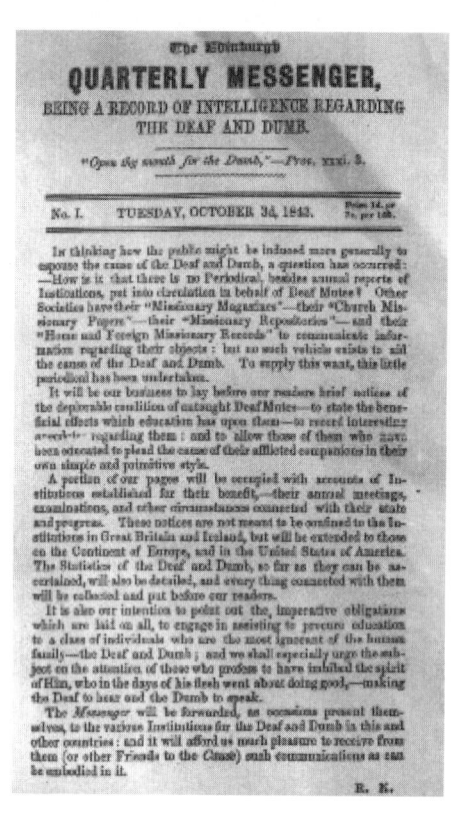

One of the First Magazines for the Deaf
Produced by the Institution for the Deaf and Dumb, Edinburgh 1843

Irene Hall
First woman Editor of the British Deaf News
Photo: Irene Hall

CHAPTER X

LITERATURE, THEATRE AND TELEVISION

Deaf Magazines

The earliest known magazine for the deaf to be published in the United Kingdom was the *Hull Deaf & Dumb Times*, a local news-sheet produced by a Deaf man, followed by the *Edinburgh Messenger*, the first issue of which appeared in October 1843. This magazine was published by the Edinburgh Institution for the Deaf and Dumb and produced by the pupils on the school's press. The editor was the headmaster, Robert Kinniburgh. It had a short life span and the last issue to appear was No.12, January 1845.

The next magazine to appear was *The Magazine for the Deaf and Dumb*, first published by the Association in Aid of the Deaf and Dumb (forerunner of the present day Royal Association for the Deaf) in July 1855, but only five issues were published, the last in 1857.

The present day *British Deaf News* can trace its origins back to 1873 when the Rev. Samuel Smith published *A Magazine Intended Chiefly for the Deaf and Dumb*. Then there followed a bewildering succession of names as the magazine changed hands several times. In 1879, the magazine was called *The Deaf and Dumb Magazine* and Mr. Alexander Strathern of Glasgow took over publication in 1881 but gave it up in 1883 due to ill-health. It was then edited by James Paul of Kilmarnock until 1885, when he handed over to Ernest Abraham who renamed the magazine *Deaf and Dumb World*. The title was changed yet again in 1887 to *Deaf-Mute World*, but only two issues were produced before Abraham was forced to close down due to heavy losses.

Into the vacuum stepped *The Deaf-Mute* in 1888, published by a new organisation called the Deaf-Mute Association, a brainchild of a J.J. Maclean and Francis Maginn of Belfast. However, proposals for the formation of a national association to be called the British Deaf and Dumb Association, together with a publication called *The Deaf and Dumb Times* meant only one issue was published.

From the appearance of the *Deaf and Dumb Times*, edited by Charles Gorham of Leeds, in 1889 the *British Deaf News* has an unbroken genealogy, although the magazine underwent a number of name changes and was merged with another magazine with a long lineage in 1955, *The Deaf Quarterly News*.

Although the first editor of the present *British Deaf News* was a hearing man, the majority of the editors of the *Deaf and Dumb Times, Deaf Chronicle, British Deaf-Mute, British Deaf Monthly* and *British Deaf Times* were deaf men up to the death of Joseph Hepworth in 1921. In contrast, the *Deaf Quarterly News* (in its various names) was always edited by a hearing person, generally a missioner, and its news generally was of more interest to those working in the welfare of Deaf people rather than Deaf people themselves.

Apart from a brief period from 1962 to 1964 when the Rev. Mark Frame edited the *British Deaf News*, no deaf person edited the magazine from 1921 to 1989 when Mrs Irene Hall was appointed editor - the first woman so appointed.

Following restructuring of the BDA in the late 1990s, publication of the magazine was transferred to a private company, Red Lizard Ltd. of Redditch, Worcestershire, who appointed another woman, Catya Nielson, as editor.

Other Magazines for the Deaf

Other magazines on deafness and Deaf people exist. Perhaps the one that is read most by Deaf people is *One in Seven* one, published by the RNID. This magazine can also trace its lineage under various titles. In the mid-20th century, it was published under the titles *The Silent World* and *Hearing*. In the 1980s, the magazine became *Soundbarrier* for a few years before a partnership with the BBC saw a title change to *See Hear!*, to match a television programme of the same name.

In 1997, the title changed again to the present *One in Seven* and was issued as a magazine to all those who paid membership subscriptions to the RNID. The current magazine is in a most attractive format, and in the view of many people, a rival to the *British Deaf News*.

Membership magazines are also issued by a number of other deaf organisations. For example, CACDP issues *The Standard* and the British Deaf History Society issues the *Deaf History Journal*. The range of magazines on offer therefore covers many different areas of the Deaf World.

In addition, many of the local Deaf associations and societies have issued, and some still continue to issue, in-house magazines giving information of particular relevance to their own localities though some covered other news of the Deaf World. One magazine, *Ephphatha*, the organ of the Royal Association for the Deaf, had a long history, having been published for over 60 years before it ceased publication with issue No. 200 in 1959.

The deafness magazine or journal with the longest continuous existence under one title is *Teacher of the Deaf*, which was first published in 1903. Other associations and organisations have their own magazine, for example Talk *(National Deaf Children's Society)*, HARK *(Hearing Concern)* but few are read by deaf people.

Teletext and the Internet

The advent of modern information technology allowing access to teletext pages on television, and from the late 1990s on the Internet, have provided Deaf people with more choices of accessing information than ever before.

The longest running Deaf teletext television magazine is *Read Hear*, published and updated weekly on BBC2. Another more limited teletext television magazine is *Deafview*, shown on Channel 4 and also updated weekly. Viewing the Read Hear pages is a must for people who wish to gain employment in working with deaf people as job advertisements are updated regularly.

It is, however, perhaps the Internet that has really revolutionised Deaf people's access to information. The rapid spread of websites belonging to a variety of deaf organisations ensures that every Deaf person who has the appropriate technology can access information of particular relevance to their enquiries. This access is not of course limited to deaf organisations. Anything from train timetables or holidays are accessible through the Internet and are particularly useful to Deaf people who are spared having to seek the information they require by other means.

Chapter X   A Pictorial History of Deaf Britain

Changing Times, Changing Titles
The RNID magazine has changed titles over the last 20 years of the 20th Century in line with perceived themes.

A typical Internet page – this one is for the British Deaf News

Chapter X   A Pictorial History of Deaf Britain

David Wright
Photo supplied by Royal National Institute for Deaf People

Dorothy Miles
Photo supplied by British Deaf History Society

Deaf Poetry, Novelists and Writers

During the twentieth century, following in the footsteps of Harriet Martineau, there have been a number of deaf novelists and authors. The best known of these was Kate Whitehead, later to be the wife of Selwyn Oxley, who built up a huge collection of Literature about the deaf. Other books written by deaf people have tended to be biographies, such as the highly humorous *Life among the Deaf* by Michael Jack.

There have been several Deaf people, who have had collections of poetry published as books, and/or who have earned part of their living as authors.

David Wright (1920 - 1994)

David Wright became totally deaf at the age of seven through contracting scarlet fever and a period of private tuition, was educated at Northampton High School for Deaf Boys (Spring Hill), then at Oriel College, Oxford.

In 1950, he won one of the last Atlantic Awards in Literature and subsequently published several books including *Monologue of a Deaf Man*, and was from 1965 to 1967 Gregory Fellow in poetry at Leeds University.

Dorothy Miles (1934 - 1993)

Dot Miles, as she was more familiarly known, was born in Mold, North Wales, and became deaf at the age of 8 through meningitis while she was at the Christ Church Elementary School in Rhyl, North Wales. After an education at the Royal Schools for the Deaf, Manchester, and Mary Hare Grammar School she became a clerical assistant in a research laboratory library and afterwards worked for a few years with deaf people in Blackburn and in Liverpool.

Dorothy then took a big decision to go to Gallaudet College (now University) in Washington, D.C. in 1957 where she graduated with a B.A. in English with Distinction.

She married a fellow student in 1958, but was divorced in 1962 and became a naturalised American citizen, working in various fields including teaching and sign language research, but her first love was drama and poetry. When the National Theatre for the Deaf was formed in 1967, she was one of the early participants and was involved in every production from 1968 to 1973, before leaving to work in California.

Dorothy Miles returned to Britain in 1977 and became heavily involved in sign language teaching, video production, the Deaf Players Theatre and also appeared on several *SEE HEAR* productions.

She was probably the foremost signed poetry performer in the world, some of these performances having been shown on television and to live audiences and had several poetry books published.

Dorothy Miles met a tragic end in 1993 when she threw herself out of her flat window, leaving the Deaf community to mourn the loss of a great contributor to its culture.

Jack Clemo (1916 -1994)

Jack Clemo was born in 1916 in Cornwall and started to go blind when he was five years old, progressing until he was completely blind when aged 39. He also became totally deaf at the age 19 and, isolated from his neighbours in the Cornish clay community of Goonamarris, he turned to literature, more particularly poetry.

Goonamarris was also a deeply religious community and Jack Clemo sometimes offended them with his own brand of view: that the way to a spiritual experience of God was through the communication of two people in sex. As Clemo's literary efforts blossomed, the cottage at Goonamarris became a kind of literary Lourdes with people coming to see the writer.

Jack Clemo married a Ruth Peaty when he was 52 years old and went to live with her in Weymouth.

Arthur Frederick Dimmock (1918 -)

One of the greatest contributors to Deaf History and journalism in the 20th century, Arthur (or AFD as he is known throughout the Deaf community) was born hearing in Whitley Bay, Northumberland, and became deaf at the age of four through meningitis. His education started at home when his mother acquired a manual alphabet chart and learnt to use it proficiently so that she could instil in him a command of English that was to stand him in good stead throughout his career. Upon admittance to the Northern Counties Institution for the Deaf and Dumb, Arthur had a command of language slightly above the average of a hearing child of the same age.

Prior to leaving the Northern Counties Institution, Arthur sat and passed three public examinations and also the University Entrance Examination but was refused admission to Durham University through being a deaf mute.

Instead, he obtained employment as a cabinetmaker and, during the war, as a patternmaker and latterly edited the *Independent Courier* and wrote widely for magazines, newspapers and even French publications for 60 years He retired in 1982 after 25 years as an industrial photographer and technical writer.

In his spare time, he organised tours for groups consisting mostly of Deaf people throughout the world for over 40 years.

For his work with Deaf people and for services to literature, Arthur was awarded several honours. These included one from the Southern Deaf Sports Council, with whom he had a long association, the Medal of Honour from the BDA, and the Communicator of the Year Award, 1995. The same year, he received an M.B.E. from the Queen. The final accolade came in 2000 with a honorary doctorate (D.Arts) from University of Wolverhampton

He was made President of the British Deaf History Society in July 2000.

Chapter X   A Pictorial History of Deaf Britain

Jack Clemo, Deafblind Poet
Photo supplied by Royal National Institute for Deaf People

Arthur Frederick Dimmock, MBE
Photo supplied by Arthur Dimmock

Chapter X   A Pictorial History of Deaf Britain

Evelyn Glennie, Percussionist
Photo supplied by Royal National Institute for Deaf People

Liz Varlow, Viola player with the London Symphony Orchestra
Photo supplied by Royal National Institute for Deaf People

Deaf Music

It is a common fallacy that deaf people do not enjoy the theatre, or even music; often this avenue offers a marvellous means for deaf people to express themselves in their own language. The main drawback has been that there has never been sufficient money or encouragement to enable deaf people to pursue careers or interests in the performing arts.

Just because deaf people cannot hear, it does not mean that they are impervious to music. Music does not depend on hearing alone, as some might think, but also on vibrations, and the majority of deaf people have a very acute feeling for noise through vibration. Deaf people have appreciated music for centuries. Hart, the sixth Duke of Devonshire, who was stone deaf, asked while on his death-bed for one final performance by his own orchestra.

There have been deaf musicians and composers, the most famous example being Ludwig van Beethoven, who was a pianist, conductor and composer of music. He started going deaf at the age of 28 and was completely deaf by his mid-forties but went on to compose some of his famous symphonies after that age.

In the early 1980s, a young deaf girl triumphed over deafness to become a professional percussionist. Evelyn Glennie lost her hearing at the age of six and was accepted into the Royal Academy of Music after a long struggle. In the years before she was accepted into the academy, many professionals showed disdain for the ability of a deaf girl to become a professional percussionist. However, the trustees of the Beethoven Fund for Deaf Children supported and encouraged her to such an extent that she was able to graduate from the Academy with distinction. She subsequently embarked on a career that saw her give performances at the Royal Festival Hall and at many other concerts.

In the 1990s, Paul Whitaker from Bradford became a professional pianist and performed several solo concerts across Britain. Also in the 1990s, Liz Varlow who became profoundly deaf at 18 was accepted by the London Symphony Orchestra as a Viola player. She is the only known deaf person to be professionally employed by a world famous orchestra.

Also in the last decade of the twentieth century, pop groups and entertainers began to recognise Deaf people's right to enjoy music and used sign language interpreters on stage to sign the songs. This proved popular with Deaf people, especially at the Gay and Lesbian Pride Festival in London. In 1997, the famous Glastonbury Festival in Somerset for the first time ever provided a "deaf area" where Deaf people could meet, relax and enjoy the summer music.

In 1999, the ex-Spice Girl and pop entertainer, Geri Halliwell, used BSL in her promotional video and stage performances. When asked why she had used BSL, she replied "Why not? I have a lot of deaf friends and it's a beautiful language."

Another activity that gained in popularity were Sign Songs, where Deaf and hearing people came together to perform, usually for charity.

Deaf Theatre

In the theatrical world, there was no professional theatre of the deaf until 1967 when the National Theatre for the Deaf was formed in the United States. In Britain it was not until 1969 when the first semi-professional deaf theatre company was formed.

Drama has always been a favourite activity amongst deaf people since the first schools and social clubs came into being. In the 1890s, many adult deaf social programmes included regular dramatic sign language performances in their social calendar. This continued through the twentieth century, with the British Deaf Association holding Drama competitions as a regular feature of their congresses.

In 1961, the Deaf Mime Group was formed by a few individuals who believed in the ability of deaf people to act and wished to provide those with the most talent with the opportunity of having professional tuition with the specific idea of appearing in BBC programmes for deaf children.

In 1962, the RNID took over sponsorship of the Deaf Mime Group. This group performed *Mario the Magician, Peter and the Magic Pears* - both in 1962 - and *The Waxworks Mystery* (1965) on BBC television, *Sganarelle*, and *The Pearl* at the Curtain Theatre in 1969. In 1969, the group was renamed The British Theatre of the Deaf, and performed at a number of theatres before going on a professional tour in 1974 supported by the Arts Council.

Since then a number of other theatrical companies have been developed starting with the Interim Theatre in 1979. A number of these are mainly educational, and include the Common Ground Dance Company. Most were supported with Arts Council funding. This development meant that more and more deaf actors and actresses came through the ranks to appear on television as well as in professional plays.

One such individual was Sarah Scott, the partially-deaf elder daughter of comedian Terry Scott, who was for a time associated with the Interim Theatre, but who is now associated with a professional Theatre which operates workshops and gives plays.

The play *Children of a Lesser God* opened in Britain initially in American Sign Language to rave reviews with an American deaf actress, Elizabeth Quinn, in the principal role. Sarah Scott took over the role for a time at the Albery Theatre, London. *Children of a Lesser God* proved to be an attractive play for a number of adult Deaf dramatic societies to perform.

The growth of interest by Deaf people in the theatre led to many theatres putting on performances signed by interpreters for local Deaf people. Although these were popular, access was not always convenient, with the interpreters being stuck to one side of the stage so that Deaf people could not always watch the performance and the interpreter at the same time.

In 1997, a project was started between Shakespeare Link and Shape Deaf Arts, which resulted in the appearance for the first time of Deaf people performing Shakespeare's plays at the Swan Theatre in Stratford-on-Avon.

Chapter X   A Pictorial History of Deaf Britain

A Scene from 'Meet My Grandfather' by the Spurs Club, 1948
Photo: The Spurs Club.

Shakespeare's 'The Taming of the Shrew'
The Swan Theatre in Stratford-on-Avon
Photo: British Deaf News

Chapter X   A Pictorial History of Deaf Britain

A Deaf Studio Audience
Studio audiences and debates are a popular feature on Deaf television programmes such as *See Hear on Saturday!* and *Listening Eye*. This picture is from *Listening Eye*, 1991.
Photo: Tyne Tees Television

SIGN ON Presenters, Tessa Padden and Francis Murphy
Photo: Tyne Tees Television

Television

Considering the length of time that television has been with us, it is astonishing that there was no specific programme for deaf people presented by deaf people until the 1980s. Through the 1960s and 1970s programmes with sign language content were few and far between, and were mainly church services.

The first regular programme aimed specifically at deaf and hard of hearing people was a weekly review of the previous week's news, called *News Review*, shown on Sundays on BBC 2. It offered a weekly summary of the news by one of the BBC's newsreaders with open subtitles and once every blue moon, usually around Christmas, it deigned to provide viewers with some titbit of deaf activity.

It was highly unsatisfactory, and the almost non-existence of genuine deaf actors and actresses did not help improve matters when television programmes were made which had a deaf character central to the plot; hearing actors and actresses were used to portray deaf people, sometimes with disastrous results.

The BBC's *SEE HEAR* programme for deaf people was the first attempt to provide a regular series which deaf people could relate to. Now titled *See Hear On Saturday!* it is still the only main regular long-running series after nearly 20 years on television. The presenters are usually native-users of BSL.

Channel 4 has shown several series of a programme called *Sign On,* formerly titled *Listening Eye,* made by Tyne Tees Television using deaf presenters. Sadly, this programme is produced rather irregularly in small doses. The programme's format was fundamentally different from the *SEE HEAR* series in that it had current deaf affairs as its regular theme, and it provided a valuable alternative to *SEE HEAR.* The same production teams at Tyne Tees have also produced several documentaries. *A Language for Ben* and *Pictures in the Mind* both earned praise from the Deaf community and from the media generally. *A Language for Ben* was the Best Educational Production (Feature Length) in the American Television Movie Awards for 1985.

Another Channel 4 programme that received acclaim was *Deaf Century* in 1999 produced to coincide with the Millennium. This was an historical documentary about the Deaf community and Deaf people and gave a valuable insight into the Deaf World for viewers.

In 1995, an annual event started when the Deaf Film and Television Festival was held. Aimed at celebrating and publicising successes in Deaf film and television, it provides an opportunity for Deaf people to share experiences and aspirations.

Very few major films or television soaps have featured the Deaf way of life or sign language in their programmes using Deaf actors and actresses, usually failing miserably to get the reality of the Deaf World across. One passable film that included a Deaf actor was *Four Weddings and a Funeral,* starring Hugh Grant, in which a Deaf actor, David Bower, also starred.

At the time of writing, there is still no nationally networked daily news programme in Britain, which uses deaf people to present the programme. It is the avowed aim of the Deaf Broadcasting Council to secure this programme.

Chapter XI   A Pictorial History of Deaf Britain

The Bomb Crater in the grounds of Donaldson's Hospital School in Edinburgh, on the morning of 3 April 1916.

This near miss rocked the School and shattered many windows and wrecked furniture inside the school. It could have been worse as many deaf children were fast asleep during the attack. One pupil, George Scott, said:

"..A German Zeppelin flew over but I felt nothing. I was fast asleep. Next morning I awoke to chaos – everything overturned, furniture all over, beds moved, tables tipped over.."

Photo: Donaldson's School

CHAPTER XI

DEAF SCHOOLS IN THE WAR YEARS

Both the First World War in 1914-8 and the Second World War in 1939-45 broke out whilst schools were still closed for the summer holidays. This proved to be a great advantage to the military authorities, which promptly requisitioned several schools for use as either military barracks, hospitals or training centres.

This happened at Doncaster with the Yorkshire Institution who lost use of one full term at the start of the 1914-8 War, and to Dundee who lost use of their Castle for the whole of the war period. At Manchester, the Non-Oral department at Clyne House was requisitioned as a military hospital, causing overcrowding in the Main School.

The same thing happened at the start of the 1939-45 War, but more schools were affected. Donaldson's School in Edinburgh became a German prisoner-of-war camp; the Royal School for Deaf Children at Margate became the headquarters of the local civil defence forces and an emergency police station. Manchester lost Clyne House (now its nursery department) yet again as a military hospital.

Despite the hardship, very few schools in the 1914-8 War experienced any horrors arising from the War itself. The East Anglian School for the Deaf at Gorleston managed to avoid getting hit when a number of German warships appeared off the coast of Norfolk and Suffolk and bombarded Lowesoft and Great Yarmouth with shells fired from the ships' massive guns.

The school that came closest to experiencing the horrors of the war was Donaldson's Hospital School in Edinburgh. On the night of 2 April 1916, air-raid warnings sounded throughout Edinburgh and at five minutes past midnight a huge explosion shook the city. A German Zeppelin had flown over the Scottish coast at Leith and dropped a bomb that by pure luck hit a bonded warehouse full of whisky. This went up in large flames, lighting up the night sky over Edinburgh.

Donaldson's Hospital and the nearby George Watson Hospital School were both large impressive buildings and the Zeppelin bombers could not resist using them as targets as they made their way across the city to the Castle. Donaldson's took a near miss, but its neighbour, George Watson, was not so lucky and had its two upper floors severely damaged. After dropping a large number of bombs at the Castle, all of which missed but hit another whisky warehouse which once again illuminated beautifully the imposing building that is Donaldson's, the Zeppelin aimed for it once again with the last of its deadly cargo.

Once again, their aim was lousy. If it had been more accurate, the toll in Edinburgh that night (there were 10 dead and scores wounded) could have included many of the sleeping Deaf children at Donaldson's.

Donaldson's lost many windows, including its most precious oriel window in the chapel, which was famous all over Scotland as one of the earliest figure-stained windows. It was never replaced.

Evacuees in the 1939-45 War

The Second World War broke out the day before the majority of deaf schools were due to reassemble after the summer holidays. As a result, half the children in many schools did not turn up.

Although some schools were quick off the mark to evacuate their children, it was not until May 1940 when the German Wehrmacht overran Holland, Belgium and struck deep into northern France that schools in danger areas began to take seriously the need for evacuation.

The Royal School for Deaf Children, Margate, evacuated to Oxfordshire where three large houses were taken over in Goring-on-Thomas and the school was able to carry on in a 'make-do' fashion.

Other schools also evacuated to the countryside. Some of the children at Donaldson's Hospital School for the Deaf went to Cockburnspath, others to North Berwick. Having lost Clyne House again, the nursery department of the Royal Schools for the Deaf, Manchester, was evacuated to Middlewich in Cheshire. The Old Kent Road Schools for the Deaf were evacuated temporarily to St. Alban in Glamorgan, before relocating at Banstead, Surrey. There, they were joined by Anerley School for the Deaf who had originally evacuated to the Royal Cross School, Preston thence to the Royal West of England School at Exeter, hurriedly evacuating the latter following the Baedeker raids on Exeter in 1942.

Anerley School was not at Banstead for long. They returned to their own school in November 1942 but had to move again, this time to Yorkshire when the flying-bomb blitz started and the premises sustained damage.

At Middlesborough, the Hugh Bell School was partially evacuated to Pickering, North Yorkshire, but a number of parents refused to let their children be evacuated.

Some schools, like Newcastle's Northern Counties School, were evacuated in early September but soon returned to their proper premises. Others, like the Leeds School for the Deaf and Liverpool School for the Deaf, went to open-air schools on the city outskirts. Liverpool later relocated to Southport. Several schools, like the one at Bristol, did not get evacuated until 1941 or 1942 when the increasing likelihood of air raids in the areas deemed it prudent to do so. Some schools stayed put and accepted evacuees, like the Royal West of England School at Exeter, a policy that nearly backfired when the school was hit in the Baedeker Raids.

The Jewish School for Deaf Children in London were evacuated to Brighton at the start of the war, but only stayed a short time as Brighton was deemed to be too dangerous for Jewish children, and they relocated to Wiltshire.

A number of deaf children were unlucky in that they had to stay at school for the whole duration of the war, neither seeing their parents nor going home for any holiday. In some areas, notably the islands off the British mainland like the Outer Hebrides, the Orkneys and the Shetlands, some deaf children lost their opportunity of receiving an education because of the restrictions on shipping.

Chapter XI   A Pictorial History of Deaf Britain

War-time Evacuees Clearing Snow at Camp, Winter 1939-40
Photo: Northern Counties School for the Deaf, Newcastle

Evacuees undergoing Gas Mask Training, 1940
Photo: Northern Counties School for the Deaf, Newcastle

Chapter XI   A Pictorial History of Deaf Britain

The Allen Homes at the Royal School for Deaf Children, Margate
Their loss caused severe accommodation difficulties for the school after being totally destroyed in the war.
Photo: Royal School for Deaf Children, Margate.

Royal School for Deaf Children, Margate, in their New War Time Home, Goring-on-Thames
Photo: Royal School for Deaf Children, Margate

The Bombing of Schools

The first bombs to fall on any British deaf school happened the day the war broke out at Margate on 3 September 1939 when a number of incendiary bombs landed in the grounds of the Royal School for Deaf Children.

As this school was the nearest to the mainland of Europe and thus within range of many of the Luftwaffe planes, it was subjected to a large number of air raid attacks. However, the greatest loss the school suffered was when the Allen Homes were totally destroyed in 1942. These Homes were used to accommodate boarders at the school and their destruction severely hampered the School's capacity after the war. The headmaster's house in the school grounds was also destroyed and the main building hit on a number of occasions.

Because the school premises were being used as a civil defence headquarters, many vehicles parked in the grounds as well as air defence positions were constantly attacked and destroyed by German planes.

Having escaped damage during the shelling of Great Yarmouth and Lowesoft by the German Navy in the last war, the East Anglian School for the Deaf at Gorleston-on-Sea was not so lucky the second time round. In a sneak raid by the Luftwaffe, several bombs destroyed part of the school. In the same raid, the headmaster's house was reduced to rubble.

Children from the Anerley School for the Deaf had a rather unfortunate time. Having first relocated to the Royal Cross School in Preston, they were then moved to the Royal West of England School at Exeter. Barely a week later, the school at Exeter was severely hit in the Baedeker Raid, many children narrowly escaping injury. They were then sent to Banstead, but had to return to their old school in Clapham shortly afterwards. They were then relocated for the fourth time to Yorkshire when the flying bomb blitz started. The school premises were then occupied as civil defence headquarters, but this did not last long either. The premises were severely damaged by a flying bomb some weeks later and it was not repaired until long after the war.

Another London Deaf school that was being occupied by the military at the time, Old Kent Road, was also badly hit in a bombing raid, causing serious accommodation difficulties for the school after the war.

As far as can be ascertained, the only causalities amongst Deaf schoolchildren happened when the Royal Cambrian School for the Deaf at Swansea was bombed. Several children were seriously hurt, but there were no deaths.

A much more serious catastrophe was narrowly avoided when a bomb went through the roof of the main building of the Royal Schools for the Deaf, Manchester, but the bomb fortunately failed to explode. At that time, over a hundred children were fast asleep in the dormitories. Clyne House, where in peacetime its nursery department was based, was severely damaged and the military hospital had to relocate.

Chapter XII   A Pictorial History of Deaf Britain

Children having Ultra-Violet Light Treatment
Photo: Royal Schools for the Deaf, Derby

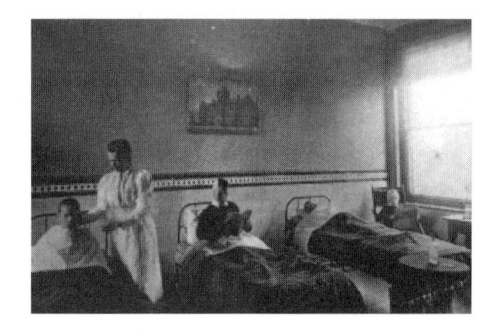

Children in Hospital
Photo: Royal Schools for the Deaf, Derby

Children in Sick Bay
Photo: Royal Schools for the Deaf, Manchester

CHAPTER XII

DEAF EDUCATION TODAY

History since 1900 - Conditions

In the early 20th century, oralism was at its most fervent in British schools. In addition, there were a number of small private schools in existence where the owner usually taught children. For example, in Wimbledon a Mrs Maria Mills ran the Oral School for the Deaf from 1896 to 1938. In Haslemere, Surrey, a Miss C. M.Parker operated the Wych School for Deaf Children from 1918 to 1925. Many Deaf leaders were concerned at the lack of education being given to deaf children. Instruction of deaf children in the acquisition of English grammar and other school subjects were being curtailed in favour of speech training.

In addition, conditions in many Deaf schools were extremely grim. There was so much poverty in the families of deaf children that tuberculosis and malnutrition was prevalent. One elderly Deaf man was to say in an interview in 1985:

> *My education was neither good nor bad. Of course, teaching was by oral methods, which was not helpful but what I remember more are the conditions in which we were educated. The food was unspeakable. Most children wore threadbare clothes and badly worn shoes in need of repair. The hearing school next door was just as bad. We were in a poor area and all children were victims of poverty. Most if not all of our parents were either out of work or badly paid. There was no money available, and I suppose it showed in the quality of school life. The building was always damp, cold even in summer and we always suffered from chilblains in winter.*

Conditions in many deaf schools continued to remain grim until well after the 1939-45 war. The memories of many of those who were at school in the mid-20th century were not of the education methods used, but the bullying that accompanied the methods plus the poor living conditions. It was not uncommon for deaf schoolchildren caught signing in oral establishments to suffer physical, verbal and emotional abuse in the establishments' attempts to stop them signing. Canings (with sticks or rulers) on the hands were frequent; some children had paper bags or sacks tied around their wrists, others were punished by losing liberty time outside classrooms doing detention that involved writing out pages of lines "I must not sign". In some schools, children's failure to pronounce words, vowels or consonants properly might lead to a cuff on the head as a punishment.

In others, the memories of their schooldays might relate to the conditions in their schools. Many were rat, mice or cockroach infested. One of the author's most vivid memories of his schooldays in the early 1950s is of cringing with fear in his bed in the school hospital ward along with other sick children watching hundreds of mice or rats scurrying across the floors in the moonlight, preventing trips to the toilet. No one stayed in the hospital ward for long if they could help it.

Cold and damp conditions did not help. One school's logbooks from 1919 to 1926 shows frequent complaints of classroom temperatures ranging from 36°F to 46°F for weeks and weeks. No wonder many children were ill.

History since 1900 – Government Reports

Some of the worst, and best, influence on Deaf Education came in the form of reports commissioned by, or legislation implemented by, the government of the day.

In the early 20th century, the government inspector responsible for overseeing Deaf Education was a Dr. A. Eichholz, who was a fervent oralist. Even he, however, was forced to concede that the oral method was not always the most appropriate method to use with some Deaf children and he had to recommend that fingerspelling should be used instead of speech to memorise facts.

Two Education Acts were important milestones in Deaf Education. The Act of 1937 lowered the age of admission to school for deaf children to five years, and the Act of 1944 raised the age at which children could leave school. The 1944 Act also contained many important provisions for the education of deaf children, leading to a slow improvement in the standard. Perhaps one of the most important provisions of this Act was where it permitted orders to set up special schools where they were needed. Under *"The Handicapped Pupils and School Health and Statutory Orders, 1945"* section of the Act, the Ministry of Education recognised and permitted the setting up of The Mary Hare Grammar School as from 1 January 1946 as a Special Secondary School for Deaf Boys and Girls.

The focus on the teaching of oral methods continued into the 1960s with the publication of the Lewis Committee Report, which came out in the summer of 1968. This survey into Deaf Education by a group of 16 people headed by Professor M. M. Lewis, Emeritus Professor of Education at Nottingham University had only one Deaf member. It's terms of reference were *'to consider the place, if any, of fingerspelling and signing in the education of the deaf'*.

The Report listed a total of fourteen recommendations, four of which suggested research activities directly connected with the use of sign language. However, there were also five recommendations that would tend to dampen such efforts, and two recommendations to improve the conditions for further oral advances in deaf education.

The overall impression given by the Report suggested that whilst the Committee were impressed by evidence submitted by advocates of sign language methods, they were unable or willing to give clear-cut advice on the subject matter.

Speaking at a conference in 1975, the Head of the Department of Audiology and Education of the Deaf, Manchester University, asserted that the Lewis Report's two aims *('to fit deaf children so far as possible to take their place in hearing society'* and *'to realise a full personal development')* meant that the oral approach was the most appropriate method in deaf education.

Three years later, in 1978, the Warnock Report came out, recommending that all handicapped children should be integrated into 'normal' education. This resulted in an increase in deaf children being mainstreamed and the closure of many special schools for Deaf children as the supply of new pupils dried up.

Forced to eat his words

Two extracts from the Logbook of the Hugh Bell School for the Deaf, Middlesbrough, commenting on the use of sign language and fingerspelling following the visit of the government inspector for deaf education, Dr. A. Eichholz. The first one (top), in June 1899, shows that the use of signing and fingerspelling was to be strictly prohibited.

> June 27th Dr Eichholtz examined the class this morning, & expressed himself satisfied with the progress made. Suggested that all the Manual lessons should be made Language ones as well. That the present Manual work be continued, but suggested rug-making for the boys, & paperflower making for the girls as pleasant work. Strictly Prohibited signing & finger spelling, & advised the offer of a Reward for those who spoke most during playtime

Eleven years later, in November 1910, Dr. Eichholz has changed his tune. Now he recommends that fingerspelling be used instead of speech to memorise facts!

> 31st of October.
> 9.11.10 A. Eichholz
> Dr Eichholz recommended that fingerspelling should be used instead of Speech, especially in memorizing facts, and more attention should be given to the writing of Series Actions.
> 9.11.10 Half holiday given by the Mayor.

Chapter XII   A Pictorial History of Deaf Britain

Mary Hare Grammar School, Arlingdon Manor, Newbury
Photo: Author's Collection

Left: **Bernard Pitcher**
Middle Right: **Spring Hill Oral School for the Deaf, Northampton**
Bottom Right: **Dene Hollow Oral School, Burgess Hill, Sussex**
Photos: Left, Bernard Pitcher; Middle Right, Author's Collection; Bottom Right, Sally Ellis

Oral Successes

Grim though the conditions were in many schools, not all schools were that bad. In Burgess Hill, a Miss Mary Hare had started a private school, which was producing some academic successes. The Dene Hollow Oral School was opened in 1916 with 45 pupils aged 3 to18, many coming from the founder's previous school in Hove. It had a homely atmosphere and provided an educational setting that was far removed from the institutional background many deaf children were forced to endure at that time.

Dene Hollow remained in existence until the death of Miss Mary Hare in 1945 and many of the pupils who received an education there have happy memories of their time at the school, a stark contrast with the experiences of many other deaf children in the large institutions.

In 1946, The Mary Hare Grammar School was approved by the Ministry of Education and in the following year, Arlington Manor at Newbury was purchased and several of the remaining pupils from Dene Hollow were transferred there, some going to the Spring Hill Oral School at Northampton.

Over in Northampton, the Reverend Thomas Arnold's school was now being run by Frederick Ince Jones and still turning out academic successes. Spring Hill Oral School's fine academic record was helped by the fact that there were never more than 25 boys in the school at any one time.

One of the students graduating from this school was a remarkable young man who went on to become Britain's first Deaf Ph.D., Bernard L. Pitcher.

Bernard L. Pitcher (1910 - 2000)

Bernard Pitcher was born deaf and received six years of private tuition at Mrs. Wehner's Private Deaf School before he entered the Spring Hill Oral School for the Deaf at Northampton. He was so successful at Spring Hill that he entered the University of London Matriculation Examination, obtaining credits or distinction in every subject that he took. As a result, he was admitted to the university where, despite enormous difficulties due to his deafness, he gained an Honours B.Sc., followed by the degree of Doctor of Philosophy in science and geology, becoming the first born-deaf man in Britain to obtain a doctorate.

After retiring to Worthing, he became secretary of the local deaf club, serving for many years.

Dr. Pitcher died in a rest home in 2000.

The oral successes at Dene Hollow and Spring Hill prompted the founding of two other schools that were to cater mainly for the partially hearing, and the education there would be based on teaching through aural and oral methods. These schools were Ovingdean Hall School in Brighton, which came about of the old Brighton Institution closing down, and Birkdale School for Partially Hearing Children in Southport. The latter came about as a result of the partially hearing department of the Liverpool School for the Deaf having stayed on at Southport after the 1939-45 war before becoming an independent school in its own right.

History since 1900 - The rise and fall of some schools

By 1900, most of the great institutions had been in existence for over half a century. Many had pupil rolls of over one hundred; some like Manchester had a lot more. The 'babe' of the Deaf schools was the Royal Cross School in Preston, opened in 1894.

After 1900, most of the Deaf schools that opened were day schools such as the Anerley School for the Deaf in London and the Thomasson Memorial School in Bolton, though there were some exceptions with the opening of some excellent boarding schools. Two of these schools were in Surrey and were designated as secondary modern types of school.

Surrey County Council opened Nutfield Priory Secondary Modern School for Deaf Children in an 1868 building set high up on a ridge in Redhill with extensive grounds. It never had more than 80 pupils at any one time and the standard of education was quite good, with a diversity of subjects being taught. Compared with the grim and unsatisfactory conditions many deaf children had to endure in older, institutionalised schools, it was a very positive step forward.

Another school that opened in Surrey was Burwood Park Secondary Technical School for Boys at Walton-on-Thames in 1955. Set in an 18th century mansion with spacious grounds in an enclosed private park just south of Walton-on-Thames owned by Lord Iveagh of the Guinness brewing family, it was opened with much publicity and hope as a technical alternative to Mary Hare Grammar School, which tended to be more academic. They shared the same entrance examination, known as the Joint Entrance Examination, which was taken by ten and eleven year old pupils all over the UK, and sometimes in English-speaking overseas countries. In what turned out to be a short life span, Burwood Park never had more than 45 pupils at any one time (girls were not admitted to this school until the late 1980s), a smaller school population than Mary Hare. Sports matches between the two schools were fiercely contested to the point of warfare and were suspended after a time.

The Warnock Report, and its aftermath, leading to an increase in mainstreamed education for deaf children decimated many Deaf schools. Nutfield Priory was one of the first to go, being closed at short notice by its owners, Surrey County Council.

Other secondary schools that fell to the march of time included the Royal School for Deaf Children in Birmingham (the former Institution), the Royal Cross School at Preston, the Llandrindod Wells School in Wales (descendant of the Royal Cambrian Institution), Anerley School for the Deaf and Maryhill School for the Deaf (formerly the Glasgow Institution/Langside School). Several famous primary schools for deaf children such as Ackmar Road School for Deaf Children also met the same fate.

Burwood Park School, after fighting for several years to stay open in the face of dwindling numbers, threw in the towel at very short notice in December 1996, sending shockwaves throughout the Deaf community. Katie Mowat of Southport (whose father was also a pupil at the school) was the last pupil to step out of the school on a very sad occasion.

Chapter XII   A Pictorial History of Deaf Britain

Group of Girls on Sports Day at Nutfield Priory School (Closed 1987)
Photo: Author's Collection

Lewis Cup Netball Winners 1976, Royal Cross School, Preston (Closed 1990)
Photo: Author's Collection

Bottom: **Pupils and Staff, Burwood Park School (Closed 1996)**
Photo: Author's Collection

Chapter XII   A Pictorial History of Deaf Britain

Left: **Royal School for the Deaf, Derby**
Photo: Author's Collection

Right: **Northern Counties School for the Deaf, Newcastle-upon-Tyne**
Photo: Author's Collection

Left: **Library Session, St. John's Catholic School, Boston Spa**
Photo: St John's, Boston Spa

Right: **Autistic Children having swimming lessons**
Photo: Royal Schools for the Deaf Manchester

The Remaining Special Schools for Deaf Children, 2000

Today, only eight of the old institutions from the 1850s still stand and serve Deaf Education. These include Donaldson's School in Edinburgh and Northern Counties School, Newcastle-upon-Tyne. The Royal School for Deaf Children, Margate (formerly the London Asylum), is still the oldest surviving Deaf school in the world. Two Royal Schools for the Deaf, at Derby and Manchester, are still in existence as is the Royal West of England School at Exeter. The remaining two schools are in Yorkshire, the St. John's Catholic School for the Deaf, Boston Spa, and the Yorkshire Residential School for the Deaf, Doncaster. Of these schools, the one at Manchester only takes in Deaf children with additional severe difficulties, i.e. autistic Deaf children.

There are only another nine special Deaf schools providing secondary education apart from Mary Hare Grammar School. These are Beverley School, Middlesbrough (a descendant of the Hugh Bell School); Braidwood School, Birmingham; Elmfield School, Bristol; Hamilton Lodge, Brighton; Oak Lodge School, London; and Thorn Park School, Bradford. All except Hamilton Lodge are day schools. Two others, Birkdale at Southport and Ovingdean Hall at Brighton, are partially hearing boarding schools and pursue a strict oral policy.

There are other schools that retain the word 'Deaf' in their title, but in reality, they are either schools or units attached to mainstream schools, or bases for peripatetic services. The Aberdeen School for the Deaf and Heathlands School for Deaf Children, St. Albans, are examples of a school within a mainstream school, whilst Garvel School for the Deaf in Greenock is an example of a peripatetic base, though it also has a primary unit. Another example of a deaf school serving as a peripatetic base is the Blanche Nevile School in London.

There are a smaller number of schools that cater only for primary deaf schoolchildren, and one or two others that cater specifically for Deafblind schoolchildren, for example St. Vincent's School in Glasgow.

Over in Northern Ireland, Jordanstown still exists but only has a primary unit and is a base as an outreach service for the Homefirst Community Trust. There is a Catholic day unit and peripatetic service at St. Francis de Sales School.

The majority of these schools have less than 50 pupils and they are able to give more individual attention to students. However, the dwindling number of pupils is a major worry for many of them and a number of the residential schools have turned to having a 6th form or Further Education facility. For example, the site at Doncaster where the Yorkshire School is still based after over 175 years is better known as Doncaster College than as the school.

The majority of deaf children are now in mainstream education and the number of units in existence has grown considerably during the last two decades of the 20th century.

Deaf Teachers Today

It is only in the last two decades of the 20th century that the devastating consequences of the Milan Congress have been overcome and Deaf people able to work in education once again. However, the majority either work as tutors of British Sign Language or as classroom support assistants, a role that was made famous by Judith Collins in the award-winning television documentary, *A Language for Ben.*

Although some Deaf people have become, and are still, employed by a number of universities as lecturers – mainly in those where the subject Deaf Studies is on the curriculum, few Deaf people have become qualified teachers. Due to the current demand for qualifications, most work mainly in Further or Adult Education, holding qualifications such as Certificate in Education, where there are good numbers of Deaf students.

Fewer still have been able to pass the stringent hurdles required to become a qualified Teacher of Deaf children. One of the longest serving teachers, and perhaps the best known, is Mabel Davis.

Mabel Davis

Born in Ayrshire, Scotland, Mabel became deaf at the age of 7 through T.B. meningitis and attended a small primary school in Dalry where there were other deaf children. She was educated at Mary Hare Grammar School where she was Head Girl in her final year. It was at Mary Hare that she first encountered British Sign Language.

After leaving school, she became a librarian. Whilst the new Alice Elliott School for the Deaf was being built at Liverpool, she offered to catalogue their library. At that time, Liverpool also ran an Evening Institute for Deaf Adults and she was asked to take on an English class for two evenings a week. Shocked at the low standard of reading and writing in intelligent Deaf adults, she became determined to be a teacher.

As she had two young children at the time, she took her first degree with Open University, then went to the Notre Dame Teacher Training College for her teaching certificate. Following this, she took her Bachelor of Education degree at Liverpool University and took the British Association of Teachers of the Deaf In-Service Diploma to qualify as a teacher of the deaf. It was a long hard road that Mabel had to struggle through to qualify as a teacher of the deaf and she started her teaching career at the Alice Elliott School for the Deaf, Liverpool in 1981.

Her teaching excellence was such that in 1986, she was appointed Vice-Principal of Hamilton Lodge School for the Deaf, Brighton, staying there for 6 years before being appointed Headteacher at Heathlands School in St. Albans. This was the first appointment of a Deaf person to a post as Headteacher since Edward Kirk at Leeds almost a century before.

In 1993, she received the RADAR People of the Year Award for services to education.

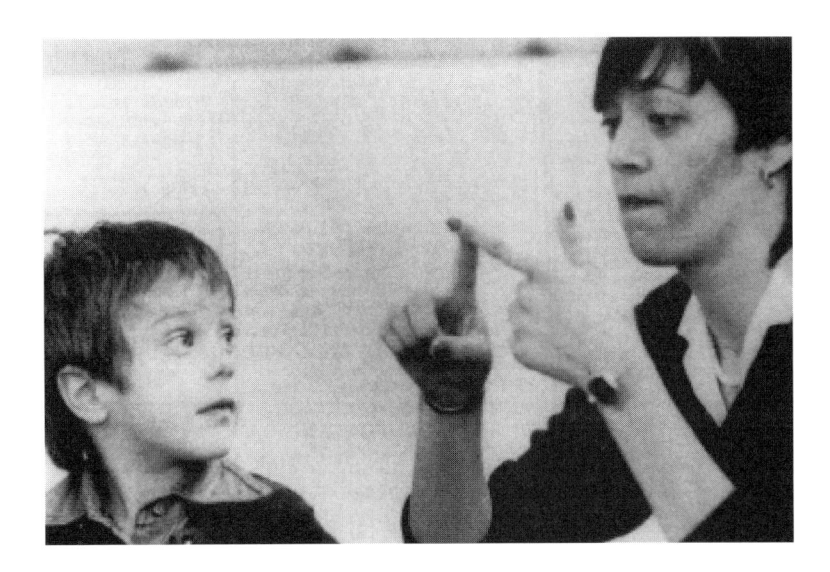

Chapter XII   A Pictorial History of Deaf Britain

Judith Collins communicating for Ben Fletcher.
A television documentary titled *'A Language for Ben'* was made about her role as classroom support assistant.
Photo: British Deaf News.

Mabel Davies
Headteacher at Heathlands School, St. Albans
Photo: Mabel Davies

Chapter XII   A Pictorial History of Deaf Britain

**Computer Class,
Doncaster College**
Photo: Doncaster College

Top: **Electronic Notetaking in class**
Bottom: **Communication Support in tutorial**
Photos: City College Manchester

**Mark Guerrieria receiving The Clive Holker Memorial Award
For Best Student on NVQ 3 Printing Course, City College Manchester**
Photo: City College Manchester

Further Education for Deaf People

One of the biggest strides made in Deaf Education was in the growth of Further and Adult Education opportunities that opened up for Deaf people in the last two decades of the 20th century.

The trend was started by residential schools at Derby, Doncaster, Margate and Exeter starting to provide further education opportunities to counter falling numbers in the deaf school population as a result of mainstreaming. Even Burwood Park School, in a desperate bid to keep open, started a further education facility in a neighbouring building owned by the estate called Norfolk House, which became a college of the same name.

Only in London, with the City Lit Institute, and in a few large cities such as Birmingham (Bourneville College) could Deaf students attend college on a non-residential basis.

The biggest boost to Further Education for Deaf people came with the publication of the Tomlinson Report in 1993, which looked into the overall provision of opportunities for those with special needs.

In 1978, the Warnock Committee report on special educational needs was a watershed for thousands of children who barely a decade before might have been deemed uneducable. Since then, Lady Warnock's children had been banging at the doors of colleges for some years. Some had opened their doors, installing wheelchair ramps and the like to make access easier but only a minority had gone further and reshaped the curriculum. Too many had left their doors shut. Strict funding rules had seen others register thousands of disabled students on the wrong courses under the pressure of legislation.

Although the Tomlinson Committee report had looked at a wide range of special needs, their recommendations were highly relevant to hundreds of deaf school-leavers and adults, particularly where the emphasis was placed on colleges having to reflect the profile of their local special needs population when drawing up strategic plans for curriculum delivery.

This meant that Deaf students would no longer be confined to a limited choice of having to go to one of the residential Deaf colleges for their further education, but could attend their local colleges with appropriate support being provided. In theory, this meant the provision of sign language interpreting, notetaking facilities, and many other forms of additional support including modification of curriculum material.

All this was to take time to build up. There was, and still is, a shortage of qualified people to undertake communication support duties, a shortage of suitably trained Deaf Further Education teachers, a shortage of qualified notetakers and just about everything else. In the years since the Tomlinson Committee report, there have been many initiatives to provide training opportunities to overcome these shortages. City College Manchester, for example, have implemented Communication Support Worker and Electronic Notetaking training courses and also TDLB and Teacher training for Deaf students. As a result, the future looks good for the majority of Deaf students in further and higher education, meeting a need that went begging for years.

Chapter XIII   *A Pictorial History of Deaf Britain*

Sir Arthur Henderson Fairbairn
He liked to be known as "The Only Deaf and Dumb Baronet" in the world.
Photo: Author's Collection

CHAPTER XIII

DEAF PEOPLE 1900-2000

Sir Arthur Henderson Fairbairn, Bart (1852 - 1915)

The year 1915 saw the death of one of the greatest supporters of the British deaf community in Sir Arthur Henderson Fairbairn, who rejoiced in the title of 'the only Deaf and Dumb baronet in the world'. The British landed gentry can look back on a past filled with special glories due to the responsibilities of their rank, and Sir Arthur Fairbairn was a man great enough to shoulder these responsibilities. Gracefully, tirelessly and successfully, he left behind some concrete examples of generosity and philanthropy as well as the memory of a genial heart and a simple soul doing good in an aristocratic manner.

Sir Arthur Fairbairn was born Deaf to Sir Thomas Fairbairn and was the grandson of Sir William Fairbairn who was a great inventor and builder of bridges and dockyards which earned him a fortune. His sister, Constance, was also born Deaf but the youngest brother, James, was not.

He was educated at the private school for the deaf run by Henry Brothers Bingham at Rugby entirely by sign language and fingerspelling, as was his sister. Neither Sir Arthur or Constance Fairbairn could speak or lip-read throughout their lives.

Sir Arthur married Florence Long in 1882, a marriage that was useful to him in social circles as his brother-in-law was a powerful Member of Parliament, but Sir Arthur's true love was reserved for British Deaf people. He was never ashamed of being deaf without speech when he moved in society and he mingled with Deaf people on every possible occasion.

He was a tireless worker for the cause of deafness, opening many missions and institutes, attending many bazaars and functions to which he always managed to bring influential friends who would spend money freely. He was a President or Vice President of many deaf organisations, including the Royal School for Deaf Children, Margate; the Charitable and Provident Society for Granting Pensions to the Aged and Infirm Deaf; London Deaf Cricket Club; the London branch of the BDDA. He was also a committee member of the Brighton Institution for the Deaf and Dumb and of the Winchester Deaf Diocesan Mission. As treasurer of the RADD, he once balanced the books, which had serious deficit, with a handsome donation.

St. Saviour's Church for the Deaf owed its new electric lighting and heating system to his generosity and he contributed to many deaf charities.

He was President of the Reception Committee of the 8th Biennial Congress of the British Deaf and Dumb Association in 1903 when he received his guests with magnificent and lavish hospitality.

Although in poor health in 1912, he accepted an offer to be chairman of the delegates to the Congress of the Deaf in Paris 1912 on their visit to London and paid for their lavish entertainment out of his own pocket.

His name lives on in the Fairbairn Centre for the Deaf, Southampton, where he was a committee member for many years.

Arthur James Wilson (1858 - 1945)

Born with normal hearing in Camden Town, London, he became deaf from scarlet fever when 12 years old. His education following the onset of deafness was self-acquired due to reading and writing.

Arthur J. Wilson was better known to thousands, perhaps millions, of his countrymen in Britain and Ireland as 'Faed' (DEAF spelt backwards), the pen-name by which he contributed hundreds of articles on cycling to magazines and edited his own magazine. He also published books on the sport.

A keen cyclist, having ridden one of the original boneshakers in 1869, he once cycled 3200 miles in a year competing in races. He founded two cycling associations - the North Road Cycling Club and Cyclists' Road Records Association, of which he was President for nearly 30 years - an unique achievement for a deaf man in a mainly hearing organisation.

Arthur J. Wilson was also the first deaf Briton to own a car (in 1896) and competed in races not only in cars or on cycles, but also on motor bikes. He was probably the first Deaf man in the world to do so. He also got another 'first' that was most unwelcome when he became the first Deaf driver to fall foul of the road traffic laws and be fined for speeding. To his chagrin, A.J. Wilson, who could speak very well and was a successful businessman, got headlines in the national newspapers describing him as 'deaf and dumb'. This may have been because he was so hopeless at lipreading that everyone had to communicate to him through the manual method. In fact, it was a condition of employment at the business he owned, A. J. Wilson & Co., that all employees be required to master the manual alphabet and at one time Wilson was employing over 200 men and women!

A keen all-round sportsman, he graduated from cycle and motor-car racing when he began to feel his age and then to speedboat racing. He owned a motor launch named *Splash*, which he lost to the Navy in the war.

Wilson became President of the National Deaf Club in 1909 and held the position for over thirty years. He also helped to found the Federation of London Deaf Sports Clubs.

During the 1914-1918 war, he used his wealth to establish the Sir Frederick Milner Hostels for Deafened Soldiers, and served as Chairman. He did magnificent work as Commandant of the London Hospitals Motor Squadron, financed largely with his own money, taking wounded servicemen for health drives, to theatres and to various other entertainments. For this work, he was made a Freeman of London, again a unique achievement for a deaf man.

He was friends with the Prince of Wales, later Edward VII, and was very well respected throughout London. He refused an offer of an O.B.E. as an insult, feeling that he deserved at least a knighthood for his achievements and voluntary work.

Married twice, Wilson moved to Leamington Spa upon his retirement in the early 1930s and helped to found Coventry Institute for the Deaf. He died in Leamington in 1945 at the age of 87.

Arthur Wilson
Photo: Author's Collection

Caricature in the *British Deaf Times*, 1912

Chapter XIII   A Pictorial History of Deaf Britain

Algernon Joel Morris Barnett
Missioner to Northants & Rutland Mission for the Deaf and Dumb for 25 years.
Photo: Arthur Groom

Reverend Mark Frame
Editor of the *British Deaf News* 1962-1965
Photo: British Deaf News

Algernon Joel Morris Barnett (1884 - 1952)

One of the larger than life characters of the early 20th century was Algernon Barnett, the Missioner for the Diocese of Northants and Rutland. Algy, as he was known to everyone in the Deaf community, was one of two Deaf brothers born in London to Jewish parents. An education in the Jewish School for the Deaf in London was followed by employment as a copy artist.

When the company he worked for went into liquidation and he became unemployed, Algy Barnett became acquainted with the Reverend Albert Smith of the Royal Association of the Deaf and Dumb in London, and was converted to Christianity. The influence of the Reverend Smith helped him to be appointed as Missioner to the Deaf and Dumb in Northampton and surrounding area in 1928.

Algy Barnett was a unique character with a permanent smile on his face, often oddly dressed but always with a bow tie that was usually askew and shoes that were rarely polished. He was a big man who loved his food and was always fond of telling stories about himself. His favourite two stories about himself concerned food. One was about the day he was caught by the Bishop of Peterborough looking into the shop window of a fishmonger in Peterborough; the Bishop asked Algy why he was looking into a fish shop and not a bookshop. The other story related to one time he visited London and made for the Lyons House named the Salad Bowl where he could help himself to huge helpings of food. Unfortunately, the chair collapsed under him and he landed flat on his back with food all over him.

Algernon Barnett was well known all over Northamptonshire and Rutland, and would plan his working days according to the bus or train timetables, as he never used a car. He also never had any office equipment except pen and paper and the décor of his office was as flamboyant as he was, full of pictures that he painted and with gaily painted walls.

Algy loved organising Dinners and Rallies, but at the last Dinner he organised, he was obviously unwell and died shortly afterwards while at work. The local church was packed for his funeral service, which was conducted by the Bishop.

Reverend Mark Frame (1899 - 1965)

Deaf at the age of six, he attended the Langside School for the Deaf and Dumb in Glasgow, following which he was apprenticed to a firm of picture engravers. Like many of his contemporaries at the time, he immersed himself in the active social life of Glasgow Deaf Social Club. During this time, he formed an ambition to be a missioner to Deaf people and applied for the part-time post as Missioner at Paisley. That gave him time to study theology at Glasgow University, following which he became the first Deaf man to be ordained as a priest in the Church of Scotland.

Like so many missioners of his time, Frame was a strong supporter of the BDDA and became Secretary after the death of Leslie Edwards in 1951. After the tragic death of K.P.McDougall in 1962, he took over as Editor of the *British Deaf News*, holding that post until his death in 1965.

George Annand Mackenzie, M.A. (1871 - 1951)

George Annand Mackenzie was born in Liverpool, one of three deaf brothers. Up to the age of 13, he was privately educated by his mother using signing and fingerspelling, as she did not agree with the oralist method used by the Liverpool School for the Deaf. In this, Robert Armour, the Deaf missioner for Liverpool, ably assisted her.

When 13, Mackenzie was sent to be educated at a hearing school where the teachers did not know what to do with him and left him to his own devices a lot of the time. Even so, he came top of the class in many subjects. After two years at this school, he left to study at the School of Art in South Kensington, where he won many prizes.

In 1901, he accepted the post of Missioner to the Deaf and Dumb in Oxford; it was here that an undergraduate suggested he should try for a University degree at Oxford, but permission was refused.

In 1906, he went to Cambridge to found the Mission for the Deaf and Dumb and this move enabled him to enter University.

His deafness debarred him from lectures and he was unable to avail himself of the help of tutors, but he persevered and he graduated in 1911, overnight becoming front-page news as the only Deaf man (then) to achieve the academic distinction of Master of Arts of Cambridge University.

George Annand Mackenzie was active in the work of the British Deaf Association and was to be Missioner at Cardiff after leaving Cambridge in 1922, retiring in 1931. He was unique amongst Deaf men of the early twentieth century.

Mayor of Wembley: Arthur Edmond (1914 - 1982)

Arthur Edmond was educated at the Royal School for Deaf Children, Margate; in his final year, he was Head boy.

Showing great courage and dedication, he started his own printing business in a small garden shed, which grew into several shops. Always active in the affairs of his local community, he became Mayor of Wembley in 1954.

Arthur Edmond always had a deep love for his old school, and in 1964 accepted an appointment to become a Governor of the School, and was elected to the Committee of Management.

In 1973, he received what was probably his highest honour, his appointment as High Sheriff of Greater London by H.M. the Queen and it was during his year as High Sheriff that he personally raised £100,000 towards his old school's costly rebuilding programme, a most remarkable achievement.

Besides these fund-raising activities, he found time to organise special tickets for the schoolchildren to attend the Lord Mayor's Show and encouraged the Variety Club of Great Britain to donate video equipment to the school, besides doing a host of other things for his Alma Mater.

Arthur Edmond is the only known born-deaf person ever to be elected a mayor and to be appointed a High Sheriff of Britain's capital city.

George Annand Mackenzie, M.A.
Photo: Author's Collection

Arthur Edmond
Mayor of Wembley
Photo: Author's Collection

Dulverton Station as it was in the 1930s
Photo: Somerset County Records Office

Albert Tarr's Memorial in East Anstey Church, Devon
The plaque is about four feet high and two feet wide, and black with age. The Carnegie Medal is embedded near the bottom of the plaque.
Photo: Author's Collection

Albert William Tarr (1881 - 1935)

When the Taunton-Barnstaple train arrived at Dulverton station on the Great Western Railway's Exe Valley Line just before 5 p.m. on Tuesday 8 January 1935, most passengers proceeded to the station exit across the tracks, although this was prohibited and a footbridge was provided. This was what a mother, Ivy Thomas, and her child did. The footbridge was at the other end of the platform and too many passengers could not be bothered to use it, despite the standard railway warning not to do so. This was particularly dangerous at this station as trains approaching on the down line could not be seen until they were 40 yards from the station due to a bend and a road bridge.

Mrs. Thomas was the last passenger to set off across the tracks, laden with parcels from her shopping trip, with the little boy tagging along behind. Most passengers had got across and exited the station when the Barnstaple to Taunton train came around the bend under the bridge.

When the driver spotted the mother and the boy on the tracks, the mother had actually already reached the other side, but the little boy had fallen behind his mother and was still on the tracks.

Albert Tarr, a 54 year-old deaf tailor without speech, was standing in the place where he always stood to catch his train home to East Anstey after finishing work. He was the only one to spot the danger to the mother and child and dashed onto the tracks in order to try and save their lives, waving his arms frantically. By this time, the driver was braking sharply and blowing a warning on his whistle. This was the first time that everyone else on the station at that time became aware of the danger and they could only watch helplessly as the child stood petrified with fright between the rails. They saw the mother drop her parcels and turn around to step back and try to reach her boy. They saw Tarr reach the mother and grab hold of her and also appear to try to push away the child, then the train hit them all.

When the train had stopped, it was found that the child's body was lying on one side of the rails, his head on the other side. Tarr was lying half on top of Mrs. Thomas between the rails. Both appeared to have been killed instantly.

Albert Tarr was unmarried and lived with his widowed mother at the tiny Devon village of East Anstey. He was an ex-pupil of the Royal West of England Institution for the Deaf and Dumb, Exeter. For his act of bravery, Albert Tarr was posthumously awarded one of the highest civilian awards that could be given for acts of heroism by civilians, the Carnegie Bronze Medal.

This Medal is embedded in a Memorial Tablet erected to Tarr in the little parish church of East Anstey and reads:

'To the Glory of God and to perpetuate the honoured Memory of Albert William Tarr of this parish who was accidently killed at Dulverton 8th January 1935 at the age of 54. Although deaf and dumb and so unable to raise an alarm, he threw himself in front of an approaching train in a valiant effort to save a mother and child. This record is made by many friends in recognition of his sacrifice. The medallion incorporated is the highest award of the Carnegie Hero Trust Fund on whose illuminated roll the heroic act is recorded.'

Other Deeds of Bravery

Although Albert Tarr is the only Deaf man to have been awarded a posthumous medal for bravery, there have been other brave deeds by Deaf people throughout the 20th century that have resulted in official recognition for outstanding bravery. Two in particular have been unique awards.

Kenneth Andrews (1919 - 1966)

One July day in 1943 at Blaconsthorpe, Norfolk, a born-deaf farm labourer named Kenneth Andrews was walking home from work accompanied by his wife, and carrying his young baby, when he saw a R.A.F. Typhoon fighter plane crash in flames. Quickly pushing his baby into his wife's arms, Andrews ran to the downed plane and saw that the pilot was trapped in his cockpit.

Without any regard for his own safety, Andrews climbed onto a wing of the blazing plane, and kicked frantically at the toughened perspex of the cockpit canopy until it shattered, then dragged out the semi-conscious pilot. Seconds after Andrews had dragged away the pilot; the plane exploded into fierce flames

Andrews flagged down a passing vehicle, and asked the driver to take the pilot to the nearest hospital and then calmly went home with his wife to have his dinner. When other people arrived at the scene and found no-one in the burnt-out cockpit, they assumed that the pilot had bailed out. Only when the pilot recovered consciousness in hospital and informed the authorities of his rescue did the R.A.F. manage to track down Andrews and make his bravery known.

The King's Commendation for brave Conduct was gazetted to Kenneth Andrews on 5 November 1943.

Andrews was killed in a road accident in 1966.

William Robertson (1937 -)

On the night of 22 June 1957, the fishing vessel *Venus Star* from Portsoy, Banffshire, Scotland, was off Loch Ewe when a fire broke out in the engine-room.

It was spotted by William Robertson, then aged 20, a deaf man who had been educated at the Aberdeen School for the Deaf, and who had only been at sea for one year.

Robertson fought his way into the engine-room to try to contain the fire with blocks of ice taken from the hold and was burned about the arms. However, the flames were near the petrol tank and the fishing vessel was in danger of being blown up so the skipper had to give the order to abandon ship.

In the confusion of fighting the fire, the dinghy had gone overboard and was drifting away, trapping the crew, Robertson did not hesitate and dived overboard and swam out to the dinghy which he succeeded in getting back to the fishing boat for the crew to get off.

By his quick thinking and brave action, Robertson saved the lives of five men and the Stanhope Gold Medal for the Year 1957 was awarded to him.

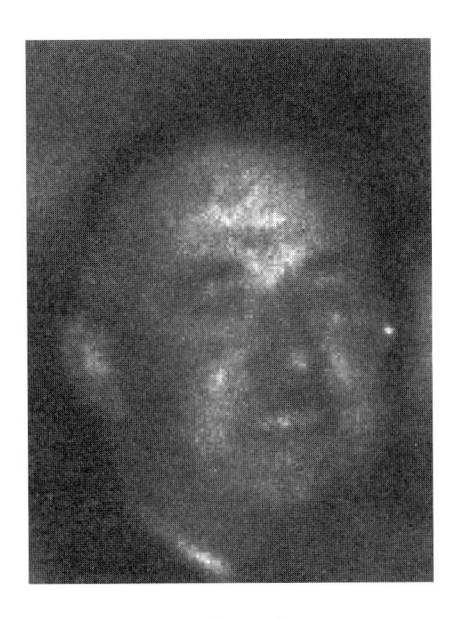

Chapter XIII   A Pictorial History of Deaf Britain

Kenneth Andrews
(blown up from a photo taken about 1960)
This is the only known picture of this shy and brave man.
Photo: Peter Gosse

William Robertson
Photo: Aberdeen & North of Scotland Society for the Deaf

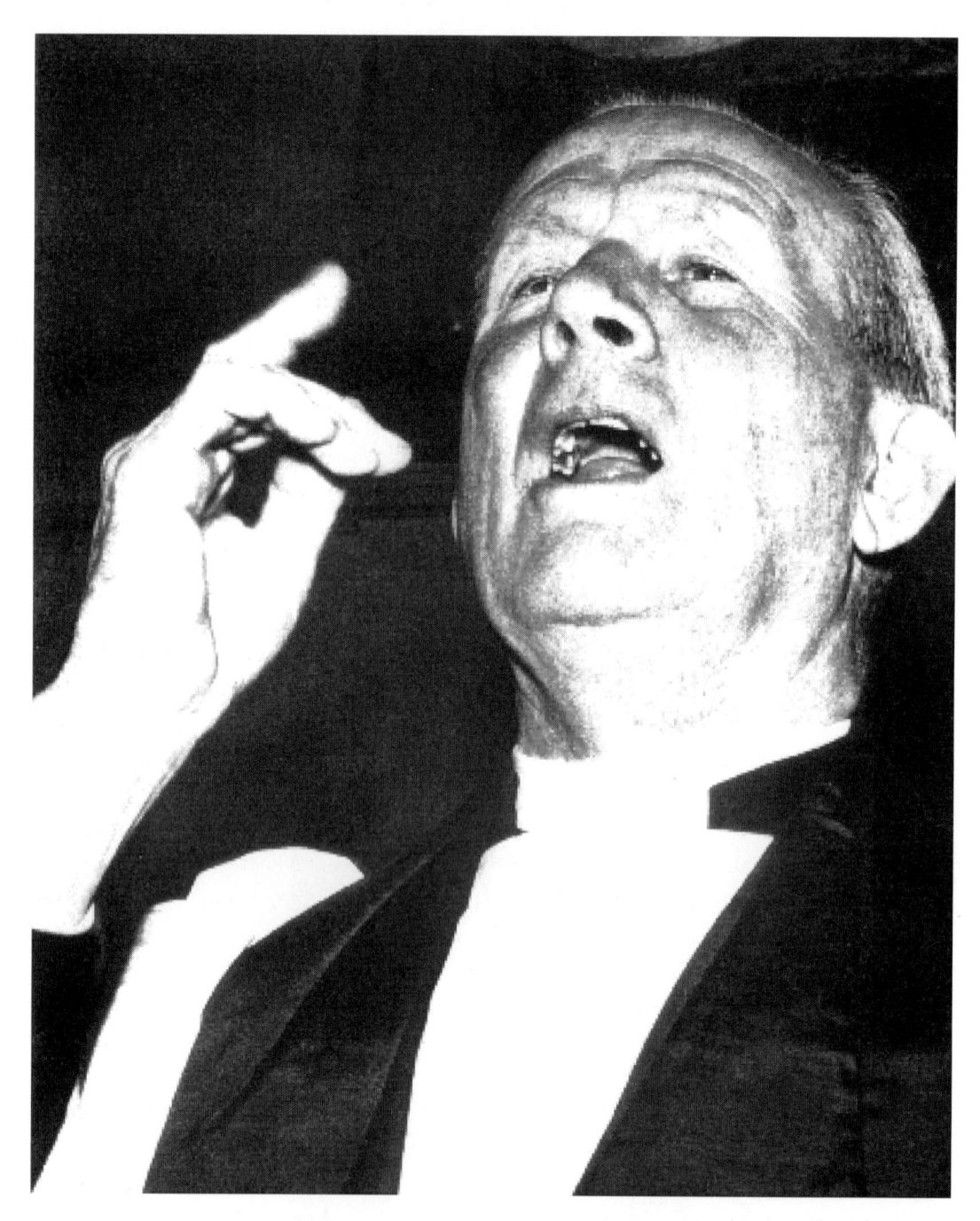

Chapter XIII   A Pictorial History of Deaf Britain

The Reverend Benjamin Morgan
Photo: Geoffrey Eagling

Reverend Benjamin Burton Morgan (1898 - 1984)

He was born Deaf at Aberystwyth, Wales, and attended the Royal School for the Deaf, Manchester, where he stayed until he was 18. After leaving school, he apprenticed in mechanical dentistry in Manchester and then worked as a dental mechanic in various parts of North Wales. However, he was never happy in his work. His ambition whilst at school had been to be a doctor or a teacher but his deafness prevented him from pursuing a career in either of these professions.

A chance meeting with Algernon J. M. Barnett, Missioner at Northampton, changed his life. Ben Morgan was to have a life long friendship with Barnett and under his influence, he met other clergymen and missioners working with Deaf people such as Leslie Edwards. Through their encouragement, he obtained at the early age of 24 the post of Missioner at Wolverhampton. Later, he became Missioner to the Deaf and Dumb of South Staffordshire and Shropshire, working from his base at Wolverhampton.

As Missioner, Morgan felt he had found his true vocation because in his work, he was able to do some teaching in his sermons to his Deaf congregations. He was a brilliant orator and would hold his Deaf audience spellbound.

Through the influence of Leslie Edwards, he became interested in the BDDA and served on its Executive Council for many years, later becoming one of its Vice-Presidents. As a member of the BDDA, his interest in education came to the fore and he constantly advocated for Further Education for Deaf people. He was instrumental in helping to start the Summer Schools, which were such a mainstay of the BDDA's programme for half a century.

In 1950, Morgan was appointed by the RADD to the post of Missioner for the Deaf and Dumb of the Guildford Diocese and the whole of Surrey. His thirst for knowledge and desire to equip himself more fully to serve Deaf people led him to seek ordination as a priest.

In February 1954, a unique event in Deaf History occurred when Ben Morgan was ordained into the ministry for the deaf, the first Deaf man since the Reverend Pearce of Southampton in 1886. Later, he was ordained as a priest by the Bishop of Guildford. He served the Deaf people of Surrey as a Chaplain until his retirement in 1963.

After retirement, the Reverend Morgan continued to interest himself with Deaf people, helping to form Surbition Deaf Club in 1958, serving as Chairman until 1962 and then as President for 16 years. He also did voluntary work in hospital work with psychiatric cases and with Deafblind people.

Ben Morgan was married to Joan Sleth-Smith, the daughter of the popular 'Zoo Man', David Sleth-Smith, a Fellow of the Royal Zoological Society, in 1938 and had two children by her.

The Reverend Benjamin Morgan died peacefully in his sleep on 3 March 1984 after a lifetime of brilliant work amongst Deaf people.

Sir James Graham, 6th Duke of Montrose (1878 – 1954)

Eldest son of the 5th Duke of Montrose, James Graham was educated at Eton where he caught diphtheria during the great floods of 1894. This was the cause of his deafness, which put paid to a planned career in the army and in politics. Deafness, however, did not prevent him from going off to South Africa and taking part in the Boer war.

It was while he was travelling to South Africa in 1899 via India that he became the first man ever to take a cine-film of a total eclipse of the sun. After the South African War, he tried unsuccessfully to stand for the South African parliament before returning home to marry Lady Douglas Hamilton.

In the 1914–1918 War, he was largely responsible for reactivating the Royal Naval Volunteer Reserve and was appointed Commander of the Clyde division, rising to Commodore in 1921 before retiring in 1927. While a naval officer, he invented and designed the first-ever aircraft carrier, the *Angus*.

On the death of his father, the 5th Duke, he succeeded to the Dukedom of Montrose and took his seat in the House of Lords. It was in that House that he scored his greatest triumph for the cause of deaf people. He informed the Labour Government of Attlee that to provide free spectacles to the partially-sighted, free dentures to those whose teeth had rotted, free artificial limbs to the disabled, but to *actually charge* the sum of £10 to deaf people for National Health hearing-aids was blatant discrimination! By his speeches, he shamed Attlee's government into changing this policy so that free hearing aids and batteries were available under the National Health Service. For many years, he served as President of the Royal National Institute for the Deaf, up to his death in 1954.

Jack Ashley (1922 -)

Jack Ashley was born in Widnes and after being elected as Member of Parliament for Stoke-on-Trent South, he seemed set for high political advancement. Tragedy struck, however, at the age of 45 when he contracted a virus infection following which he became totally deaf. His story since then has been a triumph of courage and perseverance.

He was successfully re-elected at every General Election following his deafness and managed to cope extremely well in the House of Commons, often with the best technological aids available, and became famous for his championing of disabled causes.

He was made a Companion of Honour in the 1971 New Year's Honour, became President of the Royal National Institute for the Deaf and became a familiar figure at many functions for deaf people. Possibly his most enlightening period of association with deaf people came at the Xth World Congress for the Deaf in Helsinki in 1987 where he spent ten days in his capacity as President of the RNID and found it an experience never to be forgotten, given that he did not understand sign language.

He stood down as Member for Stoke-on-Trent South at the 1990 General Election and accepted a Life Peerage, becoming Lord Ashley.

James Graham, Sixth Duke of Montrose
Photo: Royal National Institute for Deaf People

Jack Ashley
Now Lord Ashley of Stoke
Photo: Royal National Institute for Deaf People

Chapter XIII   A Pictorial History of Deaf Britain

Jock Young, with his family
Photo: Jock & Lillian Young

Murray Holmes
Photo: British Deaf Association

John Young, OBE (1926 -)

John Young was born in Glasgow to hearing parents. The youngest of three children, he went deaf through measles when three years old, and was sent to the Langside School for the Deaf in Glasgow to be educated. He was with the school when it evacuated to Dalquharran Castle in Ayrshire in 1939, and left that in 1942 to be apprenticed to the shoe trade. One of his proudest moments in the shoe trade was when he personally made shoes for the deaf Duke of Montrose who was then the President of the RNID.

After an early career that also included working for Singer (the sewing machine manufacturer) and Rolls Royce aero engines divivion, he was appointed Social Work Assistant with the Edinburgh and East of Scotland Society for the Deaf in 1981.

From the time he left school, Jock (as he was popularly known) was heavily involved in Deaf community activities. At first, this was in his native Glasgow as a member of his club's management committee then becoming Secretary of the BDA's Scottish Regional Council in 1969. He was also involved as Secretary-Treasurer of the Scottish Amateur Sports Council from 1969-1973. He was first elected to the BDA's Executive Council in 1973, and became its first-ever Deaf Chair in 1983, serving three successive terms before stepping down in 1992.

During his time as Chair of the BDA, Jock was prominent as the 'face' of the Deaf community, setting up a number of initiatives in Britain and in Europe, where he was involved in establishing the European Secretariat for the Deaf, becoming its first Honorary Director. In that capacity, he addressed the European Parliament in Strasburg, which accepted a proposal put forward that they recognise the sign languages of all its member countries.

For his services to the Deaf community, John Young received numerous awards including a honorary MA degree from Durham University, and both the BDA's and RNID's Medal of Honour. He was also awarded the World Federation of the Deaf's International Medal of Merit, and the OBE in the Queen's Birthday Honours in 1992. His last award was the BDA's Francis Maginn Award in 1998.

Murray Holmes (1946 -)

Born in Greenock, Scotland, Murray Holmes became deaf through meningitis at the age of 5 and he was educated in classes for the deaf in a local school where strict oralism was enforced and which he left with no academic qualifications whatsoever. His educational experiences have left him a strong advocate of Total Communication for which he has constantly campaigned.

He was elected to the Executive Council of the BDA in 1976, and became Vice-Chairman in 1981, and following the retirement of Jock Young, served as Chairman until his succession by Austin Reeves.

Murray Holmes was the BDA representative on the World Federation for the Deaf (WFD) and in 1983, was elected to its Bureau. At its Congress in Finland in 1987, he was elected one of the four Vice-Presidents.

Father Peter McDonough (1955 -)

One sunny summer's day in 1982, history was made when Pope John Paul held an open air Mass at Heston Park, Manchester. It was attended by an incredible number of people, at least 250,000 minimum, probably more. Millions more people watched the event on television.

Before all these watching millions of people, Pope John Paul ordained some priests, one of whom followed the service through a sign language interpreter. That man was the first deaf person in this country to become a Roman Catholic priest and probably the first ever to be ordained by a Pope.

Father Peter McDonough was born deaf of deaf parents and has a sister who is partially deaf. After a mixed primary education in partially hearing units and in ordinary state schools, his parents at last won their battle to send him (and his sister) to St. John's School for the Deaf, Boston Spa.

After leaving St. John's, he attended Salford Polytechnic where he got his engineering diploma and then decided to study Electronic Engineering at Sheffield University. However, during his first year at University, his mother died and he got a sudden calling to be a priest.

After a serious of interviews, he was sent to the English College in Valladolid, Spain, where in the company of 30 other English students he studied for the priesthood.

After a stint as parish priest at St. Mary's, Oswaldwistle, Lancashire, and also Chaplain to the Deaf in the northern part of the diocese, Father Peter is now closely involved with Henesey House, Manchester.

Reverend Vera Hunt

It is not all that common even for a hearing woman to be ordained a priest, therefore it is a remarkable event for a Deaf woman to achieve ordination, so when Vera Hunt of London became the first Deaf woman to be ordained as a priest in 1995, Deaf history was made.

Vera Hunt became deaf through meningitis when aged 7. It was actually her second attack of meningitis and although she was not expected to live, she pulled through. She was aged 11 when she finally went to school and it was to Spring Hill School for the Deaf in Northampton that she went to.

After leaving school, she worked for a Masonic regalia firm, doing embroidery work and then as a machinist for GEC after her marriage to a Deaf man she met in Slough Deaf Club.

Her involvement with the Church began at an early age, but really took off when she formed a small church in Uxbridge Deaf Club with the then Chaplain of the Royal Association for the Deaf. This led to her taking a course as a lay-helper, then a three year postal course to get her licence as a Reader. After that, she was accepted for training at the Salisbury and Wells Theological College which led to her ordination as Deacon.

Reverend Vera Hunt is now the Honorary Chaplain of the Royal Association for the Deaf, the first woman to hold the post, and works from St. Saviour's Church in Acton.

Chapter XIII A Pictorial History of Deaf Britain

Father Peter McDonough

Reverend Vera Hunt

Chapter XIII   A Pictorial History of Deaf Britain

Clark Denmark
Photo: Clark Denmark

Sharon Ridgeway with a group of Deaf & Hearing children in the Philippines
Photo: Sharon Ridgeway

Clark Denmark (1954 -)

Clark Denmark was born Deaf in Glasgow to Deaf parents. His sister Catherine was also Deaf and there is hereditary deafness in other members of the family. He went to the Glasgow School for the Deaf at Maryhill. Although the school was oral his "teachers were forced to use Sign Language" with Clark because he "was a lousy lipreader!"

Clark went to a further education college after school to gain "O" and "A" GCE levels before enrolling at Gallaudet College (USA) to study mathematics and physics at degree level. However, he left after two years when he realised that their degrees are not recognised outside the USA. He decided to return to Britain and work for his "own people".

Back in Scotland, Clark became Secretary of the Scottish Regional Council of the BDA and worked on television programmes for the Deaf, as the presenter of Channel 4's wonderful *Listening Eye* series for several years.

After working as a computer programmer with a National Health Services computer bureau covering the West of Scotland, he joined Durham University in 1985 to head the newly-formed British Sign Language Training Agency (BSLTA). The BSLTA was to see the development of trained Deaf BSL tutors over the course of the next few years.

He left Durham to join the BDA in 1992 as Director of Education. He is now Director of the Centre for Deaf Studies at Bristol where he lives with his television presenter wife Carolyn Nabarro.

Dr. Sharon Ridgeway (1957 -)

Dr. Sharon Ridgeway was in London and her deafness goes back three generations of her family, who came over to the UK from Russia and Poland when life was hard for Jewish people living there. Her grandparents also had deaf brothers and sisters. After leaving school with no qualifications, she had many different jobs including working on a kibbutz in Israel. On her return to Britain, she had a period in social work with Deaf people before getting a research post at the National Centre for Mental Health and Deafness (NCMHD) in Manchester.

She studied for a BA (Hon), MSc., and Certificate of Qualification in Social Work and obtained her doctorate (Ph.D) at the University of Manchester and now works at the NCMHD where she is a Chartered Psychologist and Head of Counselling Services.

Dr. Ridgeway is Chair of the British Society of Mental Health and Deafness, and is the BDA representative to the European Society for Mental Health and Deafness. She is also nominated Expert in Mental Health for the World Federation of the Deaf and has been listed in World Who's Who (1997). Sharon has a national and international reputation and frequently travels to present her work. Specialist interests including developing therapeutic approaches to work with deaf people and abuse of deaf children.

Sharon met Noel Traynor at the BDA Congress in Scarborough in 1995, and after a whirlwind romance, they were married six months later at Granada Studios, Manchester.

Clive Mason (1954 -)

Clive was born Deaf in Lennoxtown, Glasgow, and went to the Glasgow School for the Deaf at Maryhill before being apprenticed as a toolmaker to Chrsyler Talbot of Linwood, a job he held until the plant closed down. Even before then, he was greatly involved in the Glasgow Deaf community where he was well-known for brilliant storytelling.

This led to him being picked to partner Maggie Woolley as one of the presenters on the BBC's *SEE HEAR* programme in 1984. After the car plant he worked for closed down, Clive worked full time for the BBC for six years, doing other presentations besides working on *SEE HEAR!*

After his full time contract with the BBC ended, Clive became a lecturer in the Deaf Studies Department at the University of Wolverhampton though he still retained his links with *SEE HEAR!* By working as an occasional presenter. At the time of going to print (2000), Clive has been involved with the programme for 16 years.

Outside his involvement with *SEE HEAR!*, Clive has his started his own independent production company.

Anthony James Boyce (1937 -)

Tony Boyce was born in London and attended the Tottenham School for the Deaf and the Mary Hare Grammar School in Newbury. He went on to attend Reading University where he gained a BSc degree in Pure and Applied Mathematics and Physics.

His first job after university was as a scientific officer at the British Welding Research Station in Cambridge, where he also helped to tutor apprentices. It was there that it was suggested he should become a teacher and shortly afterwards, he saw by chance a pamphlet produced by the National College of Teachers of the Deaf (NCTD) which stated there was a desperate shortage of teachers of mathematics and science in deaf education. The pamphlet contained in small print "Any graduate is eligible to teach".

After passing the Ministry of Education medical examination and interview, Tony was immediately given a teaching post at the Yorkshire Residential School for the Deaf, Doncaster, in 1964. He was therefore the first deaf teacher of the deaf in modern times and became a threat to the NCTD because of their preference for the oral method of communication. Initially, he was refused the award of the teaching diploma because the NCTD considered him unable to pass one subject – speech teaching. However, the Department of Education and Science watched Tony teaching periodically over a period of two years and recognised his teaching abilities and awarded him the status teacher of the deaf. Tony retired from teaching on medical grounds in 1994 after helping to establish Doncaster College for the Deaf.

His varied interests include chess. He has been for a number of years President of the International Committee of Silent Chess. His other interests include gemmology (the study of precious stones) and Deaf History. He has been Chair of the British Deaf History Society since 1997.

Chapter XIII   A Pictorial History of Deaf Britain

Clive Mason.

Tony Boyce (in white coat) in his role as Chair of the British Deaf History Society making a speech.
Photo: British Deaf History Society

Chapter XIII A Pictorial History of Deaf Britain

Emile Stryker
Photo: Raymond Lee

Mika Brojer
Photo: British Deaf News

Great Deaf Men of Jewish Faith

The London Deaf community was fortunate in the late 20th Century to have a number of Deaf people of strength and character who contributed so much to the advancement of their fellow Deaf of all minorities. Two of them were closely involved with the Jewish Deaf Club but their experiences were also available to all other Deaf people in London.

Emile Stryker (1917–1990)

Emile Stryker was born in Wurzburg, Germany, and came to Britain in 1939 to escape Nazi persecution. After leaving the Jewish School for the Deaf he found employment in the clothing trade but his real interest lay in voluntary work with Deaf people. He was active in the Jewish Deaf Club and Green Lanes Deaf Club. Later, he became involved in the Federation of London Deaf Clubs and in the National Union of the Deaf.

Due to his ability to speak German, he was used by British Deaf Tour groups as a German-speaking interpreter on occasions.

Emile was heavily involved in the launch of the first World Conference of Jewish Deaf people in London 1984.

His health deteriorated in his later years and he became blind, learning the deafblind alphabet.

Mika Brojer (1946-1998)

Born and brought up in London, Mika was educated at Burwood Park School. His contribution to the London Deaf community was immense, with involvement in a diverse mixture of minorities.

He was a strong supporter of the National Theatre for the Deaf and British Sign Language. In his capacity as Advice Worker with the Royal Association in Aid of Deaf people (RAD) and the Job Club in Green Lanes, he helped Deaf people in many different ways.

His thought-provoking debates in London were attended by many grass-root members of the Deaf Community and gave rise to greater awareness of Deaf people's rights.

Many friends and admirers who would miss a man of strength and great passion mourned his death from cancer in April 1998.

Terry Riley (1944 -)

Born to Deaf parents in Manchester, Terry was educated in a mainstream school. He suffered from mastoiditis and had numerous operations from the age of 3 months and at the last operation, lost his last residual hearing, becoming profoundly Deaf. He has been involved in the Deaf community since being a baby and was secretary of St. Joseph's Deaf Club at the early age of 15. Through his love of sports he became involved with the North West Sports Council, and also the North Regional Council of the BDA, and on its split became the first Chair of the North West Area Council (BDA).

His employment varied and after 17 years as a Special Inspector executing warrants for the Gas Board, Terry's life changed dramatically when he secured a position as researcher on the BBC's *SEE HEAR!* production team in 1986. He eventually rose in the BBC ranks to become the first Deaf producer on a mainstream television programme. In 1997 Terry was awarded the RNID's "Hear for all" Media award for his outstanding television programmes *"Breaking the Silence"* and *"The Birth of a Language"*.

After being associated with the BDA at regional level for many years, he was elected as Executive Councillor for the North West Region in 1990, and then was elected as one of the three National Councillors. In July 2000, Terry was awarded the BDA Medal of Honour for his outstanding contribution to the Deaf community.

Whilst with the BDA he served on numerous committees, which opened the doors to a better quality of life for Deaf people. Terry was also involved in Europe particularly with the European Union of the Deaf and served for 4 years as Vice President. Terry has represented the BDA at World events and WFD Congresses.

His achievements were recognised when he was one of the few Deaf people ever to be the subject of the BBC's *"A Look at Your Life"* programme in January 2001.

Janet Veronica Brown (1964 -)

Janet Brown was educated at the Royal Schools for the Deaf (Manchester) from the age of four, and left with no qualifications. She then spent 5 years in Henshaw's College for the Blind, Harrogate, where she received mobility training and life skills to help her independence. This included some work experience in a hotel in Harrogate where she worked as a chambermaid.

After her period in Harrogate, she was not able to have a career due to lacking the necessary qualifications and support. However, Janet is a determined woman with a lot of motivation to learn and with the support of her husband Edward whom she married in 1992, started to attend college regularly where she has enjoyed some success, especially in word processing and working with computers.

She is a firm believer in the rights of Deafblind people and is very demanding of equal access to resources in the college she attends, earning the admiration of all staff she comes into contact with. She has also become one of the "faces" of SENSE and Deafblind UK, regularly agreeing to be photographed for their publicity material.

Chapter XIII   A Pictorial History of Deaf Britain

Terry Riley at a graduation ceremony with Janet Brown (see below)

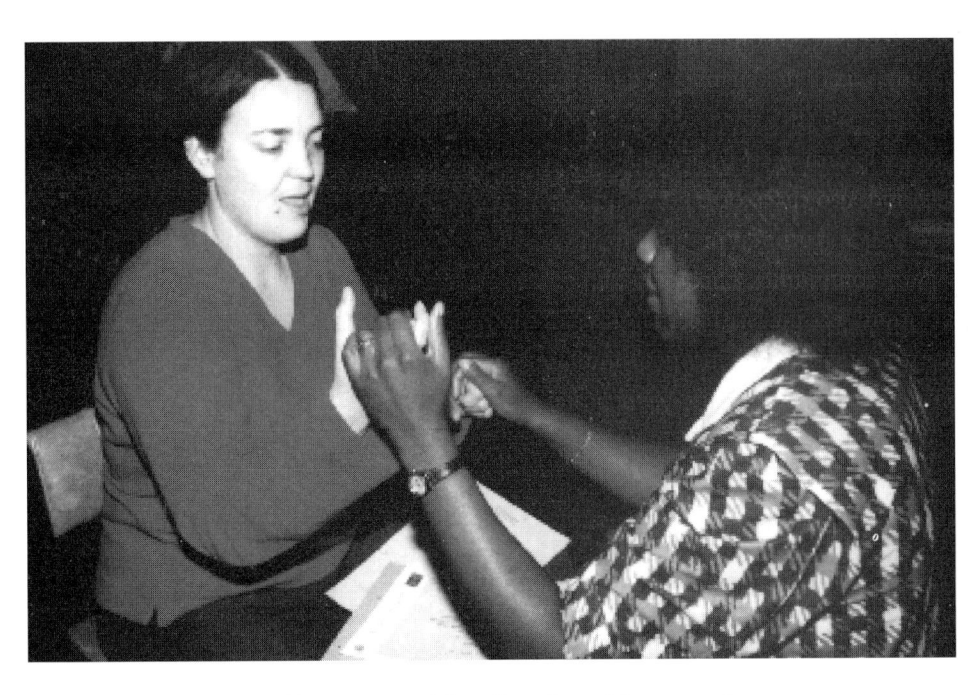

Janet Brown, receiving 'hands on' interpreting.
Both photos: City College Manchester

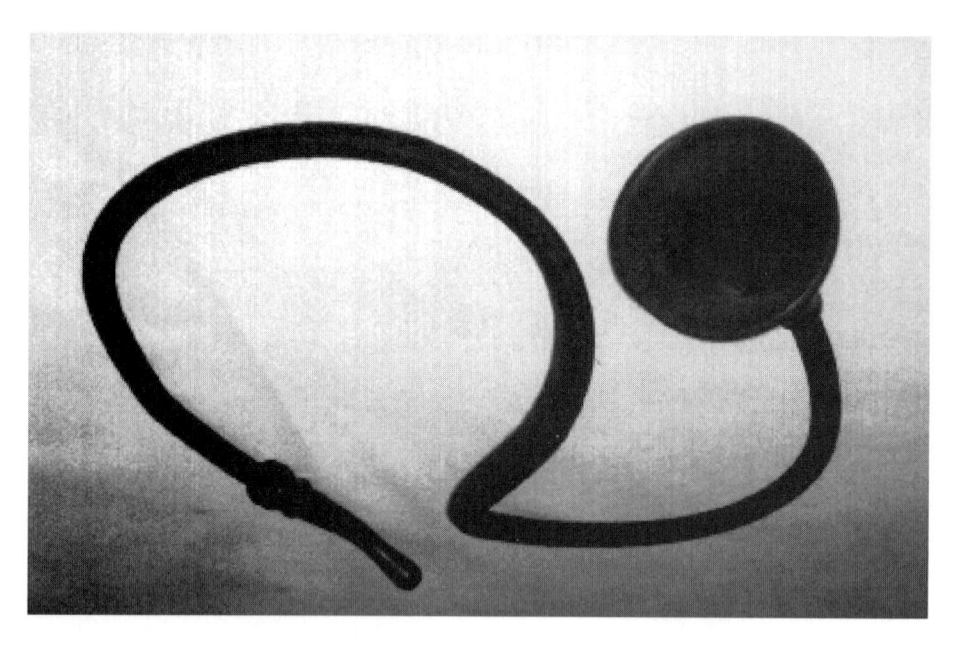

Chapter XIV   A Pictorial History of Deaf Britain

A rubber speaking tube, early 20th century
Photo: Deafness Support Network

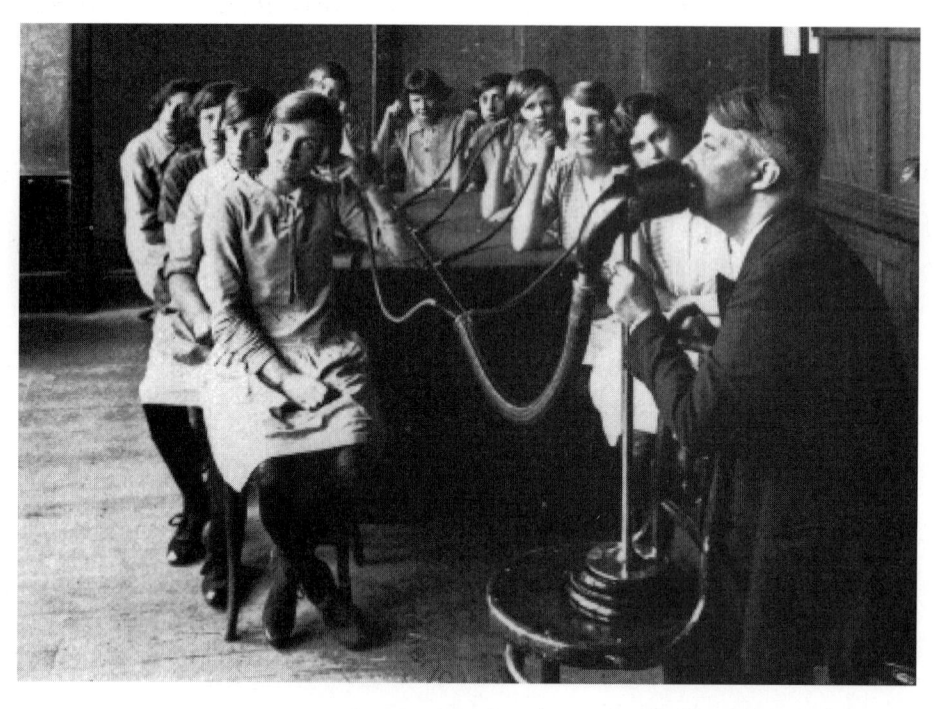

An instrument called the Multiphone in use, 1929
Photo: David Woolley Collection

CHAPTER XIV

DEAF TECHNOLOGY

Hearing Aids

Attempts to prevent the onset of deafness or to improve reception of sound through the ear go back centuries. In the 1660s for example, ear trumpets made of metal and animal horn were produced, some of which were small enough to be hidden under the wigs that were very fashionable those days. In the highly fictitious memoirs of Baronne d'Aulney written in 1675, we read of a type of hearing aid fashioned like a horn small enough to be fitted inside the ear (and thus under the hair or wig) yet still be able to amplify sound so that the wearer could hear and understand conversation whispered at the other side of the room! In 1668, Samuel Pepys noted in his diary on 2 April that he had experimented with a form of ear trumpet at the Royal Society.

Ear trumpets and the like may have been preferable to being subjected to the numerous 'quacks' who operated in those days promising to restore fading hearing. In a letter to his father, Sir Thomas Browne, his son Edward wrote to him from Paris about a curious method of treating deafness.

Here was one Sir William Meredith who, having a great desire to be cured of his deafness, a physitian* ordered him to be anointed, I suppose in order to salivation, the effect of which was that after his head was light, and hee talk'd wildly for some space, he died. (*The original spelling is retained).

Sir Thomas Browne's Works (page 65, 1664)

Few of course went that far, but the desire to amplify sound went on relentlessly. Manufactured versions of metal and plastic horns, speaking tubes and other amplifiers were disguised in fans, walking sticks, under wigs and in dinner plates. Some of the quality of sound from these acoustic devices compared favourably with some of the electronic aids we see today!

In 1819, King Goa VI of Portugal had created for himself an Acoustic Throne. It was an armchair with timber arms carved as lions with gaping mouths. Courtiers knelt before the king and spoke into the lions' mouths and the sound was conveyed up the arms through tubes to the king's ears!

Soldiers and sailors with hearing damaged by noise in the 1914-1918 War were given ear trumpets and because known as 'tin ear Joes'.

At the end of the 19th century the first electrically-powered carbon aids were made and in 1923, Marconi made a cabinet model hearing aid using valve technology. It was portable, but not wearable, made up of a microphone, amplifier and hand-held earpiece, powered by a large dry-cell battery. In 1935, Amplivox made the first wearable electronic hearing aid.

From 1949 when the NHS made the first body worn hearing aids, technology has improved to such an extent that miniature hearing aids that fit inside the ear have been developed and further strides have been made in that the first digital hearing aids have now come onto the market.

Hearing Devices & Aids: A Chronological Record

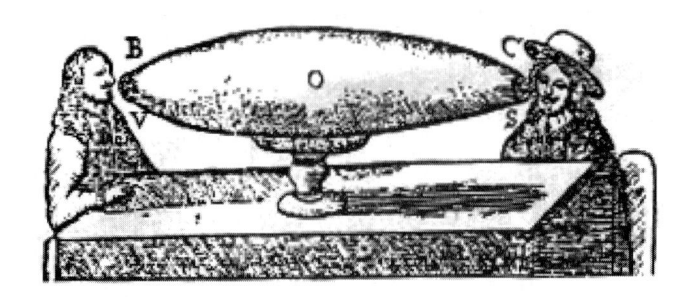

Ellipsis Otica, the earliest form of hearing device 1673

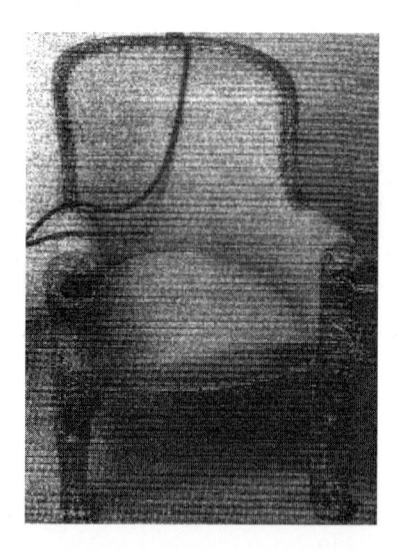

The Acoustic Throne of King Goa of Portugal, 1819

The king's subjects had to kneel and speak through the open lions' mouths, and the King listened via the hearing tube attached to the back of the throne.

Two different types of 'horns' used as hearing devices, 1870s

Chapter XIV   A Pictorial History of Deaf Britain

National Health Service battery-type body-worn hearing aids in use, 1960s

A selection of Year 2000 hearing aids, including digital models

Aids for the Home

How deaf people were woken up in the morning was always a subject for jokes and cartoons in newspapers and magazines from the 19th century through to the mid-20th century. These would range from long pieces of string tied to toes and trailed out of a window for the early morning street gas-lamp lighter to pull as he walked along extinguishing the gas lamps to cumbersome scientific devices that relied on an alarm clock to tip a glass of water over the face of the sleeping Deaf person.

The reality was, perhaps, that many Deaf people relied on an in-built sense of timing that allowed them to get up in the mornings. Others would rely on hearing family members, such as parents or children, to wake them up when the alarm went off.

The same sort of humour would apply to how Deaf people answered the door, or knew their babies were crying.

The quality of Deaf peoples' lives inside their own homes was revolutionised when James Mountcastle, a deaf man from Loughborough, patented his Mountcastle Bell just after the 1939-45 War. For the first time, they could know when someone came to their door. Around the same time, the Royal National Institute for the Deaf started up their Research and Technical department, enabling developments to be made in baby alarms and other environmental aids such as bedroom alarms that turned a light on or flashed to wake the occupants up. The first models were extremely cumbersome devices, but at least they worked.

For many Deaf people, the Mountcastle Bell, with its subsequent amendments to enable the house occupants to distinguish between doorbells and the telephone ringing and the ability to switch between day and night operation, was probably their first technical aid. It is still in use in thousands of deaf homes throughout the country, even with the advent of other modern technology.

Baby alarms, bedroom alarms and smoke alarms have developed out of recognition from the earlier cumbersome models and has become a thriving industry for a few specialist producers, extending into pager systems.

When the first television sets started to appear in peoples' homes, Deaf people also went out and bought them. However, most found them a waste of money and begrudged the licence fee they had to pay because most of the content was unintelligible to them, except for the rare programme for the deaf and hard-of-hearing. Only expert lipreaders could follow what was being said and even then, not everything was lipreadable. Only sports programmes could be watched with some degree of enjoyment. Deaf people had to wait until the mid-seventies for the development of technology that enabled teletext television to be produced. As the early teletext televisions were hideously expensive, a brief but profitable industry sprang up that produced contraptions called Nufax machines that were able to read teletext and therefore subtitles. Similarly, when video recorders became the vogue, the first recorders were unable to record subtitles, and it was sometime before special machines were on the market again at a high cost – that enabled subtitle recording. Now, no Deaf home in Britain would be complete without a teletext television and a subtitle recording facility.

A bulky 1960s Bedside Alarm

A Year 2000 Bedside Alarm.
This model allows a pillow vibrator to be attached if needed.

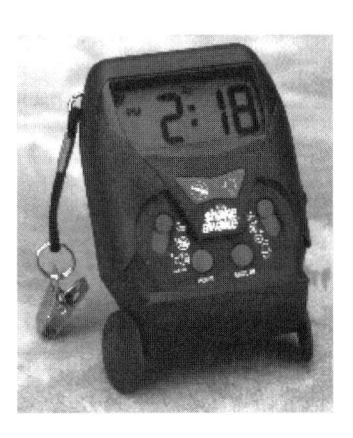

A Travelling Vibrating Alarm Clock, 2000

A Vistel Training Session being carried out by the Breakthrough Trust
Photo: Breakthrough Deaf-Hearing Integration

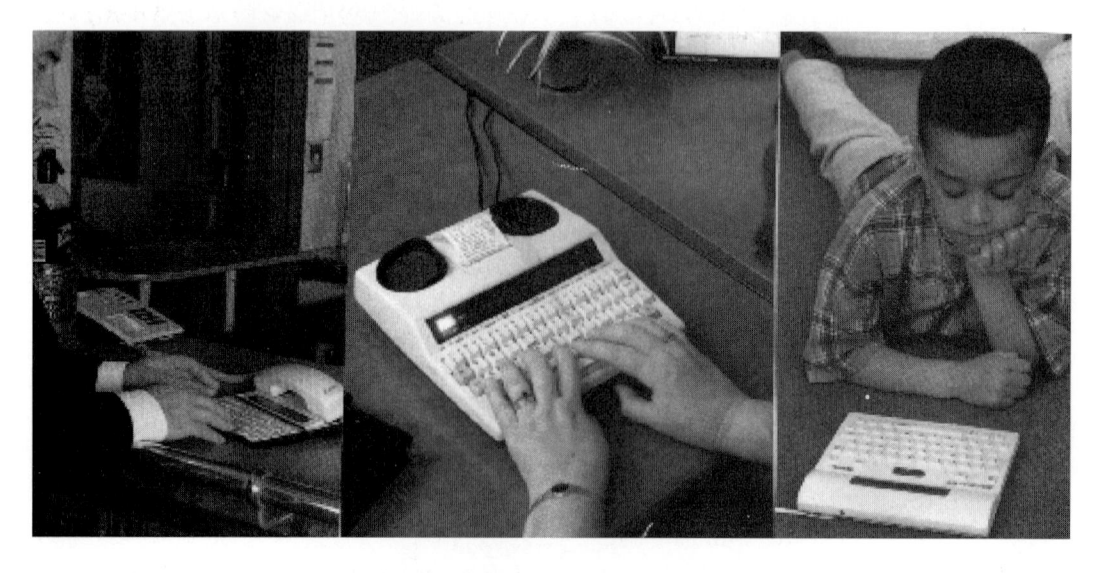

A selection of Minicoms in use, 2000

Telecommunications

When Alexander Graham Bell set out in 1876 in an attempt to devise an amplification device for his deaf wife, he ended up inventing the telephone and in the process excluded deaf people to almost a century of benefiting from his new technological marvel. Whilst hearing people made rapid progress in their lives thanks to telecommunications, Deaf people languished in poverty or as second class citizens as criterion for employment demanded the ability to use the telephone, even where it was not absolutely necessary.

Not until the early 1970s with the development of machines called Vistels (short for visual telecommunication devices) were Deaf people able to start using the telephone system. The main drawback with Vistels was that the machines were expensive and non-portable and people needed training on how to use them. Vistels were distributed by the Breakthrough Deaf-Hearing Integration who organised regular training weekends for those who wanted to know how to make the best use of the machines. The Vistel Mark II that evolved from the first model was even more expensive and so bewildering to use for most Deaf people that the majority of the machines were rented out instead of being purchased outright.

Rapid developments in new technology meant that it was just a matter of time before someone came along with cheaper, streamlined telecommunication devices. Several of them actually came along at more or less the same time, with the most popular model being the American minicom (known in the United States as a TDD). The original model imported to Britain was Minicom 3, but within a few years it was being superseded by the Minicom 5, then the Minicom 7. For most Deaf people, these machines were still expensive and tended to churn out garbled messages if there was any interference on the line.

Demand for a more portable model soon led to the development of a 'compact minicom', that could be carried around. However, access to a telephone was still needed and many deaf people grew to dislike them because of the difficulty of balancing the equipment when using public telephones. The fact it needed an electrical socket was an additional frustration as people started to discover telephone points were not always necessarily near electrical sockets!

Time, however, does not stand still and telecommunications technology continues at a rapid pace. When the fad for mobile telephones took off amongst the general population, Deaf people were not slow to discover the advantages of short message services (or text messaging). In a short space of time, the use of mobile phones took over from minicoms and other line-based textphones as the main means of communication between Deaf people. It would not be unusual, however, to find in a Deaf person's home a minicom or other textphone and a fax machine as well as a mobile phone.

The same Deaf person would also be likely to have a computer with an electronic mail facility.

The Deaf person's world in 2000 is so different from the time when the likes of Deaf pioneers like George Healey or William Agnew relied on pen and paper in the 19th century, or missioners like David Fyfe and Algernon Barnett who relied on their feet and public transport to keep in touch with their scattered clients.

A Pictorial History of Deaf Britain

PICTURE GALLERY 1 – WHO ARE THEY?

Two group photographs of Deaf schoolchildren, *c1890*
Source unknown, but believed to be from the
Brighton Institution for the Deaf and Dumb
Photos: Author's collection

**Rare 1880s photograph of schoolchildren from the
London Asylum for the Deaf and Dumb, Old Kent Road.
The seated boy in the middle (Hallett) was aged 59 in 1936.**
Photo: The Hallett Collection

Schoolboy Football Team, c1930
Source unknown.
Photo: Author's collection

Group of Deaf people, c1950
Source unknown
Photo: Author's collection

Charlie Drake, the comedian, with some Deaf schoolchildren
Date and source unknown
Photo: Author's collection

Deaf people having a picnic in 1909
Source unknown, but photograph is captioned "Brockenhurst, July 17 1909"
Photo: Author's collection

A group of Deaf people on an outing, 1930s
Photo: Hampshire, I.O.W. & Channel Islands Association for the Deaf

A group of Deaf people on a day out, 1930s
Source unknown
Photo: Author's collection

PICTURE GALLERY 2 – BDDA Groups?

A Group of BDDA People?

We can identify George Healey of Liverpool in this photograph, which dates it pre-1927 (the year of his death). Another identified is Ernest Aycliffe, also prominent in the BDDA in the 1920s.

Photo: Hampshire, I.O.W. & Channel Islands Association for the Deaf

Another group of (BDDA?) people

This is possibly at the Cardiff Congress, 1947. People identified in this photograph include R.S.Oloman, Algernon Barnett (died 1952), & Ernest Ayliffe.

Photo: Hampshire, I.O.W. & Channel Islands Association for the Deaf

Another BDDA group picture?
The venue seems to be the same as in the previous picture. The man standing up on the brickwork is K.P.MacDougall, Editor of the *British Deaf News* in the early 1950s.
Photo: Hampshire, I.O.W. & Channel Islands Association for the Deaf

A BDDA South Regional Council Rally in Southampton
Photo: Hampshire, I.O.W. & Channel Islands Association for the Deaf

PICTURE GALLERY 3 – Photographic Tours

In the 1910s, it was a popular pastime for groups of Deaf photographers to go on tours with cameras and snap Deaf life wherever they could find it.
Often these photographers accompanied the evangelist Selwyn Oxley and his Deaf wife, the authoress Kate Whitehead, who toured in a horse-drawn caravan.
The bottom photo on the next page shows the photographers taking tea with Selwyn Oxley.

Taking tea with Selwyn Oxley
All photos from the Hallett Collection.

A Pictorial History of Deaf Britain

Sport Picture Gallery

Clapham St. Bedes Athletic Club, 1930s

Balham Deaf Tennis Club, 1930s
Photos from the Hallett Collection.

Liverpool Deaf Cricket Club, 1879
Photo: Liverpool Deaf Sports & Social Club

Clapham St. Bede's Deaf Cricket Club, 1911
Photo from the Hallett Collection.

Lancashire & Yorkshire Cricket Teams, 1929

Leicester Deaf Cricket Club, 1927

Edinburgh Deaf Cricket Club, 1949
All photos in author's collection

A Pictorial History of Deaf Britain

Leicester Deaf Cricket Club, 1970s

Belfast Deaf Snooker Team, 1970s

Great Britain Basketball Team, World Games, Bulgaria 1993

Swansea Deaf Football Club, 1927
Photo: Church of the Holy Name Mission to the Deaf

A Pictorial History of Deaf Britain

Burwood Park School Football Team, 1960-1

Southampton Deaf Football Team, 1970s
There is a familiar face on the back row, extreme right. It is Austin Reeves, BDA Chair from 1996 onwards (still current at the time of print)
Photo: Hampshire, I.O.W. & Channel Islands Association for the Deaf

Using the Videophone
Photo: Deafness Support Network

The Internet
Bound to play a large part in Deaf people's lives.

CHAPTER XV

THE DEAF COMMUNITY: THE FUTURE?

We have looked into the past. Let us now look into the future. Where will the Deaf community be at the end of the next century, in the year 2100? Questions abound - will it still be here or will it go the way of the mammoth, or the Aztec and the Inca, or the South American Indian? To answer these questions, one penultimate question must first be tackled - how strong is the Deaf community's desire to survive in the 21st century?

The desire to survive as a group, apart from requiring a strong infrastructure and leadership, relies on the determination of every Deaf individual to keep the community going. Deaf History tells us, amongst many incidents and examples throughout different eras, about the amazing determination of Deaf people to survive both as individuals and as part of a community sharing the same language, mentality and culture. The terrifying period when Oralism was welding absolute power and those Deaf people who suffered under this particular reign of terror confronted the banning of sign language with defiance and they triumphed. There are examples in the past showing the resilience and determination of Deaf individuals battling for equal rights and equal participation. The Deaf person, as an individual, will always be around until the end of the world. For as long as there are Deaf people existing in the future, Deaf communities will also exist. No matter what vast leaps in science and technology in their endeavours to eliminate deafness will bring, deafness itself will pursue every Deaf person relentlessly – and that is part of the structure of Nature. Nature and the world exist on the reconciliation of opposites – day and night; summer and winter; great and small; the wise and the stupid; the deaf and the hearing, and so on and this balance will always be maintained.

Future technology will aid, more than hinder, Deaf people. Not a few years ago, the idea of a Deaf person using a mobile phone sounded absurd, but many Deaf people use it nowadays. New innovations such as mobile-cams are not far off and Deaf users will be able to sign to each other via the hand-held mobile-cam. The cinema will be able to offer captions via specially designed spectacles that would read invisible open captions on the screen. Revolutionary changes in communication technology would enable Deaf people to work via the Internet from home, on the same pay as their hearing counterparts. There are much more obviously, but all that would still hinge on the Deaf community's greatest hindrance – the attitude of hearing people.

Attitudes of hearing people to deafness and the Deaf community will be of utmost importance. There will always be hearing people in the mould of Alexander Graham Bell (who once proposed that congenitally Deaf persons should be prohibited from marrying each other by law), and Dr. David Buxton, one-time headmaster of the Liverpool Institution for the Deaf and Dumb, who forecast in 1889 that *"..sign language would soon die out.."*. However, the Deaf community has always proved that it can resist such attacks. With the right support from majority of the hearing population and its own determination, the Deaf community will continue to exist.

Adapting to Change

The Deaf community, in order to survive, must be adaptable to change. Oralism will be outdated as respect and interest in sign language among the hearing population grow. BSL, once it has been recognised as an official language, will become acceptable. Under the new Human Rights Act, it will be illegal for oralists to ban it. Deaf clubs will flourish to cater for hearing people's interest in Deaf Studies and communicating with the Deaf – and the Disability Discrimination Act will grow into a powerful legal tool. However, members of the Deaf community must show flexibility and respect to other Deaf individuals who wish to have Cochlea Implants, or bionic ears. Even the development in genetic surgery should be viewed in a positive light if it improves the healthy well-being of those who could be multi-disabled as well as being Deaf. After all, when it comes to the issue of human rights, one cannot be choosy and decide that one can have that right but not that right. Deaf people must respect the right of others to choose, even if it disagrees with their views and principles – after all, those who choose to have implants or bionic ears would still be, first and foremost, deaf persons.

Although there are some fears over the future of existing deaf programmes when analogue television ceases in 2007, there is a possibility that, with the advent of digital television, a number of individual channels catering for the needs of the Deaf will spring up, thus generating employment to Deaf people.

Organisations *for* the Deaf will no longer exist as such. As they begin to listen to Deaf people, the balance of power with shift to the membership and its demands and they will become organisations *of* Deaf people once Deaf members develop their confidence in themselves and demand not only the best but their rights.

There were Deaf people in A.D. 1000, and long before that too. Deaf people have proved their resilience by surviving various forms of oppression for thousands of years. Deaf people will still be around in A.D. 2100, though perhaps society at that time will be virtually unrecognisable from what it is now.

Whatever each Deaf person in Britain believes, there is no doubt there is still a future for the Deaf community. However, because of all the likely changes, it is all the more important that our Deaf History is preserved and recorded for our future generations to look back upon with genuine pride in our heritage.

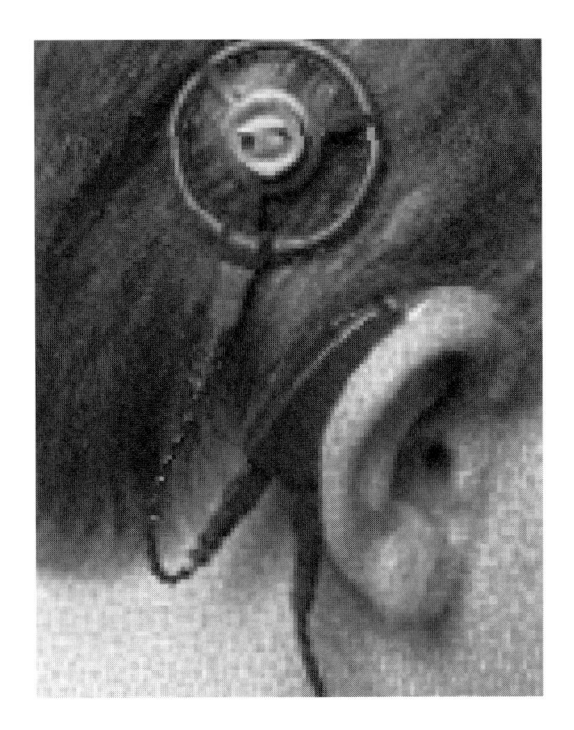

Cochlea Implants

People with implants are still *deaf* people. The Deaf community has to be flexible enough to accept them.

ABOUT THE AUTHOR

Peter Webster Jackson was born in 1944 to hearing parents in Redruth, Cornwall, and became seriously ill with meningitis in 1948 whilst living in Kiel (Germany) where drugs and hospital facilities were still in short supply. As a result of becoming deaf, Peter was sent to the Royal Residential Schools for the Deaf (Manchester) in 1950. There he found other children like himself, and became exposed to British Sign Language. His childhood memories of the Manchester school were of grim conditions, extreme cold in winter, rodent and bug infestation and appalling food. Nonetheless, the friendship and comradeship developed with other pupils of his generation remains with him to this day.

In 1955, Peter sat the Joint Entrance Examination for Mary Hare Grammar School and the new Burwood Park School and was one of the first boys to enter Burwood Park. Despite it's oralist approach, Peter has many fond memories of his time at Burwood Park. He considers that the school helped him, as it did many others, to develop qualities of leadership and independence.

After leaving school, Peter worked as a clerk with the Refuge Assurance Company in Manchester for 21 years, rising to a position as Deputy Chief Clerk of its Overseas Department. During his time there, Peter served for two years as union representative – a difficult period at a time when the use of sign language interpreters was unknown.

In 1982, the British Deaf Association set up in conjunction with the University of Durham a fellowship in memory of its late General Secretary, Allan Brindle Hayhurst, and on 1st January 1983, Peter commenced his new duties as Research Fellow. He was never to look back and after four years in Durham, Peter set up as a freelance consultant and part-time lecturer. He was responsible for setting up AIDS AHEAD, which sought to disseminate information about HIV and AIDS to deaf people.

Around the same time, the BDA commissioned Peter to write a book on the history of Deaf people in Britain. His first book, *Britain's Deaf Heritage*, was published in 1990 during the BDA's Centenary Year.

By then, the work involved with AIDS AHEAD had grown to the extent where Deaf people with HIV and AIDS were being supported through a network of befrienders and counsellors set up for the purpose. AIDS AHEAD also diversified into other health promotion and health prevention areas, and became the BDA's Health Promotion Department, with Peter as Director. During this period, Peter was part of the BDA's Senior Management Team and also achieved what he regards as his greatest accolade, being voted unanimously for two years running as the Chair for NAHAW, a nation-wide organisation of 500 professionals working in the field of HIV & AIDS. He was the only Deaf person in the organisation.

Following the restructuring of the BDA in the mid-1990s due to its financial difficulties, Health Promotion was one of the causalities and Peter reverted to being a freelance consultant and part-time lecturer, as well as writing a series of books on Deaf crime. Most of his current part-time work is with City College Manchester, and most of his consultancy work is devoted to fundraising and project planning for a number of organisations. The total value of funds raised for these charities and organisations is in excess of £1million.

In his spare time, he is involved with the British Deaf History Society and is currently its secretary. He has also been involved with Deafness Support Network as Chair of Vale Royal Deaf Centre.

Twice married, he has a grown up son, Wayne, from his first marriage. He now lives in Winsford, Cheshire, with his second wife, Maureen

Peter & Maureen Jackson

FOOTNOTES

[1] The first school for the Deaf in the world (see page 52, Chapter III: also page 111, Chapter V).

There has always been controversy over where the *first* school for the Deaf was started. In the past, some Deaf historians (especially Americans) have always insisted that this was in France by the Abbé de l'Epée in 1760. However, recent research suggests that Thomas Braidwood started teaching deaf children a few months before l'Epée. This research is supported by others who assert that although l'Epée gave shelter to two deaf children in 1760 he did not formally start teaching them (and other deaf children) until 1762/3.

If this is correct, then Braidwood's Academy was the first Deaf school in the world.

BIBLIOGRAPHY

Journals, periodicals and Newspapers

Aberdeen Press & Journal 1987
American Annals for the Deaf
Bath Chronicle 1791-1794
Bath Guide 1818-1831
British Deaf & Dumb Times 1889-1908
British Deaf Monthly 1896-1903
British Deaf Mute & Deaf Chronicle 1891-1895
British Deaf News 1955-2000
British Deaf Times 1903-1954
City News (Manchester) 1880
Daily Mail 1962
Daily Telegraph 1878
Deaf & Dumb Magazine 1879-1885
Deaf & Dumb Times 1889-1891
Deaf News 1950-54
Deaf Quarterly News 1905-1950
Deaf History Journal
Deaf History Journal Supplements
Elgin Magazine 1831
Ephphatha 1896-1959
Evening Argus 1983
Gentlemen's Magazine 1883
Glasgow Evening News 1891-1907
Glasgow Evening Times 1871-1893, and 1995
Glasgow Herald 1871-1895
Glasgow Mail 1890
Greenock Telegraph 1976-1982
Hearing 1977
Journal for the History of Astronomy 1979
Leicester Mercury 1988
Liverpool Daily Post 1943
Liverpool Review 1887
Magazine for the Scottish Deaf 1929-1931
Medical History 1973
One-in-Seven Magazine 1997-2000
See Hear! Magazine 1992-1997
Silent World 1954
Somerset County Herald 1889
Somerset County Gazette 1899
Soundbarrier 1987-1992
Talk 1972
Telegraph Sunday Magazine 1987
The Christian Leader 1890
The Edinburgh Messenger 1843
The Guardian 1982
The Northampton Independent 1927
The Teacher of the Deaf 1906-1956

The Times 1986
Volta Review 1946-1948
West Somerset Free Press 1935
Woman 1982

Television Programmes and Videotapes

British Deaf Association (1994) *The Living Heritage of the Deaf Community*
Deaf Century, Channel 4 (1999)
Listening Eye series (1986-1994)
SEE HEAR! (1981-1998)
See Hear on Saturday! (1998-2000)
SIGN ON (1994-1999)

Annual Reports, School Magazines, Publicity Brochures, Internet Websites

Aberdeen & North East Scotland Society for the Deaf
Ashgrove School for the Deaf (Penarth)
Breakthrough Deaf-Hearing Integration
British Association of Teachers of the Deaf
British Association of the Hard of Hearing
British Deaf Association
Burwood Park School
Council for the Advancement of Communication with Deaf People
Coventry & Warwickshire Association for the Deaf
Deafness Support Network
Donaldson's School for the Deaf
Doncaster College for the Deaf
Federation of Deaf People
Edinburgh & East of Scotland Society for the Deaf
Hamilton Lodge School for Deaf Children, Brighton
Hampshire, Isleof Wight & Channel Islands Association for the Deaf
Hearing Concern
Hearing Dogs for the Deaf
Heathlands School for Deaf Children, St. Albans
Hugh Bell School, Middlesbrough
Glasgow & West of Scotland Society for the Deaf
Leicester and County Mission to the Deaf
Mary Hare Grammar School
Norfolk House College
Nottingham & Nottinghamshire Society for the Deaf
Nutfield News (Nutfield Priory School)
Royal Association in aid of Deaf people
Royal Cross School, Preston
Royal National Institute for Deaf People
Royal School for Deaf Children, Margate
Royal School for the Deaf, Derby
Royal Schools for the Deaf, Manchester
Royal West of England School for the Deaf, Exeter
SENSE
SHAPE Deaf Arts

St. John's Catholic School for the Deaf, Boston Spa
Tayside Association for the Deaf
Sussex Diocesan Association for the Deaf
Warrington & District Society for the Deaf

Typewritten Notes, Personal Records

Algernon Barnett (Arthur Groom)
Anerley School for the Deaf (Bernard Allery)
Ashgrove School for the Deaf (Ashgrove School, Penarth)
Baedaker Raids (The late Canon A. Mackenzie)
Benjamin Morgan (Geoffrey Eagling)
Bourton House (R. Parris)
Breakthrough and David Hyslop, OBE (Gillian Winstanley)
British Theatre for the Deaf (RNID)
Drama and the Deaf (RNID)
Deaf Mountaineering Club (Irene Hall)
Dene Hollow School (Sally Ellis)
Doreen Woodford
Erica Cox (Patricia K. Wrighton)
Freeford Manor Records
Geoffrey Eagling
National Deaf Club Records (Melinda Napier)
Northampton School for the Deaf (Northampton County Records Office)
Raymond Lee
R.W. Hallett
Spurs Club Records (Richard Goulden)
Unpublished Thesis (Colin M'Dowell)

Personal contributions

Arthur Dimmock, MBE
Edward Brown
Jeffrey McWhinney
John Young, OBE
Sarah Jane Cooke
Sharon Ridgeway
Terry Riley

Official Records, Archives and Manuscript Collections

Bedfordshire Historical Records Society (Finberg papers)
Bedfordshire Records Office
Cambridgeshire Records Office
Cambridge University Library indexes
Central Public Library (Manchester) indexes
Cheshire County Records Office
Cornwall Records Office
Dorothy Osborne Letter Collection, British Library
Egerton Mss., British Library
History MSS. Commission Report, British Library

Kent Records Office
National Galleries of Scotland indexes
National Portrait Gallery indexes
Norfolk County Records Office
Northampton County Records Office (file no.ZAB799)
Popham Mss., Somerset County Records Office
Public Records Office
Scottish Records Office
Seaforth Mss., Scottish Records Office
Somerset County Records Office
Sorina Reserata, British Library Collection
Staffordshire Records Office
The Royal Humane Society
Tonkin's Mss., Cornwall Records Office

Inscriptions on Memorials, Gravestones etc.

Fishermen's Memorial, St. Geraldine's Church, Lossiemouth, Morayshire.
Foundation stone, preserved at Royal School for Deaf Children, Margate.
Gravestone in St. Andrew's Parish Church, Walberswick, Suffolk.
Members' List, Edinburgh & East of Scotland Society for the Deaf.
Tarr Memorial, East Anstey Parish Church, Devon.

Dictionaries and Reference Books

Burke's Extinct & Dormant Baronetcies, Burke's Peerage (Genealogical Books) Ltd, 1841.
Dictionary of British 18th Century Painters, Antique Club, 1981.
Dictionary of British Animal Painters, F. Lewis, Publishers, Leigh-on-Sea, 1973.
Dictionary of British Artists 1880-1940, Antique Collectors Club, 1952.
Dictionary of British Artists Working 1900-1950, Eastbourne Fine Art, Eastbourne, 1975.
Dictionary of British Historical Painters, F. Lewis, Publishers, Leigh-on-Sea, 1979.
Dictionary of British Landscape Painters, F. Lewis, Publishers, Leigh-on-Sea, 1952.
Dictionary of British Marine Painters, F. Lewis, Publishers, Leigh-on-Sea, 1967.
Dictionary of British Miniature Painters, Faber & Faber, London, 1972.
Dictionary of National Bibliography, Vol. Nos. III, XIII, XVIII, XXI, XXII, XXXV -1888 edition.
Dictionary of Painters of Miniatures, Philip Allan Co, London, 1926.
Dictionary of Victorian Painters, Antique Collectors Club, 1971.
Encyclopaedia of Boxing, 7th Edition Hale (London), 1983.

Publications

Alker, Doug (2000) *Really not interested in the deaf,* D.Alker Publications
Arrowsmith, John Paunceforth (1819) *The Art of Instructing the Infant Deaf & Dumb,* British Library Collection.
Ashley, Jack (1975) *Journey into Silence,* Bodley Head Press, London.
Atherton, Martin, Russell, David and Turner, Graham (2000) *Deaf United,* Forest Books, Coleford.
Battiscombe, Georgina (1984) *Queen Alexandra,* Constable, London.
Boyce, Anthony J. (1996) *The Leeds Beacon,* British Deaf History Society Publications.
Boyce, Anthony J. & Lavery, Elaine (1999) *The Lady in Green* British Deaf History Society Publications.

Braddock, Gilbert C. (1975) *Notable Deaf Persons,* Gallaudet College Alumni Association, Washington DC, USA.
Brown, Peter (1994) *Banton* British Deaf History Society Publications.
Bulwer, John (1644) *Chirologia,* British Library Collection.
Bulwer, John (1648) *Philocophus, or the Deafe & Dumbe Man's Friend,* British Library Collection.
Buxton, Dr. David (1854) *Anedotes and Annals of the Deaf & Dumb,* W. Fearnall & Co, Liverpool.
Buxton, Dr. David (1857) *On the Marriage and Intermarriage of the Deaf & Dumb,* W. Fearnall & Co, Liverpool.
Cameron, A.D. (1986) *The Man Who Loved to Draw Horses,* Aberdeen University Press.
Caw, James L. (1975) *Scottish Painting,* Redwood Burn Ltd, Trowbridge.
Devenshire, The Duchess of (1982) *The House - A Portrait of Chatsworth,* Papermac.
Dimmock, Arthur F. (1991) *Tommy,* Scottish Workshop Publications.
Dimmock, Arthur F. (1993) *Cruel Legacy,* Scottish Workshop Publications.
Dimmock, Arthur F. (1996) *Arthur James Wilson* British Deaf History Society Publications.
Dixon, Conrad (1987) *Ships of the Victorian Navy,* Ashford Press.
D'Orazio & Edwards (1971) *Who's Who in Wrestling,* Paul, London.
Farrar, Abraham (1901) *Arnold's Education for the Deaf,* Simpkin, Marshall & Co, London.
Firth, George (1988) *Chosen Vessels,* Papyrus Printers, Exeter.
Francis, Dick (1986) *Lester,* Michael Joseph, London.
Gannon, Jack R. (1981) *Deaf Heritage, A Narrative History of Deaf America,* The National Association of the Deaf, Maryland, USA.
Geikie, Walter (1841) *Etchings Illustrative of Scottish Character & Scenery,* McLachlan, Stweart, Edinburgh.
Grant, Brian (1990) *The Deaf Advance, A History of The British Deaf Association 1890-1990*, The Pentland Press Ltd, Edinburgh.
Greasley, Rev. W. (1923) *The Siege of Lichfield,* Constable, London.
Groce, Nora Ellen (1985) *Everyone Here Spoke Sign Language,* Harvard University Press, Cambridge, Massachusetts.
Harwood, Rev. Thomas (1806) *The History of Lichfield,* Cadell & Davies, London.
Herdman, Robin (1988) *History of Northern Counties School for the Deaf, Newcastle 1838 - 1988,* Northern Counties School for the Deaf.
Holt, Emily (1879) *Margery's Son,* J.F.Shaw & Co., London.
Jackson, Peter W. (1990) *Britain's Deaf Heritage,* The Pentland Press Ltd, Edinburgh.
Lee, Raymond & Hay, John (1993) *Bermondsey 1792,* National Union of the Deaf, Feltham, Middlesex.
Lee, Raymond (1996) *Walter Geikie* British Deaf History Society Publications.
Masters, Brian (1980) *The Dukes,* Bland & Briggs, London.
Miles, Dorothy (1988) *British Sign Language, A Beginners Guide,* BBC Books, London.
Montgomery, George W. (1988) *Past, Present & Future, the Story of a School,* Donaldson's School for the Deaf, Edinburgh.
Outhwaite, Daphne (1985) *A History of the Centre for the Deaf, Bristol 1884 - 1984,* Deaf Information Project, Bristol.
Oxley, Selwyn (1921) *The Deaf of Other Days,* Ferrier & Co, London.
Popham, F.W. (1976) *A West Country Family: the Pophams from 1150,* Olivers Printing Works, Battle, Sussex.
Roe, W.R. (1917) *Peeps into a Deaf World,* Bemrose, Derby.
Wright, David (1969) *Deafness, a Personal Account,* Allen Lane, The Penguin Press, London.

Other Reports

Report on the International Congress, Milan 1880 (Arthur A. Kinsey)
Report of the Royal Commission on the Education of the Blind & the Deaf & Dumb (HMSO 1889)
Report of the Working Party of the Higher Study Group on the Further & Higher Education for the Hearing-Impaired (HMSO 1982)
The Report of the Lewis Committee (HMSO 1969)

NAME & SUBJECT INDEX

Aberdeen & N.E.Scotland Deaf Society (includes the Deaf Centre)	142,143,200,211
Abraham, Ernest	231
Ackers, Benjamin St. John	36,37
Adams, Paul	229
Agnew, William	45,90,128,144,146,147,159,166,299
Alker, Doug	180-182,197
American Sign Language	45
Anderson, Crawford Carrick	225,229
Anderson, Duncan	139
Andrew, Prince	178
Andrews, Kenneth	274,275
Armour, Robert	270
Arnold, Thomas	30,33,37,68,69,106,135,255
Arrowsmith, Thomas	86,87,90
Ash, Harry	42,90,100,101
Ashley, Jack	278,279
Atkinson, Alexander	59,132
Ayrshire Mission to the Deaf	161,162
Bain, Charlotte	116,117
Baker, Charles	30,60,68,72
Baker, Henry	29,51,52,68
Balham Deaf Centre	308
Banton, George	56,57
Barland, James	64
Barnett, Algernon Joel Morris	148,268,269,277,299,304
Bastin, Cliff	226,227
Bath Institute for the Deaf	152
Beethoven, Ludwig Van	239
Belfast Institutes & Centres	143,155,165,311
Bell, Alexander Graham	70,71,115,299,315
Bilibin, Alexander	100,101
Bingham, Henry Brothers	60,161,265
Birmingham Institute for the Deaf	143,151,155,159
Blackwood, Alexander	94
Bone, Edward	6,7,23,26,42,199
Bonn, Leo	180,181
Bourneville College	263
Bower, David	243
Boyce, Anthony J.	286,287
Braidwood, John	59,93
Braidwood, Thomas	1,30,52,55,56,59,60,68,85,93,112,320
Breakthrough Deaf-Hearing Integration	178,188,189,298,299

Brennan, Mary	46
Bristol Deaf Centre	151,153
British Association of Teachers of the Deaf	185,260
British Deaf Association (includes British Deaf & Dumb Association)	42,44,45,46,49,97,98,106,120,131,135, 144,151,155,156,160-179,181,182,185, 186,189,193,194,197,206,207,208,211, 221,231,236,240,265,269,270,277,281, 285,290,304,305,313,318
British Deaf History Society	105,109,192,193,232,236,269,286,287, 319
British Deaf News	231,232,233,268,269,305
British Deaf Sports Council (also British Amateur Deaf Sports Association)	194,195
British Society for Mental & Health & Deafness	285
British Theatre of the Deaf	240
Brojer, Mika	288,289
Brown, Janet	290,291
Bulwer, John	1,8,22,23,26,27,29,51,198,199
Burke, James	214,215,217
Burns, Matthew Robert	62-64,94,140
Burnside, Marion	126,127
Butler, Tim	222
Buxton, Dr. David	37,41,315
Byres, Harry	217
Cambridge Deaf Centre	270
Campbell, Duncan	23,29,50,51,199
Campbell, Jean	115
Cardiff Deaf Centre	143,270
Carew, Richard	1,7,26,199
Cavendish, William Spencer	118,119,239
Caves, David	217
City College Manchester	262,263,291,319
City Literary Institute for Deaf People	181,184,263
Clapham St. Bede's Centre for Deaf People	151,161,202,204,205,308,309
Clarke, Nobby	222
Clemo, Jack	236,237
Collins, Judith	260,261
Communication Support Workers	262,263
Sarah Jane, Cooke	228,229
Council for the Advancement of Communication with Deaf People (CACDP)	46,49,186,187,208,232
Coventry College	187
Coventry Deaf Centre	151,159,204,266
Cox, Erica	229
Creasy, John	55,56,60
Cressener, John	20,51
Cricket	170,213,218,219,228,229,265,309-311

Crosse, Richard	77,78,80-83,85,199
Cubis, Pat	216,217
Dalgarno, George	29,51,55
Daniels, Susan	184,185
Davidson, Thomas	90,96,97,147,161,200
Davis. J	143
Davis, Mabel	47,260,261
De Leon, Pedro Ponce	26
Deafblind UK	290
Deaf Broadcasting Council	192,193,243
Deaf Caravan & Camping Club	208,209
Deaf Connections	159
Deaf Direct	159
Deaf Magazines	40,109,132,148,165,166,169,193, 230-233,267
Deaf Mime Group	240
Deaf Mountaineering Club	208,209
Deaf Tribune Group	46,197
Deafness Support Network	159,319
Deafway	159
Defoe, Daniel	23,28,29,51,199
Denmark, Clark	284,285
Dent, Rupert	90,98,99,147
Derby Deaf Centre	213,216
Deuchar, Margaret	46
Diana, Princess	174,175,178
Dimmock, Arthur F.	197,224,236,237
Disability Discrimination Act	211,316
Docharty, Edwin	144,148,149
Docharty, James	144
Downing, Sir George	12,23,29,199
Drake, Raymond	226
Drysdale, Alexander	64,143
Dundee Deaf Centre	64,65,143
Dutton, Martin	90,106,107
Dyott, John	1,10,11,23,199
Edinburgh & East of Scotland Society for the Deaf (includes the Deaf Mission/Centre)	94,139,159,161,200,213,218,281,310
Edinburgh Congregational Church	31,63,90,94,95,115,138,139,199
Edmund, Arthur	270,271
Education Acts	75,190,252
Edwards, Leslie	169-171,269,277
Eichholz, Dr. A.	252,253
Elliott, Dr. Richard	36,37,165
Ernest Ayliffe Home (The)	174,304
European Union for the Deaf	175,281,290
Evelyn, John	1,23,29

Exeter Deaf Centre	152
Fairbairn, Sir Arthur H.	264,265
Farrar, Abraham	41,132,134,135
Federation of Deaf People	48,49,196,197
Ferguson, Alexander	136,137
Ferrers, Benjamin	76,77
Football	144,178,181,200,211,213,218-222,225,226,301,312,313
Fordham, George	217
Forster, Jane	29,51
Frame, Rev. Mark	170,231,268,269
Fraser, Alex	226
Fyfe, David	148,149,299
Gallaudet University	45,165,166,235,285
Gardiner, Craig	228,229
Gardner, Keith	229
Gaudy, Framlingham	18-20,29,51,77,198,199
Gaudy, Sir John	19-21,23,29,51,77
Gawen, Joseph	90,104,105,192
Geikie, Walter	30,56,90,92-94,139,140,199
Glasgow Deaf Centre (includes the Adult Mission to the Deaf)	90,91,109,139,144-147,159,161,200,201,212,213,218,219,269,281,286
Glennie, Evelyn	238,239
Goodricke, John	52,110,111
Gorham, Charles	164,165,169,174,231
Gostwicke, Sir Edward	8,9,23,29
Gostwicke, William	8,23,29
Graham, Sir James (Duke of Montrose)	147,278,279,281
Great Yarmouth	151
Green Lane Deaf Centre	289
Griffiths, William	143
Groom, Jane Elizabeth	39
Guerrieria, Mark	262
Guild of St. John of Beverley	148
Hacket, John	8,29
Hall, Irene	230,231
Hallett, H.G.	300
Halliwell, Geri	239
Hawthorne, Mike	229
Hayhurst, Allan Brindle	44,45,169,174,318
Haythornthwaite, Roland	195
Healey, George	45,143,161-163,166,170,299,304
Hearing aids	292-295
Hearing Concern	186,232
Hearing Dogs for the Deaf	194,195
Hebblethwaite, Paul	228,229

Heiniecke, Samuel	1,68
Henesey House	282
Hepworth, Joseph	231
Herriot, James	140,141,200
Hockney, David	90,109
Holder, Dr. William	1,15,29,51,68
Holmes, Murray	174,280,281
Howard, John	72
Howe, James	88-90
Hull Deaf Centre	155,159
Hull, Susannah	37
Hunt, Rev. Vera	282,283
Hunter, William	56
Hyslop, David	188,189
Interim Theatre	238
International Congress on the Education of the Deaf	46,47,197
Internet	232,233,314
Isted, Ambrose	120,121
Jack, Michael	235
Jackson, Maureen	319
Jackson, Peter	318,319
Jewish Deaf Club	289
Joanna, Princess	1-3,26
Johnson, Dr. Samuel	52
Johnson, Malcolm	222,223
Kempe, John	6,7,23,26,42,199
Kinniburgh, Robert	30,59,64,115,231
Kinsey, Arthur A.	37
Kirk, Edward A.	30,38,72,73,260
Kitto, John	124,125
Kyle, Dr. J.	46
Ladd, Paddy	197
Lane, Harlan	46,197
Lee, Martin	225
Lee, Raymond	197
Leeds Deaf Centre	143,155,161,200,218,219
Leicester & County Mission to the Deaf (includes the Deaf Centre)	143,158,159,170,204,218,310,311
L'Epée, Charles Michel de	1,111,320
Lewis Committee Report	252
Listening Eye	242,243,285
Liverpool Deaf Centre	143,161,162,200,204,213,309
Livingstone, Peter	216,217
Lowe, John William	122,123
Lucas, Samuel Bright	130,131,161
Macdonald, Alexander	148

Macdonald, Harry	154,155
MacDonough, Father Peter	282,283
MacDougall, Kenneth P.	269,305
MacDougall, William	169-171
Mackenzie, Francis Humberstone (Lord Seaforth)	52, 112,113
Mackenzie, George Annand	270,271
Maginn, Francis	45,135,161,164-166,231,281
Manchester Deaf Centre (includes the Adult Missions to the Deaf)	46,140,141,151,155,159,161,200,201, 212,213,218
Martha's Vineyard	12,23,29,199
Martineau, Harriet	126,127,235
Mason, Clive	286,287
McLean, Jimmy	226
McWhinney, Jeffrey	178,179
Milan Congress	30,34-39,41,71,148,161,203,260
Miles, Dorothy	234,235
Milla, Maria	251
Mitchell, William Frederick	98,99
Moray House College	46
Moreton, Joseph	71,72
Morgan, Rev. Benjamin	276,277
Mountcastle, James	296
Muir, James	169
Murphy, Francis	242
Nabarro, Carolyn	285
National Assistance Act, 1948	156,157
National Association of Teachers of the Deaf	72,185,286
National Centre for Mental Health & Deafness	285
National Deaf & Dumb Society	120,131,160-2,166
National Deaf Children's Society	119,184,185,208,232
National Deaf Club	148,149,151,203,266
National Theatre for the Deaf	235,240,289
National Union of the Deaf	46,193,196,197,289
Neilson, Catya	231
Nesbitt, Billy	226
North, Jane A.	90
Northampton Deaf Centre	268,269
Northwich Deaf Club (Vale Royal)	158,159,319
Norwich Deaf Centre	151
Nottingham Deaf Centre	143,159,165
Oloman, R.S.	304
Osborne, Dorothy	1,8,29
Oxford Deaf Centre	202,270
Oxley, Selwyn	135,235,306,307
Padden, Tessa	242
Parker, C.M.	251

Patrick, George Percy (Lord Carberry)	120,121
Paul, James	45,160,162,166,169,231
Pearce, Rev. Richard Aslett	130,131,143,277
Pearce, Thomas	151
Pearson, John Andrew	108
Pepys, Samuel	1,12,13,23,29,199,293
Perkins, Candy	224,225
Piggott, Lester	102,226,227
Pitcher, Dr. Bernard	254,255
Pitchforth, Roland Vivian	90,102,103,109
Plantagenet, Princess Katherine	1-3
Pollock, Cecilia	203
Pontypridd Deaf Centre	159
Pope John Paul	282
Popham, Alexander	14-17,20,23,51
Pullen, Gloria	47
Queen Alexandra	128,129,144
Queen Victoria	31,45,59,119,128,131,144,147
Quinn, Elizabeth	240
Rattray brothers	64
Reading Deaf Centre	156,202
Reeves, Austin	174,193,281,313
Reynolds, Sir Joshua	77-79
Ridgeway, Sharon	284,285
Riley, Terry	290,291
Robertson, William	274,275
Roche, Sampson Towgood	78,81,85,199
Rowland, Harry	148
Rowlands, J.	143
Royal Association in aid of Deaf People includes the Royal Association for the Deaf & Dumb, etc.)	63,97,120,131,139,140,161,166,203, 231,232, 265, 269, 277,282,289
Royal Commission for the Education of the Blind, the Deaf and the Dumb	41,74,75,135,166
Royal National Institute for Deaf People	109,147,177,180-183,186,189,197,232, 233,240,278,281,290
Scott, Robert Menzies	108,109
Scott, Sarah	240
Scouts	204,205
SEE HEAR	178,197,232,235,242,243, 286,290
SENSE	190,191,290
SHAPE Deaf Arts	108,109,240,241
Shaw, Kathleen Trousdell	90,104,105
Sheffield Deaf Centre	143,213,216
Shirreff, Alexander	52,85
Shirreff, Charles	52,78,81,84,85,101,199
SIGN ON	242,243

Smith, Rev. Albert	269
Smith, John Guthrie Spence	109
Smith, Rev. Samuel	131,132,140,143,231
Socrates	26
South Staffordshire & Shropshire Society	277
Southampton Deaf Centre	143,150,151,202,265,313
Sport	144,148,156,165,194,200,203,213,219-229,263,266,281,289,290,308-312
Spurs Deaf Club	155,203,241
St. John of Beverley Deaf Centre	159,204
St. Joseph's Deaf Club	290
St. Saviour's Church & Deaf Centre	31,90,97,105,120,123,128,131,138,140, 143, 161,166,200,265,282
Stainer, Rev. William	31,39
Stockton-on-Tees Deaf Adult Mission	161
Stoke Deaf Centre	143,202,205
Stokoe, Dr. William	45,46
Strachan, James	182,183
Strathern, Alexander Fairley	132,133,231
Street, Herbert C.	155
Stryker, Emile	288,289
Summer Schools	173,206-208,277
Sunderland Deaf Centre	159
Surbiton Deaf Club	178,277
Swain, Mary	155
Swansea Deaf Centre	155,312
Tarr, Albert	272-274
Tavaré, Frederick Lawrence	132,133
Technology	292-299, 314-317
Telecommunications	70,71,182,189,296,298,299,314,315
Television	178,182,197,211,232,240,242,243,285, 286,290,296,316
Thomson, Alfred Reginald	90,101-103,109
Tilsye, Thomas	4
Tomlinson Report	263
Torquay Deaf Centre	152
Townsend, Rev. John	55,56
Trood, William H.H.	90,91,96,97,109,147
University of Bristol	285
University of Cambridge	135,270
University of Durham	45,49,236,281,285,318
University of Glasgow	269
University of Leeds	235
University of Liverpool	260
University of London	135,255
University of Manchester	135,252,285
University of Nottingham	252

University of Oxford	235,270
University of Sheffield	282
University of Wolverhampton	236,286
Ure, William	139
Uxbridge Deaf Centre	282
Vale Royal Deaf Centre (Northwich)	158,159,319
Van Praagh, William	68
Varlow, Liz	238,239
Veditz, George W.	25
Wallis, Dr. John	1,15-17,23,51,68
War	150-156,203,204,221,222,244-247
Warnock Report	252,256,263
Watson, Dr. Joseph	55,56,60,123
Watson, Dr. Thomas	56,97
Weeble, James John	136,137
West Ham Deaf Centre	161,204,205
Weymouth Deaf Centre	152
Whalley, Daniel	15-17,20,23,51
Whitaker, Paul	239
Whitehaven Deaf Centre	159
Whitehead, Kate	235,307
Wigan Deaf Centre	155
Wilkins, Rev. John	29
Williams, Ian	228,229
Wilson, Arthur James	148,266,267
Wilson, John	108,109
Winchester Diocesan Mission to the Deaf	131,265
Winter Games	225
Wise, Dorothy Stanton	90,106,107,128
Wolverhampton Mission to the Deaf	98,277
Wood, John Philp	114,115
Woodhouse, Stanley	197
Woolley, Maggie	197,286
Workhouse	75
World Federation of the Deaf	281,285,290
World Games	194,220-225,312
Wrestling	217
Wright, David	234,235
Young, Jock	174,280,281

SCHOOLS INDEX

Aberdeen School for the Deaf	63, 64, 259, 274
Ackmar Road School	256
Airdrie Day School for the Deaf	71
Anerley School for the Deaf	152,246,249,256,
Asylum for the Deaf & Dumb, London	See Margate
Beverley School for Deaf Children, Middlesbrough	259
Birkdale School for Partially Deaf Children	255,259
Blanche Nevile School for the Deaf	259,286
Braidwood's Academy for the Deaf & Dumb	30,52,53,56,59,60,85,86,93,111,112,115, 320
Braidwood School, Birmingham	259
Brighton Institution for the Deaf & Dumb	131,166,253,265,300
Bristol Institution for the Deaf & Dumb	63,131
Burwood Park School	108,203,256,257,263,289,313,318
Donaldson's School for the Deaf	58,59,108,170,244,245,246,259
Doncaster College	259,262,263,286
Dundee School for the Deaf	63,64,65,143
East Anglian School for the Deaf	226,245,249
Edinburgh Institution for the Deaf & Dumb	30,34,57-59,64,93,94,115,132,136,230, 231
Elmfield School, Bristol	63,259
Garvel School, Greenock	71,259
Glasgow Schools (includes the Institution & the Langside and Maryhill Schools)	34,60,132,139,147,162,213,256,269, 281,285, 286
Greenock Academy	70,71
Hamilton Lodge, Brighton	229,259,260
Heathlands School, St. Albans	176,229,259,260
Hugh Bell School	246,253,259
Jewish School for Deaf Children	66,67,246,269,289
Jordanstown Schools for the Deaf (includes the Ulster Institution)	60,143,178,259
Leeds School for the Deaf	30,38,72,73,246,260
Leicester School	71
Liverpool Schools (includes Crown Street & Alice Elliott Schools)	37,41,60,61,139, 246,255,260,270,315
Llandrindod Wells School for the Deaf (formerly the Royal Cambrian Institution)	249,256

London Day Schools Board	39,55,71,75
Mary Hare Grammar School (includes Dene Hollow)	178,181,203,207,236,252,254-256,259, 260,286,318
Maud Maxwell School, Sheffield	217
Northampton School (includes Spring Hill School & Ince Jones Oral School)	30,33,68,69,101,106,135,235,254,255, 282
Northern Counties School for the Deaf, Newcastle-upon-Tyne	60,74,204,236,246, 247,258,259
Nottingham School (Ewing School)	71
Nutfield Priory School, Redhill	256,257
Oak Lodge School for Deaf Children, London	67,259
Old Kent Road School	55,246,249
Oral School for the Deaf (Wimbledon)	251
Ovingden Hall School, Brighton	255,259
Royal Cross School, Preston	32,204,246,249,256, 257
Royal Residential Schools for the Deaf, Manchester (includes the Manchester Institution)	34,39,60,61,75,98,132,213,235,245,246, 249, 250,256,258,259,277,290,318
Royal School for Deaf Children, Derby	63,119,250,258, 259,263
Royal School for Deaf Children, Edgbaston	30,34,60,61,190,256
Royal School for Deaf Children, Margate (includes the London Asylum for the Deaf and Dumb in Bermondsey & Old Kent Road)	36,37,43,54-57,63,75,97,98,101,102,105, 120,123,140,165,207,245,246,248,249, 259, 263,265,270
Royal West of England School for the Deaf, Exeter	32,60,61,75,97,136,152,153,162,166,246, 249,259,263,273
St. John's Catholic School for Deaf Children, Boston Spa	66,67,75,258,259,282
St. Vincent's School for the Deafblind, Glasgow	67,259
Thomasson Memorial, Bolton	256
Thorn Park School, Bradford	259
Wych Oral School for the Deaf	251
Yorkshire Residential School for the Deaf	30,34,60,61,68,72,86,106,140,143,213, 245,259,263,286